THE HISTORY OF
AMERICAN BANDSTAND

THE HISTORY OF
AMERICAN BANDSTAND

It's Got A Great Beat And You Can Dance To It

By Michael Shore
with Dick Clark

BALLANTINE BOOKS • NEW YORK

Library of Congress Catalog Card Number: 85-90579

ISBN: 0-345-31722-X

Cover design by James R. Harris

Cover photograph by Paul Schutzer, *Life* Magazine,
© 1958 Time Inc.

Interior Design by Michaelis/Carpelis Design Assoc., Inc.

Manufactured in the United States of America
First Edition: November 1985

10   9   8   7   6   5   4   3   2   1

To my wife, Susan. I give her a 100.
—MS

To "Pop" Singer . . .
and all the kids who have ever danced
on the show . . .
—DC

ACKNOWLEDGMENTS

First of all, a super-colossal thank you to the man who made it all possible, who gave this book a reason to be in the first place—to Dick Clark, for his time, kindness, and assistance, and just for being Dick Clark.

And to Kari Clark, for her unstinting consideration, energy, and professionalism, and for her sheer relentless niceness—she redefines the phrase "beyond the call of duty."

And to Jeff Kopp, Larry Klein, Barry Glazer, and Chris Cavarozzi of Dick Clark Productions; to Mary Dyer of the Smithsonian Institution; Connie Francis and Frank Fiore; Chubby Checker and Tony DiLoro; Fabian Forte; Frankie Avalon; Ian Wilson and Mike Peters of the Alarm; John Oates and Robin of Champion Entertainment; Bill Russell of WPBI-TV; Joy Raines and Gary Smith of Bresee-Smith and Associates; Ted Hacker and Joe Bonsall of the Oak Ridge Boys—more giant-sized thanks.

Extra-special thanks to all the *Bandstand* "regulars" who gave so unselfishly of their time, their help, their information, their memories and memorabilia—the stuff of their very lives: Bob Clayton, Justine Carrelli Muzzi, Kenny Rossi, Arlene Sullivan, Kathleen "Bunny" Gibson, Carol Scaldeferri, Joanne Montecarlo, Betty Romantini, Joe Fusco, Ed Kelly, Frank Brancaccio, Lydia Bebau, Yvette Jimenez, Bill Cook, Bobby Baritz, Joanne Orgel, Damita Jo Freeman, Kim Schreier, Sue Bowser, Deb-E Chaffin, Luis Novoa, Rob Frias, and Dawn Sheppard. This book—and the show it's about—couldn't have happened without you.

More hefty thanks to the two people I know of who *should* have been *Bandstand* regulars, but weren't: Dave Frees and Katy K.

Finally, to my editor at Ballantine Books, Risa Kessler (and her assistant, Bonnie Bader) whose patience, energy, devotion, and kindness rival Kari Clark's; to my parents, Joyce and Lester Shore, without whom I wouldn't be here; and to my wife Susan, whose patience, energy, devotion and kindness surpass everyone else's—my deepest undying gratitude.

—Michael Shore

C O N T E N T S

I N T R O D U C T I O N

In 1952 *Bandstand* arrived on the public's doorstep . . . much like a stray puppy. It was underfed (economically!); not too handsome a beast . . . but full of "personality."

At first, nobody paid much attention to the new arrival . . . but it hung around. Slowly, it became part of the family. The kids fell in love with the show first . . . then, their young mothers did . . . to be followed by the rest of the home audience. That "stray puppy" grew up to be stronger and healthier . . . and more handsome. It endeared itself to several generations.

From a local fill-in TV show to a regional network program to a national network presentation, *American Bandstand* became part of Americana.

Hardly a day goes by that someone doesn't say to me something like . . ."I grew up with you" or "Whatever happened to Bob and Justine?" or "the little girl with the blonde streak" or "Famous and June" or "Deb-E" or anyone of their favorite dancers.

Not many people have had the same job most of their adult lives. *American Bandstand* has been my "job" ever since I grew up; come to think of it, I grew up with *American Bandstand*; just like most everybody else.

My three kids all danced on the show from the time they were toddlers to the time they were teenagers. Some of the other young people who have danced over the years have become long-time friends. The same applies to many of the artists who have appeared on *American Bandstand*. It hasn't been possible to get to really know all of them—there have been more than 10,000 musical appearances on *American Bandstand* since 1952. (That means, literally, thousands of artists.) Some of them have become lifelong close friends. We see each other frequently, exchange family photos, talk over old times and new times . . . the stuff that makes for fond relationships.

I know I'm a very lucky person, blessed with good health and a wonderful family. For the past ten or fifteen years I've secretly made

American Bandstand a part of that family. It's like my fourth child—I watch it, nourish it, and carefully protect it. God forbid, as has happened on some occasions in the past, someone tries to do anything to it that would cause harm. They have to reckon with my protective instincts . . . it's a little like the natural reaction of any animal or human parent when one of its offspring is endangered!

I'm often asked one of two questions: "How long are you going to stay with *American Bandstand*?" or "How long will it last?"

The first answer . . . I'd like to continue to do the show as long as possible and then pass it on to another, but realize that I'll be around in the background, like any good parent, as long as I'm alive and kickin'.

The second answer . . . *American Bandstand* will be on TV as long as there is television. Now that we have so many alternative methods of distribution, it will always have a TV home. It's an infallible formula; I don't honestly believe that "people watching" and interest in young people, especially, will ever disappear.

I can't tell you how happy I am the publishers decided to print this book. I'm a real history buff. The past is a cherished thing. It shows us our roots and indicates the future. Like any family album, the book is full of photos, memories, and family trivia. If you're like I am, one of those who "grew up with *American Bandstand*," I hope you'll enjoy it.

The above is a well-known French proverb. Its translation is "The more things change, the more they stay the same." Perhaps nothing bears out the truth that lies at the heart of this cliché as well as the history of *American Bandstand*.

For that history is much more than just the story of the longest-running, most steadfastly unchanging format in American network television history. If that fact alone weren't enough, consider that *Bandstand* is a TV show about popular music, and hence about popular culture itself. As of this writing, *American Bandstand* has been on network television for more than twenty-eight years, and it was on locally in Philadelphia and a regional network for five years before *that*. In that time, the show has been on some 6,000 hours, has spun more than 65,000 records, has presented nearly 10,000 performances, and has had more than 600,000 teenagers dancing before its cameras. The show won its first Emmy award indirectly, for Best Editing of the 1978 Twenty-fifth Anniversary special. The Thirtieth Anniversary special in 1983 won the same award. *American Bandstand* itself has won the 1981 Emmy for Best Direction, Daytime Variety; 1982, for Program Achievement; and 1983, for Best Show, Daytime Variety.

Awards and statistics such as those are nice, but they can't even begin to *really* tell the *Bandstand* story. How do you honor a show for somehow managing to survive, unchanged and intact, for all those years, when it's a product of the ever-changing world of television and, furthermore, it's about the ever-changing tapestry of pop and rock music and all its attendant pop-cultural manifestations? Think of all the history that's been chronicled on *American Bandstand*: all the music and the performers; the dances, the clothes, the hairstyles; the modes of public behavior; the relationships between the sexes and the races. The history of this show is the history of a world, of generations, and of the ways they chose to express themselves.

Consider again that while the stars and their fans and the fads and trends came and went, *American Bandstand* has remained, virtually unchanged, through all those many years. The show has survived every fad it covered or helped spawn. It's outlasted all of its scores of imitators (in fact, it continues to inspire clones in various guises to this day, and in all likelihood will continue to do so even after it—*shudder*—is gone). *Bandstand* was here before Elvis Presley and the Beatles. They're gone.

It's *still* here.

Dick Clark sees the show's incredible longevity and consistency of format this way: "One reason the show has survived for so long, and will probably continue surviving till God knows when, is . . . well, obviously there's a secret formula I don't want to divulge too much of, but the bottom line is the show is all about people-watching. And that will never go out of style. But the analogy I always like to use is that *Bandstand*'s format is like a window in your home. You open your window shade and look out the window, and you see the whole world passing by in a half hour or whatever, you know? The *window* is always there, it's fixed, but what passes by, what you see *through* it, is always changing. That's why the show doesn't really get old. It just sits there and everything *within* it keeps changing. *American Bandstand* is the window, and the street it looks out on is the thoroughfare of popular culture."

There are *other* things that have survived the years. For instance, Dick Clark has been using the same microphone for as long as anyone can remember—perhaps even as long as the show itself has been on the network airwaves. As *Bandstand* producer Larry Klein says, "That microphone—the long, thin one—is obviously Dick's talisman, his good-luck charm. As long as he sees it there in the studio, he's comfortable. Unbeknownst to him, though, every few years we remove the parts inside it and change them as microphone technology improves. But the outer case stays the same."

American Bandstand is nothing less than an

American cultural institution. To prove it, a few years ago Dick Clark donated some of the show's artifacts—the original podium and backdrop—to none other than the Smithsonian Institution!

Who would have thought it all possible back in August 1957, when *American Bandstand* made its debut on the ABC television network? In all likelihood, nobody—except, perhaps, for the millions of young and young-at-heart who've always made up the show's true believers: its viewing audience. They never knew much about ratings or statistics or figures or formats. They knew what they liked, and they liked *American Bandstand*. And they liked it *despite* the conventional wisdom. As Dick Clark recalls:

"I remember when we were first trying to sell ABC on the idea of picking up the show on the network. One executive said, 'Who the hell wants to watch a bunch of kids dancing in Philadelphia?' I remember what all the critics wrote about the show when it first went out on the network: 'Who the hell wants to watch a bunch of kids dancing in Philadelphia?' But then I also remember a Madison Avenue advertising executive who was sent down to check out the show for a sponsor, not long after we'd gone network. When we picked him up at the train station, he was muttering things like 'Who the hell wants to see a bunch of kids dancing in Philadelphia?' He felt like he'd been banished to Siberia. But after his first afternoon in the sponsor's booth at our studio, he'd caught the eye of a cute girl with a ponytail. After the second day, he began getting into some of the dance steps. After the third day, he began humming some of the tunes. Then he went back to New York. A week later I got a copy of the memo he wrote about the show for his bosses. It was only three lines long, and I'll never forget it. It read: 'It's a great show. We ought to buy it. Don't ask me why.' "

Or, as British rockers the Who sang in a tune nearly ten years later in the mid-sixties, "I Can't Explain." The wording might be different, but the core sentiment is the same: teenage excitement, something so simple and obvious it needs no explanation. Perhaps that's the key to the everlasting magic of *American Bandstand*: The show is in essence a fountain of youth. Given our modern fascination with youth, it's no wonder *Bandstand*'s ratings have remained

consistently high ever since it went on the network. Dick Clark's status as America's Oldest Living Teenager has long passed into legend and hardly needs comment.

Indeed, one has to wonder if it's even necessary to detail the longest-running, most steadfastly unchanging format in the history of network TV. Who by now is not familiar with a typical *Bandstand* show? If, however, you've been trapped in a cave on a desert island for the past thirty-some years, here's what we're talking about: an hour's worth of teenagers dancing to the latest pop and rock hits in a TV studio, with Dick Clark hosting the proceedings like a benevolent, unassumingly friendly uncle; a countdown of the Teen Top Ten; a Rate-a-Record segment, which produced what is probably *the* most renowned *Bandstand*-associated quote, "It's got a good beat and you can dance to it. I'll give it a [fill in your grade]"; maybe some special dance segments, like a Spotlight Dance (where three particular couples are featured out of the hundreds in the studio), or a Ladies' Choice, or a Snowball (where one couple leads off and the rest gradually join in); maybe a contest here and there; a roll call of the kids in the studio and their ages and/or hometowns and/or high schools; and a couple of lip-synched performances by pop and rock stars of their latest hits. And that's it. The format is simplicity itself—deceptive simplicity, as those aforementioned comments from suspicious network executives and TV critics indicate. But it's undoubtedly that simplicity, as well as the fountain-of-youth teen culture that makes up the show's content, that combine to give *Bandstand* such incredible longevity. To quote Dick Clark again:

"It's really a perfect balance: The subject matter keeps changing, the music and the kids and the clothes and the dances, but the format in which all that is presented stays the same. In the beginning, I don't think anyone had any idea of just how perfect that mix was. Certainly the critics were never very kind to the show, but that never bothered me. Critics are only a handful of people. The rest of the world, the real people out there in the viewing audience, have always stuck by us, and that's what counts."

What else counts? Plenty. Keep in mind that *Bandstand* was the first network television show exclusively devoted to rock'n'roll music. Consider this roster of stars—fifty-two in all, one for every week of the year—that Dick Clark recalled off the top of his head, all of whom made their network television debuts on *American Bandstand*:

Paul Anka, Frankie Avalon, Chuck Berry, James Brown, the Carpenters, Johnny Cash, Chubby Checker, the Coasters, Sam Cooke, Creedence Clearwater Revival, Jim Croce, Bobby Darin, Dion and the Belmonts, Fats Domino, the Doors, the Drifters, the Everly Brothers, the Fifth Dimension, the Four Seasons, Bill Haley and the Comets, Buddy Holly, the Jackson Five, the Jefferson Airplane, Gladys Knight and the Pips, Cyndi Lauper, Brenda Lee, Julian Lennon, Jerry Lee Lewis, Loggins and Messina, the Mamas and the Papas, Barry Manilow, Johnny Mathis, John Cougar Mellencamp, the Platters, Prince, the Rascals, Otis Redding, Lionel Richie, Smokey Robinson and the Miracles, Kenny Rogers, Linda Ronstadt, Neil Sedaka, the Shirelles, Simon and Garfunkel, Donna Summer, the Supremes, the Talking Heads, the Temptations, Three Dog Night, Conway Twitty, Dionne Warwick, and Stevie Wonder.

Before getting along with our story, this seems as good a place as any to note the way that this book will cover the show's vast history. The book is divided into chapters by decade, and each decade/chapter is further subdivided according to the specific aspects of the show: the music featured on it; the "regulars," the kids who attended the show and who, especially in the fifties, became surprise celebrities themselves; the dancing displayed on the show; and the clothing and hairstyle trends invented or popularized on the show (which were many). In the fifties, when the show was at the height of its

popularity and impact, the life-styles of millions of viewers were strongly affected by what they saw being done, being worn, and so on, on *American Bandstand*. Because of that, the fifties chapter will also include a special section on the fans of the show, who were quite remarkable in the fervor of their devotion. There will be occasional discussions of *Bandstand*'s Bloopers and Practical Jokes (to borrow a certain well-known phrase). Finally, because of the incredible number of performers and hit tunes introduced or featured on the show, an appendix at the end of each chapter will list every Top 100 record performed on the show through the years. And there *were* a *lot* of them.

Want to find out more? Read on . . . and bear in mind that *American Bandstand* made rock'n'roll safe for America, and made America safe for rock'n'roll. The last thirty years would be unimaginably different without it.

THE '50S

PRE — NETWORK:

For most of us, it all began on Monday, August 5, 1957, at 3:00 P.M., when *American Bandstand* was first telecast nationwide. But the show's history actually goes back several years earlier—to September 1952, to be precise. That was when a show called *Bandstand* made its local debut on WFIL-TV, Channel 6, in Philadelphia.

The show was hosted by popular WFIL radio disc jockey Bob Horn. Horn had been eager to get into the new medium of television for some time. When WFIL executives George Kohler and Roger Clipp decided over lunch one day that they needed some sort of new, locally originated show, they called Bob Horn. What they offered Horn was, ironically enough, an early version of music videos. Dick Clark recalls:

"Horn's radio show was called 'Bob Horn's Bandstand,' so they kept the name for the TV show. But at first, the show was nothing more than Horn hosting a series of Snaders. Those were short musical performance films, some from the Snader Musical Films Library, which had contemporary pop stars like Bing Crosby, Patti Page, and Frankie Laine. These films were early versions of the music videos you see today on TV and, yes, even on *Bandstand*. They were mostly straight performances; maybe the singer'd be walking through a park or along a beach, and there might be some primitive special effects, like superimpositions of dancing feet over a big band horn section. A lot of those films used to be shown in Soundies, which were movie jukeboxes in bars and restaurants. Again, they were primitive versions of the video jukeboxes we have today.

"It's particularly ironic that *Bandstand* started out as this early version of music videos, be-

Keeping track of the action on the TV monitor behind the scenes at WFIL-TV.

HOUND DOG - Elvis Presley
CANADIAN SUNSET - H.Winterhalter
BE BOP A LULA - Gene Vincent
CASUAL LOOK - Six Teens
CAN'T WE BE SWEETHEARTS - Cleftones
STRANDED IN THE JUNGLE - Jay Hawks
THEME-PROUD ONES - Buddy Morrow
READY TEDDY - Little Richard
LOVE ME TENDERLY - Steve Gibson
SOMEBODY'S GOTTA LOSE - Hi-Fi's

cause they're all the rage nowadays, but back then the Snaders were known as 'FIL's Folly.' They were considered certain death, a real bore. Horn was not happy about having to sit there and introduce a series of Snaders along with the occasional in-person guest artist, but he had no choice. He wanted to get into TV, and this was his shot.

"But within two weeks or so, everyone, including the station executives, had to agree that the show was no more than a dull time killer. So they finally brought a bunch of kids into the studio to dance to the latest records."

They had gotten that idea from a successful radio show on WFIL's competition, WPEN: Joe Grady and Ed Hurst's "950 Club," a weekday afternoon show in which the two hosts spun records, discussed local events, and invited teenagers into the studio to dance to the records they spun. Grady and Hurst even let the kids come on the air to introduce themselves and talk about what schools they went to and the like.

Dick Clark behind the first of the legendary *Bandstand* podia.

There was always a lot of activity in front of—and behind—the cameras.

A snowy day outside the studio, as seen on the television screen by a fan.

In October 1952, the new *Bandstand* format debuted. But the station execs, in keeping with the Grady and Hurst format, forced Horn to take on a partner: Lee Stewart, known around town as a very reliable radio pitchman. Horn would play straight man to Stewart's joker, an arrangement with which neither man was really comfortable and for which neither was too well suited.

But the show went on, and it was a success. After having promoted the new format for a week with on-air spots, WFIL found its Studio B,

at Forty-sixth and Market streets (now American Bandstand Boulevard) in Philadelphia, jammed with hundreds of teenagers for its initial broadcast on the first Tuesday of October 1952. In fact, there were so many kids waiting to get into the tiny bandbox of a studio—which could fit only two hundred or so—that Horn and Stewart had to show a few Snaders every half hour or so; while the Snaders ran, they emptied the studio and refilled it with more kids. After the first broadcast, WFIL found its switchboard jammed with hundreds of calls from viewers who, to everyone's surprise and amazement, loved to watch a bunch of kids dancing in Philadelphia!

Bandstand's format was already pretty well worked out. Horn and Stewart stood at a podium before a painted backdrop that looked like the inside of a record store. The studio's dance-floor space was surrounded by roll-out pine bleachers, just like a high school gymnasium (which made it that much more natural for the

1959: Some Russian athletes and their chaperones visit the *Bandstand* set.

schoolkids who came to the studio to dance). Horn and Stewart spun records, introduced one or two guest artists who'd lip-synch their hits —Horn would croon "We've got com-pa-nyyyy!" to signal their arrival—and the kids would dance. And that was it. Simplicity itself —and it worked like a charm.

However, all was not well on *Bandstand*. Horn and Stewart were an odd enough couple as it was, but Horn barely disguised his own distaste for the duo format and constantly lobbied to have Stewart removed from the show. Yet they lasted together until 1955, when Horn and the show's producer, Tony Mam-2a-rella, finally convinced WFIL brass to drop the team format.

During that time, Horn himself had formulated what millions of people would henceforth associate with his eventual replacement, Dick Clark. Dick remembers, "Horn was very arrogant and standoffish unless he thought you could be of use to him. He was not a particularly pleasant man to work with, and there was little love lost between him and everyone else at the station. But as a professional TV man he had a unique sense of what was going on that nobody else really had at the time. It's funny that most people think of *Bandstand* as being synonymous with rock 'n' roll, because for the first few years it was on the air, there really *was* no rock 'n' roll music yet. If you look back through the old program logs of the show, you find that the first real case of rock 'n' roll on the show came in late 1954, when Bill Haley and the Comets appeared. But up until then, it was sweet pop music: Peggy Lee, Patti Page, Nat King Cole, Frankie Laine—the kind of stuff rock 'n' roll supposedly rebelled *against*."

But, as Dick Clark goes on to explain, Horn not only had devised a reliable format—he also had his nose in the air and readily sniffed the winds of change that were a-blowing:

"Horn knew he'd struck gold with the kids, so he went with his instincts based on their reactions. He knew about the waves that dee-

jays like Alan Freed were making by playing rhythm and blues music for young audiences, so Horn quickly began programming more rhythm-oriented music. Horn also invented Rate-a-Record, and he instituted the idea of the guest stars coming on to lip-synch as an on-air promotion. As personally unpleasant as he may have been, it was he who came up with the format that influenced my own life and career forever. Who knows where I'd be without him and *Bandstand*?"

Dick Clark had found his way to WFIL the same year that *Bandstand* premiered. He'd first gotten interested in radio as a fan of Arthur Godfrey and other talk-show deejays while a

A publicity composite.

sophomore in Mount Vernon High School in New York. The year was 1944, and Clark was fifteen years old. He landed odd jobs at radio stations around New York State. At Syracuse University he majored in advertising, minored in radio, and worked at the student radio station. In his senior year he worked at WOLF radio in Syracuse, starting as a weekend relief announcer; within a month he was on full-time and had his own country music show until his graduation in 1951. He landed a job as a summer replacement announcer at WRUN in Utica, where his father was station manager; to avoid charges of nepotism, he changed his on-air name to Dick Clay. He then wrote TV commercials, moved scenery, and hosted a country music show as Cactus Dick on Utica's only TV station, WKTV, which was located on a mountaintop (''We'd freeze our asses off getting up there in the

winter,'' Dick recalled in his autobiography, *Rock, Roll and Remember*).

Dick then got two offers: one to do TV in Schenectady, New York, and one to do radio at WFIL in Philadelphia. Though he was dying to get right into TV, he went instead with the bigger market and held out hope. By 1952 he was doing station IDs, commercials, and news for WFIL-AM; then he got his own show, ''Dick Clark's Caravan of Stars,'' spinning pop records. He also did an occasional TV commercial, and in order to get more exposure, he commuted to New York to sell Schaefer beer on a wrestling show—until company owner Rudy Schaefer himself saw Clark on TV one night and roared, ''Get him off, he's too young to drink beer!'' Dick Clark's legendary clean-cut, guy-next-door image was already established.

In the fall of 1953, the name of Dick's radio show was changed to ''Bandstand'' to identify

Fire Prevention Week on *American Bandstand*.

with Horn's successful TV show. Horn would pop in from Studio B every afternoon to do the opening and closing of the show, then announce that he had to get to the TV *Bandstand* and would leave Clark to do the rest of "his" radio show. This situation failed to endear either man to the other.

In late 1955, while Horn was on vacation, Tony Mammarella (who usually stood in for Horn) couldn't make it one day. Dick Clark stepped in as substitute host of the TV *Bandstand* for the first time.

Then fate stepped in and nudged musical-television history on its way to being made. Right after his substitute host spot on *Bandstand*, Dick Clark called a Cleveland station and offered his services for a proposed similar show. The Cleveland station manager rudely told Clark he was not interested. Soon afterward, in the spring of 1956, Bob Horn's career screeched to a halt. He was arrested for driving while intoxicated—in the midst of an anti-drunk driving campaign by WFIL's owner, the *Philadelphia Inquirer*. Horn was, of course, fired immediately.

Station executives may have been breathing secret sighs of relief at the trouble Horn had gotten himself into; now, they wouldn't have to suffer his arrogance, and they could try to find someone younger and better looking, someone who might relate to the kids in a more genuine and less stilted fashion. But the sighs of relief soon gave way to consternation: Who would replace Horn as host of their hottest show?

In an arrangement that all concerned knew would be only temporary, Tony Mammarella —who knew the show and the kids and was a personable man—acted as *Bandstand* host for a few months. In July 1956, Dick Clark was given the job. His first official day as regular *Bandstand* host was Monday, July 9, 1956. The number-one tune on the Teenage Top Ten that day was "Stranded in the Jungle" by the Jayhawks, an indication that rock 'n' roll music had already come to stay, and had found a

home on *Bandstand*.

At first Dick Clark was not really at home with this new, big-beat sound. As he wrote in *Rock, Roll and Remember*: "I really didn't understand the music Horn played on *Bandstand*." But Clark brought more to the show than his unflappable, low-key delivery: he brought an open mind. As he went on to write in *Rock, Roll and Remember*: "The more I heard the music, the more I enjoyed it; the more I enjoyed it, the more I understood the kids."

Those may seem like rather unremarkable words now, but one has to realize that back then, rock 'n' roll had already been denigrated far and wide as the devil's music, a scourge on our nation's youth. For someone like Dick Clark to react to it the way he did was little less than remarkable. But that open-mindedness, that unforced naturalness, that genuine sincerity, is the special magic which, along with his All-American good looks and down-to-earth demeanor, enabled him to become America's Oldest Living Teenager. In his new position, Dick Clark simply did what came naturally. And the rest, as they say, is history.

While we're on the subject of remarkable —even courageous—open-mindedness back in those days, *Bandstand*'s audience was racially integrated the same year the show went network. Dick Clark insisted on it, and Tony Mammarella joined him in pressing WFIL's management to let them have their way. As Dick Clark explains it, "Look, it was just too painfully obvious that rock 'n' roll—and by extension *Bandstand*—owed its very existence to black people, their culture and their music. It would have been ridiculous, embarrassing *not* to integrate the show." And this was at a time when issues like racism and segregation were not even discussed publicly. They were practiced —not questioned or argued with. This was at a time when the powerful and pioneering rock 'n' roll deejay Alan Freed had his own New York–based, *Bandstand*-style TV show promptly canceled when the cameras caught Frankie

Lymon dancing with a white girl.

Bill Russell was lighting director on *Bandstand* back then. He still works for the same Philadelphia station today; WFIL has since become WPVI-TV. Russell recalls that "when the station had gotten this tarnished image with all the Bob Horn business and decided to go after a new image, Dick fit the image they wanted. He *was* that image: the clean-cut, all-American guy next door. From what I could see, that really *was* Dick Clark. The other remarkable thing about him, though, was that as a worker he was a perfectionist. He made very high demands on himself, and he expected the same of everyone else. I've heard some people say that he's a hard man to work with or work for because of that, and it can be intimidating if you're not prepared for it. But if you know what you're doing, you'll be fine. I never had a problem working with him, either personally or professionally. I've only seen one other person in all my years in TV who was as good as Dick as far as having that sheer gut instinct for everything that was going on in a studio, and believe it or not that was Joan Crawford. Dick was uncanny. He could be up there doing whatever he had to do and if, for instance, he knew that in a couple of minutes he'd have to speak into another camera, and if as often happened the kids' jostling for camera position kept the camera from getting to its mark at the proper time, Dick could instinctively ad lib right on the spot just the right amount of time until the camera got there. Ask anyone who works on a TV crew: that's magic. It just makes everyone's job so much easier. And he was always amazing doing sponsor spots. But then it wasn't till later that I found out about his little trick with the tape machine."

Dick Clark's "little trick" was something he'd learned back at WKTV in Utica from Bob Earle,

Doing the Cha-lypso c. 1958.

The kids get together for a snowball fight outside the studio on a snowy day.

then the station's newscaster and later host of the popular TV show "GE College Bowl." Earle had a tape machine he named Elmer, which he'd place on the floor behind his news desk. He'd tape the evening's news before going on the air, then run an earplug from Elmer up his pant leg, under his jacket, and up the back of his neck to his ear. He would then simply recite the news as he heard it, without batting an eyelash! While that is a clever trick, one should try it oneself and see how difficult it really is in order to properly respect Clark's ability to make use of the ploy.

Joanne Montecarlo was one of several regular dancers on *Bandstand* who made the transition from the Bob Horn days to the Dick Clark era. She comments on the difference between the two as hosts:

"They were as different as night and day to me. I'd been going to *Bandstand* regularly with my sister Carmen when Bob Horn was host. My father was very strict, and he always gave me a hard time about going to the show. Then when all that business happened to Bob Horn, my father forbade me from going back again. A

few months later Tony Mammarella called my house, and told my father that they were getting this new host who was a clean-cut family man, Dick Clark, blah-blah-blah. Well, between Tony and my mother, my father was finally convinced. Carmen and I went back to the show on Dick's first day as host. I remember coming back home afterward and expecting the usual treatment from my father, but he said nothing at all. I thought something else *really* terrible must have happened. When I finally got up the courage to ask, he just shrugged and said, 'Oh, that Clark fellow seems okay, I guess' —which, for my father, was like bestowing sainthood! But it fit: Dick was, to me, a perfect balance between being personable and remaining professional at the same time. He was always nice and respectful to everyone on the show, but he was never *too* nice. He never favored anyone over anyone else—he always treated everyone very fairly as far as I could tell. Part of the problem with Bob Horn was that he was not a very attractive or young-looking man to be hosting such a show, so Dick had him beat there. Bob Horn also had a half dozen or so of his own handpicked regulars whom he favored, when in fact there were twenty or thirty kids going to the show regularly, and he just ignored everyone else. Dick, on the other hand, personalized the show somehow. I remember him always standing at the studio door after the show, telling us all to get home safely. That was very nice, and something he certainly didn't *have* to do. But that was just the way he was. He seemed to take a genuine interest. And he never talked down to us. You always felt he was on your level without forcing the issue."

Adds Betty Romantini, another regular dancer in those early years: "That same sort of nice, down-to-earth demeanor Dick had on camera was the same way he was off camera. When he was around, you just felt everything was in control. He set a good example, and everyone else just followed it. He always maintained his cool, his professionalism, yet at the same time

Dick Clark chatting on the ever-present telephone while the action continued on the dance floor.

he was always as personable as he seemed on air. He rarely got flustered or upset. In fact, the only time I remember him getting upset was once when someone was guesting on the show and as they sang, some kid up in the bleachers —who, thank God, was not a regular—threw a penny at the stage. Dick saw it happen and knew where it had been thrown from, but he waited until a station break. Then he climbed up in the bleachers. A deadly silence filled the whole studio. Dick was just *livid*. But all he said to that poor kid—who must have been wetting his pants!—was 'How *dare* you do something like that to someone who is serious about what they are doing.' I'll never forget that—the one time I saw Dick Clark even come close to losing his cool.''

Despite all these pluses, Dick Clark did have one other obstacle to surmount on his very first day as *Bandstand* host. There were several kids who'd been regulars under Bob Horn on the show, and they resented the change in hosts. They and their friends picketed outside Studio B with placards that read ''Bring Back Bob!'' and ''No Bandstand Without Bob Horn'' and ''Dick Clark Go Home!'' Dick handled the situation in his customary fashion, with professional directness and personal sincerity. He went outside and spoke to the kids in the street, explaining that the change in hosts had not been his idea but a simple matter of circumstances. He expressed the hope that the kids wouldn't hold it against him personally. Receiving no reply, he shrugged and said, ''Look, I have a job to do. I'm going back in the studio to do the show. You're all welcome to come in, too, if you like." He went back in the studio, somewhat shaken and uncertain, until he reached his podium and turned around—and saw the protesters entering the studio, depositing their placards by the door.

Dick Clark was already well on his way to becoming Philadelphia's Oldest Teenager. Now all that needed to happen for the story to be complete was for the show to go network, so the rest of America could see what had Philadelphia so excited.

John Oates was one youth excited by *Bandstand* (both before and during Dick Clark) while he was growing up in a Philadelphia suburb in the fifties. Now, of course, he's half of Hall and Oates, the enormously successful duo who are easily the biggest rock act ever to come out of the Philadelphia area. He remembers vividly the role *Bandstand* played in his life:

"I go back to the Bob Horn days with *Bandstand*, which is giving away my age, but . . . without hesitation, I would say that the show had a very, very, *very* big influence on my life. I mean, that show had such an impact on the music business, it set the tone and the pace for teenage style and attitude and everything else all across America. Did I come running home from school every day to catch it? Damn right. I'd check out the music, and the kids, their clothes, their moves, learn some dances. . . . Everybody knew the kids. The regulars were like, to us, a gang of pals that you met every day in a certain place. It just so happened that the place was TV.

"I remember the holiday shows, like at Christmas, when they'd take the show out to the ice rink at Drexelbrook Country Club outside Philly, or they'd dress up the studio to look like a ski lodge with all the trimmings, and a big table with eggnog and punch bowls. In fact, our 'Jingle Bell Rock' video was sort of a tribute to that era—*Bandstand* used to play 'Jingle Bell Rock' every Christmas, without fail. And I remember seeing guys like Fats Domino and Chuck Berry and Jerry Lee Lewis on *Bandstand*, and just . . . not knowing what to *do* with myself in my little living room. I remember the autograph table they had. There was this one guy, I wish I could remember exactly who it was, but I'll never forget how amazed I was at how fast this guy was able to sign his autograph. And now I know why!

"You know, it's funny, but as little kids growing up in the sticks outside Philadelphia, Daryl and I never even tried to go to Philly and get into the studio to be on the show. We were just too far out of town, and we knew that by the time we got in the lines'd be around the block, forget it. That's why they had the same regulars on the show, because those kids happened to go to the schools, like West Catholic High or whatever, that were located right near the studio in South Philly. I remember once all of us in school were really excited because these two guys had cut class so they could catch the train to Philadelphia to be on *Bandstand*, and we all ran home that day to turn on the show and see if they were there or not, and there they were! It was *tremendous*! But they caught hell in school the next day, and school officials got tougher on us because of it, so nobody else dared to try it.

"But now that Daryl and I have been on the show as *performers*, well you can just imagine the kind of satisfaction and fulfillment that gives us. We still watch the show whenever we get a chance. 'n fact, lately I've been thinking that maybe music is going back in a way to what it was like in the glory days of *Bandstand*. In those pre-Beatle sixties, rock 'n' roll and dancing really went hand in hand, and I think we lost some of that as the sixties went on, and totally lost it in the seventies. I feel that now we're getting back to it. To *me* it's *always* been that way, with rock and dancing. I never lost that feeling, and I'm sure *Bandstand* has a lot to do with that."

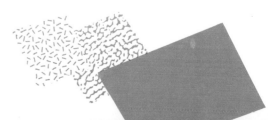

With Dick Clark at the helm, *Bandstand*'s ratings climbed even higher. For the first time, the show's regular teenage dancers—including Joanne and Carmen Montecarlo, Betty Romantini, Joe Fusco, Frankie Lobis, and Justine Carrelli—began getting fan mail from local viewers in the Pennsylvania/Delaware/southern New Jersey area. And lines began forming regularly outside Studio B, even on days when it was *not* known that a big-name star would be on the show. The letters came in a trickle and the lines weren't long, but they were a start. Dick Clark and Tony Mammarella knew they were on to something, and they began trying to sell the ABC television network on the idea of picking up the show nationally. At the time, there were already many local popular music-and-dance shows, many of them not unlike *Bandstand*, scattered around the country. But there was nothing like it on network TV. The only thing that came close was the long-running "Your Hit

Parade," a cavalcade-of-hits show with a cast of house singers doing renditions of popular tunes. But "Your Hit Parade" steered clear of rock 'n' roll and the rhythm and blues that had already become staples of the *Bandstand* playlist. The show's deceptively simple format, coupled with the older generation's suspicions of rock 'n' roll music, made it harder on Clark and Mammarella than they expected.

"I remember Dick," says Bill Russell, "peddling himself back and forth between Philadelphia and New York with a kinescope of the show under his arm. That's how ABC finally bought it. He just wouldn't give up. He believed in it, more than anyone else did. He persuaded them to give it a shot and of course nobody expected the darn thing to do anything. They asked me what chances I gave it on the network and I said, 'Oh, I think it might last a few weeks.' Just goes to show you how reliable *I* am for predictions!"

AMERICAN
BANDSTAND

After several months of such gambits —months in which more and more of the rock 'n' roll records *Bandstand* played became smash hits and the first recordings to cross over to each of the then-segregated popular, rhythm-and-blues, and country-and-Western charts at the same time—ABC finally bit. They made their decision in the summer of 1957, and on Monday, August 5, *Bandstand* became *American Bandstand* and was telecast on sixty-seven stations coast to coast.

Just as the local *Bandstand* had been, *American Bandstand* was broadcast Monday through Friday in the afternoon. But where the local *Bandstand* lasted two and a half hours, from 2:30 to 5:00 P.M., *American Bandstand* was seen only from 3:00 to 4:30 P.M. nationally. Viewers in the show's original local audience noticed something else different about the show once it went national: ABC had sent some set designers down to Philadelphia to remake the look of the studio. Gone was the old record-store-interior backdrop, replaced by a tick-tack-toe-style grid that contained frames for about a dozen gold records. There was also a map of the American continent cut out of a piece of blue, glitter-spangled cardboard. At the start of the show, the camera would shoot the dancing kids packing the studio through the cut-out map, then pull back to reveal the entire map with the kids dancing inside. Then the show's title would be superimposed on-screen. Since Dick Clark found it awkward to have to keep introducing himself to the viewers at home at the start of the show, it wasn't long before Charlie O'Donnell was hired as announcer. Charlie stayed with the show as Dick's sidekick for more than a dozen years. The show did keep the same theme song—"Bandstand Boogie," written especially for it by Charles Albertine and arranged in swinging big band style by Les Elgart. (The local *Bandstand*'s theme had originally been "High Society" by Artie Shaw and his band.)

Here's how *TV Guide* described the new show: "Dick Clark is host of this new hour-and-a-half variety and audience-participation program. He introduces top vocalists and movie personalities who will sing their hit songs and perform their specialties on the program. There will also be dance contests for the audience."

All of which was accurate enough, but it soon turned out to be a major understatement. As far as introducing top singers and performers, well, *American Bandstand* had them all. Only the biggest of the biggies, Elvis Presley, failed to make an in-person appearance on the show in those years. Chuck Berry, Buddy Holly, Bill Haley and the Comets, Paul Anka, Neil Sedaka, Jerry Lee Lewis . . . you name an original rocker from those fabulous fifties, and they made it onto *Bandstand* at one time or another.

And as for the dance contests, well, *American Bandstand* had them by the dozens. In fact, the regulars with their dancing, their hairstyles and clothes, and even their relationships, became arguably more important to the viewing audience than even the music that was played and the performers presented on the show.

Justine Carrelli, a *Bandstand* regular from the Bob Horn days who was also there that first fateful network day (and who with her beau Bob Clayton made up *the* most popular of the show's many popular couples), chuckles as she recalls it: "That first network show had to be the first, last, and only time I can recall ever seeing Dick Clark acting the least bit nervous." In *Rock, Roll and Remember*, Dick described at length his horrible case of nerves, as well as the good-natured pranks the crew pulled to try and defuse his tension. None of their tricks worked. But something else happened midway through that first *American Bandstand* show that told Dick Clark "calm down—we're gonna make it."

Because the din of records being played in the studio was so loud—to ensure that kids could dance easily, and to improve the guest's lip-synchs—Dick Clark had a telephone on his podium that connected him to the control room at the back of the studio. Just after Dick had read the name of one affiliate station carrying the show from a map of the continent near his podium, Tony Mammarella called him on the podium phone. He told Dick that earlier he'd been caught on camera on that phone, and that a few minutes later WFIL had gotten a call from a viewer who wanted to talk to Dick Clark. The viewer was calling from St. Louis.

Of course, we know through hindsight that Dick Clark needn't have worried. In fact, a few days after the first nationwide telecast, ABC called to confirm their initial estimate that the show had a solid audience of some 20 million viewers nationwide. In all the years since, the show's ratings have never flagged from that high standard.

On September 28, 1957, *TV Guide* ran a feature article, the first of many through the years that have attempted to demystify the *American Bandstand* phenomenon. The story began by noting that "police in Carbondale, a small city in Pennsylvania, were puzzled when they found only a few teenagers on the streets and in play areas after school hours. Finally the chief checked with the high school principal on possible school activity. He found instead that many of the youngsters were attending *Bandstand* parties at home while watching TV's dance-party show originating from Philadelphia's WFIL-TV." Little did they realize at the time that such scenes were being played out across America every weekday afternoon.

The story pointed out that "Dick Clark, a handsome, 27-year-old hi-fi fan and the show's host since July, 1956, estimates he sees 300,000 teenagers annually with never a disciplinary problem." The article went on to mention the show's audience dress code—coats and ties for the guys, girls dressed "in modest good taste—no slacks, tight sweaters, or low-cut gowns." And it quoted Dick Clark on this subject: "'We don't try to preach to anybody, but we help to set a good example for the people watching at home.'" *TV Guide* also

mentioned the existence of "committee members," teenagers who regularly attended the show who "show the way" in "the matter of manners and attire" for all other teens attending the show. More on that "committee" later.

That first *TV Guide* feature concluded with Dick Clark himself explaining the show's mysterious popularity: "'*Bandstand* is about 90 per cent music and dancing. The folks at home get a bang out of watching the boys and girls have a good time. Everybody likes to watch young folks having fun. That's the secret of its success.'"

On October, 19, 1957, *TV Guide* reviewed *American Bandstand*. And while the article could have been more complimentary, perhaps, it was far from the typical hatchet job. It opened with guest performer Bobby Charles on a recent show telling Dick Clark:

"Man, the teenagers around the country eat you up. The deejays around the country tell me, 'Dick Clark has got us dead.'" Mr. Clark (possibly envisioning a nation littered with the corpses of his colleagues) muttered that he hoped this wasn't true. Embarrassment aside, there is evidence that Bobby Charles was simply calling a turn of events. *American Bandstand* is a 90-minute program of records, fan mail, chit-chat, and interviews . . . and, except that it lacks a commercial between every record, it is brewing for TV the same cup of tea that 'deejays'—the czars of the music industry —have been brewing for radio since the thirties.

As TV's first national disc jockey, Clark is handsome, youthful, glib, unruffled, and addicted to the professional weakness of playing whatever noise his audience wants to hear. He offers about 35 records per show, most of them the brassiest rock and roll that New York, Hollywood and Nashville can produce.

What distinguishes *Bandstand* as a TV program, however, is that Clark (or somebody at WFIL-TV) has come up with the answer for the question of what to watch while the records are spinning. During *Bandstand*, dozens of teenagers from the Eastern Seaboard jam the studio. They pair up and dance and, thanks to some camera work by director Ed Yates that would do credit to any TV spectacular, there isn't a one of those amateur and largely anonymous supporting players who isn't worth watching.

Clark makes no bones of the fact that *American Bandstand* is a sort of smorgasbord to which the viewer can turn for such samples as he has time or appetite for. "You housewives," he says on camera, "roll up the ironing board and join us when you can."

In 90 minutes you may catch sight of Patti Page furiously signing autographs, or of some high school girl on the sidelines reverently mouthing the lyrics of Patti's latest record. It would be hard to say which slice of modern life is more interesting.

Indeed, those last lines hit the nail right on the head. To most *Bandstand* viewers, the kids constituted *Bandstand*'s main attraction.

But before getting down to specifics, some more details on the show's history through the fifties. Within weeks of its national debut, the music-industry trade magazine *Billboard* was regularly running front-page stories on the show's success in breaking hit records and artists. Those same articles noted the scores of imitators of *Bandstand* springing up all over the country: Buddy Dean had one in Baltimore, Robin Seymour had "Detroit Bandstand," there was one in Santa Barbara. . . . this cloning, a natural function of television programming, would continue unabated through the sixties, with such off-the-wall imitators as "Clay Cole's Disk-o-tek" and "The Lloyd Thaxton Show." These two, with their more unstructured formats,

would find more favor later on with hard-line rock critics who were suspicious of *Bandstand*'s domesticated look and feel, but none of them had what it took to outlast the original. Even today, there are new-wave versions obviously based on the tried-and-true *Bandstand* formula.

There were also some programming changes wrought around, and even within, *Bandstand*'s unusually extended time slot. On November 18, 1957, Johnny Carson's game show "Do You Trust Your Wife?" (later "Who Do You Trust?") came on in the middle of *Bandstand* from 3:30 to 4:00 P.M., with *Bandstand* on from 3:00 to 3:30 and back again from 4:00 to 5:00. This bizarre arrangement lasted until October 13, 1958, when "Do You Trust Your Wife?" moved to 3:30, and "Beat the Clock," a game show hosted by Bud Collier, came on from 3:30 to 4:00. *Bandstand* was then on only from 4:00 to 5:00 P.M. This set-up stuck until early 1962, when *Bandstand* moved to a 4:30 starting time. But in those early days, ABC always had an unbeatable one-two afternoon punch, as *American Bandstand* led directly into "The Mickey Mouse Club." In those years, Dick Clark would always close out the show by saying, "The mouse is coming," and give his trademark little salute before signing off.

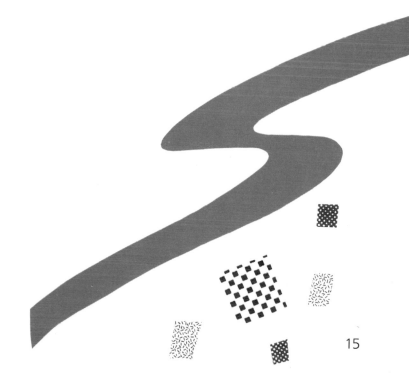

Dick Clark on the ukelele accompanying Annette Funicello and Paul Anka.

"I don't make culture. I sell it. I'm the storekeeper. The shelves are empty. I put the stock on. I make no comment pro or con."
—Dick Clark

Dick Clark meant it when he said that, so of course there is truth in his statement. But it doesn't really tell the whole story. Perhaps Dick wouldn't enjoy being saddled with such a lofty label, but to extend his metaphor, merely by stocking *Bandstand*'s shelves with the music and performers it featured, Dick Clark and *American Bandstand* have a singular, hallowed place of importance in the annals of rock 'n'

roll. This aspect of the show's history cannot be overemphasized. And if there is an axe to grind, it's the too-readily-accepted notion that *Bandstand* was an innocuous show that denatured rock 'n' roll with its dress and behavior codes and its institutionalizing of the lip-synch. Never mind that lip-synching was already a standard practice for convenience' sake before *Bandstand* ever went on the air, nor that lip-synching is still standard practice in all TV and film. (By the way, the only artist in the history of the show *not* to lip-synch was blues giant B.B. King, in the seventies; as producer Larry Klein put it, "He requested to play live. I looked at him and considered who he was, and *couldn't* tell him to lip-synch. So he performed live and it was great.") It's important to remember that *Bandstand* was the *first* network television show devoted to rock 'n' roll music and its attendant culture. As such, and especially considering its instant, mammoth popularity, the show played a key role in spreading the rock 'n' roll gospel to living rooms across America. Perhaps *Bandstand* did *domesticate* the music somewhat. But there's no rewriting the past, nor is there any argument over the fact that the show played a crucial role in popularizing the music. It's a fitting irony indeed that *Bandstand* started out as a primitive form of music videos, because their immense impact on the contemporary music business is the only phenomenon comparable to *Bandstand*'s effect on popular music, especially in its glory days of the fifties.

Such was the show's impact on music that, as Dick Clark recalls, "Al Martino and other people would come on the show whenever they needed a hit." Over the long run, *Bandstand* has been taken for granted by many people, especially critics who would probably leap on a quote like the preceding one as further evi-

Bo Diddley, c. 1958.

dence of the show's familiarized more-pop-than-rock orientation. But any examination of the facts proves how wrong those critics are: The show has always been commendably eclectic and up-to-date, and, best of all, its selection of artists has always been basically color-blind and mindless of category, unless the category be music that is popular.

Witness the opening of that very first network show. Dick Clark smiled into the camera and said, "Hi, I'm Dick Clark. Welcome to *American Bandstand*. You and I have got an hour and a half to share together with some of my friends here, lots of good music, and our special guest stars. With us today is the 'I'm Gonna Sit Right Down and Write Myself a Letter' man, Billy Williams. The Chordettes will be here too. Right now, let's do a whole lotta shakin' with Jerry Lee Lewis."

And there you had it: The first record spun on the first network installment of *American Bandstand* was none other than Jerry Lee Lewis's immortal barn-burner "Whole Lotta Shakin' Goin' On." Those first two guest stars were also indicative of the way the show unassumingly mirrored contemporary pop music tastes. Billy Williams was a moderately successful rhythm-and-blues singer of the fifties, but his mere presence on a national TV show was significant at the time. In those days, black performers got short shrift on network TV, especially in the afternoon hours, and R&B music fared even worse. The Chordettes, on the other hand, were a saccharine quartet of female singers

(left to right) Pat Boone, Sal Mineo, and Bobby Darin on their way into the studio, 1958.

whose recordings were pop, certainly not rock, except perhaps by association. Even then the connection was tenuous and forced. But in those naïve days, the Chordettes represented the old guard, the sweet music that was featured in the local *Bandstand*'s earliest, pre–rock 'n' roll days. And while such music may have been under a mounting attack from rhythm and blues and rock 'n' roll, it was still vastly popular, even with younger listeners. The explanation? Simple: it all sounded good to the kids, and the rock 'n' roll audience was still a good ten years or so away from the self-consciousness that might have told them to sneer at such "white bread" pop.

But the fact remains that when rock 'n' roll came along, *Bandstand* was there to present it to a willing audience of millions. And if the

Dick Clark with Polly Bergen.

17

THE MUSIC

Connie Francis,
1958.

show did in fact domesticate the music a bit for mass consumption, well, that was the only way to get it across. Dick Clark explains:

"You know how long we fought to keep that music alive? How hard we fought? I mean, so many assassins . . . they wanted to kill rock 'n' roll. In 1959 there were the Congressional pay-ola hearings, which were a huge trumped-up witch-hunt, an excuse to try and kill this thing. The old licensing organizations, Congress, and that whole adult generation, they all despised rock 'n' roll. Hated the music. Hated the kids. I mean, if they saw you walking around with haircuts like they had back then, they'd try and lock you up. That's how bad it was. You know, the reason I wore a coat and tie and had the dress code for the kids was not because I'm such a big fan of coats and ties and dress codes and formal wear. *It helped us pass the music through as legitimate*. They saw the show and said, 'Gee, those kids look nice, and they're all dressed up. . . .' Those kids who came in the early days of *Bandstand*, they didn't come in a coat and tie. But we made them do that, and it was the greatest sleight of hand that ever happened. Because the adults looked in and said, 'Well, that guy who's doing that, he looks like a nice fellow, he looks harmless.' And that's how we slid it across in the Eisenhower period.''

Let's admit it: Dick Clark is a rock 'n' roll hero. He goes on to explain: ''The flip side, sort of, of that whole fifties attitude came in the sixties. With the British Invasion. I had my Caravan of Stars package tours, and I was booking those new British acts who were causing so much excitement. I'd go to the immigration office and say, 'I need some help getting these acts into the country—Herman's Hermits and the Animals.' And the lady at the immigration desk would look at me like I was a lunatic. But if I had said 'I need to get the Budapest String Quartet and the London Philharmonic over here,' then no problem, of course.''

Dick Clark and
Conway Twitty, c. 1959

Jerry Vale at
the autograph table.

19

THE MUSIC

Frankie Avalon
with Dick Clark,
1958.

Mary Ann
Mobley, then
Miss America,
dances with
a member
of the
audience.

The music that was featured—the thirty-five records spun per show and the two or three guest appearances per show—were all selected by Dick Clark and Tony Mammarella in the show's tiny, cramped office at WFIL. That office was barely big enough to hold three desks —one for Dick, one for Tony, and one for Dick's secretary, Marlene Teti—and the piles of records that promo men brought by the office every day of the week. Soon after the show went national, the office was further crammed with stuffed animals and other unsolicited gifts that viewers sent in by the score. Dick eventually had to hang all the stuffed animals from the office ceiling just so people could have room to move around in there.

Dick and Tony based their playlist, as well as their Teen Top Ten countdown board selections,

20

partly on what were being reported as the hottest records in the trades, partly on what they heard from the promo men and from other radio deejays, but mostly on whatever sounded to them like potential hits. It's truly amazing just how right their instincts usually were (as a close study of the appendices will indicate). Even more remarkable is that *Bandstand* frequently spun records and brought on guest stars weeks before their songs reached any national hit charts.

Here's Dick Clark from the January 9, 1958, *Bandstand*, introducing the Teen Top Ten countdown:

"It's a funny thing, but people who maybe don't follow music too closely will take a look at this thing and say, 'What is *that?*' Take this thing here, 'Get a Job,' they'll look at that and say, 'What are you talking about, what is this thing "Get a Job"?' Because we have it on here about *six weeks* before it gets on, you know—we won't mention any names—but before it gets on the big lists. And they'll say, 'You're out of your mind, whoever heard of a top tune like that?' Because it's about six weeks ahead of every other one. This is the reason why the *American Bandstand* Top Ten is six weeks ahead

of every other one, it's the authentic list, because you let us know through the mail, you write to us, we see about four hundred thousand people in person every year.... It's a pretty accurate thermometer, or pulse, of the music business. This is how we see them shaping up this week, and once again thank you for letting us know the records you like, because that's the fastest way of knowing what makes up the hit list. *American Bandstand*, P.O. Box 6, Philadelphia, 5. From the bottom to the top, this is how they shape up this day, January 9, 1958: at number 10, it's Mr. Pat Boone and his hit, 'April Love.' At 9, 'Get a Job' by the Silhouettes. The Chantels with 'Maybe' in at number 8, Roy Hamilton's 'Don't Let Go' number 7, number 6 Billie and Lillie with 'La Di Dah,' the Diamonds with 'The Stroll' at number 5, 4 is 'Raunchy' by Bill Justis, George Hamilton IV is 3 with 'Why Don't They Understand?', and up at number 2, Jerry Lee Lewis with 'Great Balls of Fire.' And here is today's number-one song"—canned strings swelled dramatically as Dick slid the flat cover out of its place over the name of the top teen tune and its performers—"'At the Hop,' Danny and the Juniors!"

There's a great story about Dick Clark and "At the Hop." It turns out that Dick Clark was personally responsible for saving that classic from near-certain oblivion and making it a surefire hit! Here's what happened: In the summer of 1957 two songwriters named Artie

Andy Williams, 1958.

Fabian, c. 1958, as seen by a fan who took this picture from the television screen.

Singer and Larry Brown came to Dick (as songwriters, producers, managers, and promo men were frequently wont to do). They had a song called "Doing the Bop," based on one of the latest fad dances popularized on *Bandstand*. They played it for Dick and asked him what he thought. He told them that the bop was almost over as a dance craze, and that by the time they recorded and released it, it would probably flop, which would be a shame because it had a great beat and fine music. As Singer and Brown grew dejected, Dick suggested they rewrite the lyrics to tell a story about what went on at a record hop. "You could even call it 'At the Hop,'" he told them. Dick then told them some stories about what he'd seen at the record hops he'd

hosted, and from these anecdotes Singer and Brown rewrote the lyrics. The rest, to repeat the cliché once more, is history.

If you ask Dick Clark what hit records were played or personally performed on *American Bandstand*, he'll instantly reply, "All of 'em." And if you ask him whether there was any particular *modus operandi* to that playlisting —for instance, whether it was ever a conscious move to balance one black rhythm-and-blues star with one white exponent of sweeter pop music—he'll tell you, "No, never. We just went with whoever was available that either had a hit, or was about to have a hit, and it was as simple as that."

So, when we look over the *Bandstand* guest roster, we can just chalk this incredible list up to luck, fate, and a killer instinct for what was hit-bound for the youth of America.

Even before 1957 was over, the show had hosted the following: 15-year-old Paul Anka with "Diana," his first hit and his first number one—it's worth noting that Anka was among the very first rock-generation performers—and probably the first white rock performer (Chuck Berry, at least, came before him)—to write as well as perform his own songs, an honor usually reserved by most revisionist rock critics for

Bobby Darin with Dick Clark.

Buddy Holly; rockabilly giant Gene Vincent with "Lotta Lovin'" and "Wear My Ring," both Top 40 hits; Jerry Lee Lewis with the classics "Whole Lotta Shakin'" and "Great Balls of Fire"; Buddy Holly and the Crickets with their first hit and only number-one record (believe it or not), "That'll Be the Day" (billed thus by *TV Guide* on Monday, August 26, 1957: "The Crickets, a vocal group, offer 'That Will Be the Day'"!); Johnny Nash with his first hit, "A Very Special Love"; Dale Hawkins with "Susie Q"; Jimmie Rodgers with his smash "Honeycomb"; country star Webb Pierce; the Everly Brothers in their network TV debut with their second hit and first number-one record, "Wake Up Little Susie"; The Rays with the doo-wop classic "Silhouettes";

Jackie Wilson, fresh from doo-wop/soul group the Dominoes, with his first solo hit, "Reet Petite (The Prettiest Girl You Ever Wanna Meet)," which was written by future Motown Records chief Berry Gordy, Jr.; Johnny Mathis, who was always frightened to death to be on the show yet who was perennially adored by the show's female audience members, with "Chances Are," one of his best-remembered smashes yet only his third hit; Thurston Harris with the thumping, oft-covered "Little Bitty Pretty One"; the Five Satins with "To the Aisle," the follow-up to their evergreen hit of 1956, "In the Still of the Night"; Carl Perkins, who had no chart hits in 1957, reprising his rockabilly classic "Blue Suede Shoes"; the Sparkletones with the nonsensical, sartorially slanted rockabilly gem "Black Slacks"; the one and only Chuck Berry with the incomparable "Rock and Roll Music"; Danny and the Juniors with "At the Hop," their first hit; Frankie Avalon with his first hit, "De De Dinah"; and pop crooner Jerry Vale with his third hit, "Pretend You Don't See Her."

Little Anthony, 1958.

Duane Eddy with Dick Clark, 1958.

Dick Clark interviews Fabian as he sits with the kids in the bleachers.

Remember: that's only in the five months from August through December 1957. *And* we forgot to mention that on the Friday, November 22, 1957, Thanksgiving show, the guests were a New York singing duo billed as Tom and Jerry—later to be known by their real names, Paul Simon and Art Garfunkel. They lip-synched their only hit as Tom and Jerry, ''Hey Schoolgirl,'' which reached number 49 on the charts just as 1957 turned into 1958.

Then there was the ''Philadelphia phenomenon.'' Starting in 1958, a batch of clean-cut, good-looking young white kids became hugely popular teen idols, largely through their frequent exposure on *Bandstand*. They included Frankie Avalon, Fabian (Forte), Bobby Rydell, Paul Anka, Bobby Darin, Connie Francis, Annette (Funicello), and Freddy Cannon. The ''Philadelphia phenomenon'' got its name partly because some of the teen idols came from the Philadelphia area (actually, only Avalon, Rydell, and Fabian did; Francis was from New Jersey,

Dick Clark chats with Johnny Mathis, 1957.

Darin from the Bronx, Cannon from Massachusetts, and Anka from Canada), and partly because some of them recorded for such Philadelphia-based record labels as Chancellor and Cameo-Parkway. But *Bandstand* was the main, most consistent connection here.

It's curious the way "serious" rock critics have always torn their hair out in trying to figure out why the teen idols caught on when audiences of the time, in their considered opinions, should have known better. After all, the teen idols came to fame in the late fifties, just as the first wave of "real" rock 'n' rollers seemed to have been vanquished—Elvis Presley joined the Army; Little Richard gave up rock for God; Jerry Lee Lewis married his own prepubescent cousin, causing a scandal that nearly ended his career; Buddy Holly died in a tragic plane crash; and Chuck Berry was jailed for an alleged violation of the Mann Act. The reign of the teen idols lasted until the British Invasion of 1964. Today, these rock critics inevitably dismiss the years 1958 to 1963 as fallow ones indeed for "real" rock 'n' roll, arguing that the teen

Dick Clark presenting a gold record to Tommy Edwards for "It's All in the Game," 1958.

idols' music was far safer, tailored more to adult tastes, and nowhere near as flamingly uninhibited and revolutionary as that of the first wave that preceded it.

But then, as Dick Clark himself has said, the critics are only a handful of people, who all too rarely reflect popular taste. *American Bandstand* was and always has been in the very business of reflecting popular taste; thus, it played a key and historic role in the advent of the teen idols. That meant that once more the show was an integral part of recent pop-cultural history. And that is that.

The current criticism of the teen idols also misses some facts. For one, it's unfair, really, to lump performers like Paul Anka and Bobby Darin in with the teen idols, since both obviously possessed enough talent and charisma to

Dick Clark interviews Jack Bailey, then host of the very popular "Queen for a Day" television game show.

Joni James, 1956.

have made it easily without any hype, even if they did happen to ride the crest of the teen-idol wave.

Furthermore, while it's true that the teen idols were all clean-cut and white and good-looking and altogether less threatening than those who preceded them, there was something fascinating about their appeal. They partook of a similar balancing act to *Bandstand*'s own seamless merger of consistent format and ever-changing content. The teen idols *were* white—but they were also heavily *ethnic*, specifically Italian. Thus, while ostensibly ''safe,'' they also had a particularly exotic appeal to Middle America. Frankie Avalon was born Francis Avallone. Bobby Rydell was born Robert Ridarelli. Bobby Darin was born Robert Walden Cassotto. Freddy Cannon was born Frederick Anthony Picariello. Connie Francis was born Conchetta Franconero. Fabian Forte and Annette Funicello dropped their ethnic surnames for mass consumption. By the same token, it's also true that most of the *Bandstand* ''regulars''

Dick Clark with Danny & the Juniors, 1958.

26

who became so phenomenally popular in the late fifties and early sixties were themselves of ethnic descent: think of the names—Justine Carrelli, Joanne Montecarlo, Betty Romantini, Carol Scaldeferri, Frani Giordano, Pat Molitierri, Frank Brancaccio, Joe Fusco, the three Beltrante sisters, Kenny Rossi. . . .

Finally, history has shown that the original teen idols were simply the first wave of a phenomenon that has continued to resurface in each succeeding decade. In the sixties, it was the Monkees; in the seventies, Shaun Cassidy; in the eighties, Duran Duran. All of them have been accused by rock critics of merely being pretty faces seriously lacking deep rock credentials, yet all of them have been embraced by the masses. Who's right? Does it matter?? Look back again at the quote from Dick Clark at the top of this section. And be reminded once more that *Bandstand*'s job is *not* music criticism, and that that is the way it should and must be.

The show's commendably unblinkered eclecticism cannot be overemphasized, especially here.

Even as *Bandstand* was giving the teen idols a big helping hand, it was also consistently featuring such performers as, say, Link Wray, the guitarist whose 1958 instrumental hit "Rumble" is popularly considered the first heavy-metal song ever (with its slow, heavy, low-down beat, heavily distorted guitar, and ominous feel), twang-guitar king Duane Eddy, Eddie Cochran, Little Willie John, Fats Domino, Johnny and the Hurricanes (along with Wray's Wraymen and Eddy's Rebel Rousers, one of the first purely instrumental rock combos), LaVern Baker, Ronnie Hawkins (the Canadian whose backup group the Hawks would later become the Band), the Clovers, the Platters, the Coasters, the Drifters. . . the list, like the beat, goes on and on. Just check out the appendix of chart tunes performed on the show to be amazed by the completeness and range of *Bandstand*'s hit list. There was far more happening than just the teen idols, and *Bandstand* covered the entire spectrum admirably.

Fabian, who was reputedly discovered by Bob

The Fontaine Sisters perform on a New Year's Eve show, 1957.

Marcucci of Chancellor Records sitting on his South Philly doorstep, recalls those days:

"It all started for me back in Dick Clark's office when I was brought in to meet him. He heard a record of mine, one of my very first ones—maybe it was 'I'm in Love' or 'Really Blue,' I don't remember for sure. Those were my first records, and they were all flops. Now I don't know exactly what Dick thought of those records, but he did pass judgment on me, and the upshot was that he made arrangements for me to be on the show. That's where it all started for me. I was really a literal nothing until I was on *Bandstand*. Without that exposure I never would or could have gone on to anything else.

"I'd been watching the show at home whenever I could, but that wasn't too often. Usually, I had to work, so I could never think about going on the show as a dancer or a regular or anything. Which is why, when I did go on the show, it was in the capacity of working, to help my career. Which it certainly did. It started my career off and really, really helped to make it. It would not have happened without Dick Clark and *American Bandstand*, and you can quote me on that.

"It was always incredible to be on that show. I mean the first time I was on the response was *immediate*, like the next *day* as far as calls and record sales and all. Every time I was on we'd start selling a lot more records the very next day, like clockwork.

"It got pretty crazy in that little studio sometimes. The kids were great, especially the regulars, but sometimes...well, I remember once they brought me *and* Frankie Avalon in at the height of our popularity, and the place just went nuts. They had to hide us away and then take us out the back door, and we still ended up having the police come down to clear things up. The kids just went crazy, I really thought I was going to get hurt. Frankie and I barely got to our cars in one piece.

"Through it all, Dick Clark was a very comforting, understanding presence—almost paternal, even though he really wasn't that

much older than me. But he knew what he was doing so well—he never made a big deal of anything or got too excited—just having him there made everything a lot saner. There'd be all this chaos in the studio, but he'd be calm like the eye of the hurricane at the center of it all, and it all seemed somehow under control. Whether it really *was* or not I can't say. He had a very calming effect on me in particular, as I recall."

Frankie Avalon won't forget those days, either:

"*Bandstand* was an incredibly important part of my career in so many ways. It represented so many millions; virtually the whole record-buying public would see you in one shot. The response from a single appearance on that show was so amazing, so fast, so extensive, it was incredible.

"Dick Clark ran a tight ship. People thought I got on *Bandstand* just because I was a kid from Philadelphia. But I had made several records

Young Johnny Crawford demonstrates a few Western rope tricks for Dick and the audience.

that flopped, that didn't get me on the show, before I finally did make it. You had to make a chart somewhere, or get a letter of request for whatever reason, to be eligible to get on the show. They didn't want to just plug ringers. They were for *real*, and up to a certain point, I wasn't. It wasn't until 'De De Dinah' that I got on the show, really. After one shot on the show doing that song, fan mail came to the station for me by the thousands within a week.

"After my third appearance on the show, I couldn't just walk in the studio door anymore. I had to have a police escort. It was *bedlam* in there—after a while I couldn't even sit down at the autograph table anymore. They'd have me escorted right in and right out by the police just before and just after my performance. It was

Ronnie Burns (son of George and Gracie) spends a little time in the bleachers.

The legendary Bill Haley & the Comets, 1957.

always so nuts inside that little studio, it all just blurs in my memory into total teenage madness.

"The most important thing was learning to lip-synch. It's not as easy as it looks. The hardest thing is not to lose your composure and poise and feel foolish. *Bandstand* was fantastic in training me that way. When I got to Hollywood and had to lip-synch in all those beach movies, they couldn't believe how easily I worked. That's another way that *Bandstand* helped my career that most people probably don't realize—being on camera before a live audience."

It seems that Connie Francis has the fondest memories of all. "One day, with the flick of a switch, I became a star," she recalls. "The day started off like any other New Year's Day I can ever remember . . . but it would prove to be unlike all the rest.

"Precisely at 4 P.M. on January 1, 1958, I excused myself from the dinner table. Like 8.5 million other loyal teenagers, I turned on our sixteen-inch black and white Motorola TV set to ABC's *American Bandstand*, and its host and my idol, Dick Clark. *American Bandstand* had become a way of life for most of us. It literally changed the face of the American popular music scene, and Mr. Clark's young Philadelphians, the kids who danced on the show, set all the trends.

"I heard Dick Clark mention something about a new girl singer. 'So what else is new?' I thought, 'another girl singer. Ninety-seven million females in the country, and ninety-five percent of them sing songs.' 'There's no doubt about it,' predicted Mr. Clark, 'she's headed straight for the number one spot.' I began feeling sorry for myself, and envious too. 'Good luck to her,' I thought.

"And then Mr. Clark just happened to play a song called 'Who's Sorry Now?' MY 'Who's Sorry Now?' Well, the feeling was cosmic, just cosmic! Right there in my own living room it became Mardi Gras time, kickoff at the Superbowl! The ruckus I raised was startling enough to tear thirty-odd ravenous Italians away from their mountainous portions of manicotti, and everyone knows that's no mean feat.

"We all have milestones in our lives, and more often than not we realize them only in retrospect. This milestone wasn't like that at all, because I recognized it in five seconds flat! I shall always consider Dick Clark my creator, my mentor, and certainly the single most important influence on my career and therefore my life. If my friend Dick Clark hadn't happened along, there simply would have been no career."

"In my show right now," says Connie in 1985, just before she embarks on an American tour, "I do my hits the way I've never done them before. Right after the start of the show, I go offstage and change into a fifties poodle skirt with initials on it; while I'm changing, a huge video screen is lowered over the stage. As footage from *American Bandstand* plays on the screen, I begin singing:

There was a party, and there were millions of teens,
Who gathered daily in front of black and
*   white screens,*
To do the lindy, along with Bob and Justine,
Oh, that was Bandstand.
Fabe and Frankie, they made the girls go insane,
And it was groovy, to wear a ring on a chain,

Those special feelings, that only songs can explain,
On Bandstand.
How lives can turn on one little spin,
It was New Year's Day, I watched it begin,
The day Dick Clark changed my life in a minute,
On Bandstand . . . .

"Of course, that's sung to the *Bandstand* theme, and on the screen is the footage showing Dick Clark introducing my record for the first time, with a title over it reading 'January 1, 1958.' It's a very poignant moment.

"Dick Clark is a unique human being. Probably the most hardworking person in the world. One of his secrets is that he treats everybody exactly the same way, with the same deference and respect. In the end I have to say that I have never met anyone else like Dick Clark in my life, and in this business I have never had a better friend."

On the December 16, 1957, *Bandstand*, Bobby Darin chatted with Dick Clark after singing "Don't Call My Name," a record that failed to chart for him (he wouldn't have his first hit, "Splish Splash," until June 1958). Darin expressed similar feelings of amazement and gratitude to Dick and the show, but he did it even as the teen-idol phenomenon was just beginning to happen:

BOBBY DARIN: How you feel, Dick?
DICK CLARK: Jim-dandy!
BD: I haven't had the chance to see you since the show went network. I wanna congratulate you on a really great thing: you have no idea—you probably do by now—of what's been happening all across this country. Every city I've visited throughout the land, you know they said the best show on television in the afternoon, by far, is Dick Clark's *American Bandstand*.
DC (*laughs*): Give that man a gold star, would you please?
BD: It's the truth man, it really is.

And it really was.

Arlene Sullivan and partner as seen by a fan at home.

Dick Clark and Tony Mammarella had to be sure that, rain or shine, they would have at least a certain number of kids in the studio for *American Bandstand*. So just as the show was going network, they instituted the Committee, whereby certain "regular" attendants of the show were given certified status with membership cards. They had to abide by certain rules: there was the dress code and the age limitation—

no younger than fourteen, no older than eighteen. But there were also benefits: Committee members got to go to the head of the long lines of kids waiting to get into the studio, flash their membership cards or show their familiar faces, and walk in ahead of everyone else.

Dick and Tony needn't have bothered, really. From the moment the show went national, there were long lines down the block outside WFIL's Studio B. Hundreds of kids, mostly from the Eastern Seaboard but some from as far away as Cleveland or Minneapolis, waited patiently for their chance to get into the show of their dreams. By the same token, being a Committee member rapidly evolved from being something of a job into being a blessed member of an elite society. Those regulars always got much more fan mail than any of the performers who appeared on the show. As the aforementioned *TV Guide* review noted, viewers found those regular kids every bit as appealing, if not more so, than the stars they'd ostensibly tuned in to watch.

Sorting their mail (center to right): Justine Carrelli, Little Ro, and Arlene Sullivan.

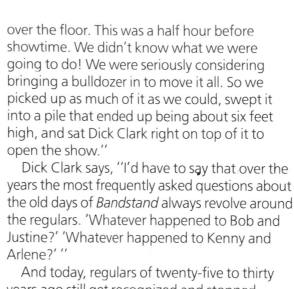

over the floor. This was a half hour before showtime. We didn't know what we were going to do! We were seriously considering bringing a bulldozer in to move it all. So we picked up as much of it as we could, swept it into a pile that ended up being about six feet high, and sat Dick Clark right on top of it to open the show."

Dick Clark says, "I'd have to say that over the years the most frequently asked questions about the old days of *Bandstand* always revolve around the regulars. 'Whatever happened to Bob and Justine?' 'Whatever happened to Kenny and Arlene?' "

And today, regulars of twenty-five to thirty years ago still get recognized and stopped frequently for autographs. Says Bill Cook: "It kills me. Won't people *ever* forget? I was on a cruise to Rio a couple of years ago, and this woman comes up to me and says 'Aren't you Billy Cook from *American Bandstand*?' " Adds Joanne Montecarlo, "It's really something the

Within a few months of the show's network debut, the mail was coming in for the regulars at the rate of 15,000 letters a week. That's right, 15,000 letters a week. And not only letters—there were all sorts of unsolicited gifts, ranging from toys, stuffed animals, and cookies to clothing, jewelry, and watches. If, say, Kenny Rossi or Billy Cook happened to be speaking with Dick Clark during a typical *Bandstand* roll call and happened to mention that he liked tie clasps or cuff links, by the following week thousands of tie clasps and cuff links poured in through the mail.

"One time," says Bill Russell, "someone got the bright idea to bring out a week's worth of mail and show our viewers what we were getting. But the instructions got messed up, and instead of just bringing out the *bags* of mail, they dumped the mail *out* of the bags all

Dick Clark chats with Kenny Rossi.

Carmen Jimenez (third from left) and friends bob for apples.

way that show follows you around. I work at Bamberger's and I have these kids that work for me and their parents used to watch me on *Bandstand*, and I mean it just follows you all your life. These kids keep coming up to me and saying 'My mom remembers you from *Bandstand*.' And then customers come in and *they* look at me and they go 'Aren't you . . .?' It really amazes me.'' And Justine Carrelli laughs, ''All over the country today, wherever I go, people still recognize me and say, 'Didn't you used to be, um, Justine, on *American Bandstand*?' I always reply, 'Used to be? I still *am!*' ''

Bob Clayton and Justine Carrelli were probably the single most popular couple in the show's history. Bob was tall, blond, ruggedly handsome. Justine was a petite, vivacious platinum blonde. On *Bandstand*, they became America's sweethearts.

Justine recalls how it all started:

''One day when I was about twelve, twelve and a half years old, I was just hanging out at Tilden Junior High School in Philadelphia with the older girls I always tried to pal around with. I was a skinny, scrawny little thing, but kinda cute I guess, and popular for whatever reason. The better-built girls were always getting their shots in at me. So one day these girls were saying how they'd just been to *Bandstand*, and why

didn't *I* tag along one time? It was like Cinderella with her three stepsisters. They didn't really think I'd come along, or that if I did I'd ever get in. Now, this was while the show was still local, and Dick Clark was just starting as the host.

''So I prepared myself, got the nicest stockings,

Betty Romantini, Tanya Kreizman, and Linda Marks. (left to right)

Ronnie Verbit.

Carole Scaldeferri as seen by a fan.

all the way home and when I got there I cried to my mother that I'd be a laughingstock at school from now on. So my mom said, 'Now, now, we'll think of something. . . .I've got it: Why don't you go back and take your older sister Mary's birth certificate!' So I did—and I got in! I must have been fourteen for about two years on that show. I don't even think Dick Clark ever knew that!

"Joanne Montecarlo was one of the hottest regulars on the show back then. I took my cues on dressing and dancing and all from kids like her. I grew up on that show, really. I was already becoming a pretty big regular on the show myself when Bob Clayton came along. He came to the show specifically to meet me, you know."

Indeed he did. Bob watched the show in his home, in Wilmington, Delaware. It was the summer of 1956. Bob recalls:

"At the time, Wilmington had its own *Bandstand*-type show, with Joe Grady and Ed

did my hair up, put on all the heavy duty makeup to make myself look as old as possible. And when we got to the studio there was a *big* line outside. I finally got to the door and this guy there, Bob the Cop we all called him, turned me away. I didn't look fourteen. I cried

Bandstand's most famous couple: Justine Carrelli and Bob Clayton.

Justine Carrelli and partner on TV.

can she dance.' So I went to the studio the very next day and I managed to get in and I was being very cocky, I went right up to her and said, 'Before this summer's over, you're gonna be my girl.' I stopped going to Grady and Hurst from that day on, I became a *Bandstand* regular, and sure enough we *were* going out by the end of that summer. And then when *Bandstand* went national it all just exploded. We became national TV stars, for no other reason than that we happened to be in the right place at the right time. It was wild. I remember one time Justine said on one show how she loved tiaras. The next week someone sent her a *diamond* tiara in the mail! It was just unbelievable, how intense the viewers were with the regulars.

Hurst, and I used to dance on that. Then one day I came home and turned on the TV and watched *Bandstand* and saw Justine there, and I didn't want to do anything but go there and dance with her. I was a fanatic about dancing in those days, and something about the way she looked and the way she moved really caught my eye. I just sat there and thought, 'Gee, God,

''I lucked out in school. I had a two thirty to three study hall for four years in a row, so I'd always get out early, cut out of Wilmington about two thirty and haul ass in my car to the studio. I'd always make it there in record time,

Another famous couple: Arlene Sullivan and Kenny Rossi.

by three or five after. At that time the road from Wilmington to the studio was two lane, one lane each way, and it was always full of these eighteen-wheeler trucks, and I'd be there zig-zagging in and out of all these trucks. Man I *moved*. I just had to get to that studio as quick as I could.

"It was just all about fun for us, pure fun. We were never looking to get famous or get fan mail or anything like that. That was all gravy on top of just going and dancing and having fun. I mean we'd dance for two and a half hours on that show, and then if we could we'd go back out later that night and dance some more. And on weekends? More dancing, of course! And when they started the dance contests on the show, that just intensified everything with the fans who watched us. Those dance contests were really more popularity contests than any-thing else. I mean we were all pretty good dancers and all, but who could say who was really better than anyone else? It just came down to popularity."

Kenny Rossi and Arlene Sullivan were the show's next most popular couple. Arlene tells her story.

Justine Carrelli.

The membership card (back and front) that a fan received upon joining the Bob Clayton Fan Club.

Bob Clayton Fan Club

Member _____

City _____

State _____

Club President _____

NATIONAL FAN CLUB   1204 S. BROAD STREET   PHILA. 46, PA.

"I used to sit at home with my mother and watch *Bandstand* back when it was local, before Dick Clark even came on. Then one day I met Justine Carrelli at a neighborhood party and she was talking about how she'd just begun going on the show herself. I said, 'Oh, I watch that show all the time. Do you think if I came down I could get in too?' She said, 'Sure, why not come down and try?' So I went down a few days later and I lucked into meeting her on Market Street, right there outside the studio. I got in because of her. She was already a regular, and even though there was a long line of kids waiting to get into the show, the regulars could always walk right up to the door and show their Committee card and get right in ahead of everyone else. Boy, was *that* a real status symbol!

"So I got onto the show, and I found that all the regulars were very very nice—they were very open to meeting new kids, when you would've thought they'd be kind of jealous or something about it all. The idea of going on the show was just that it was fun, and we loved to dance, and maybe it would make us a little cooler than some of the other kids in school. But I don't think any of us ever went into it with

our eyes open to what was going to happen.
None of us went to the show consciously thinking 'I'm gonna become a regular, and get lots
of fan mail, and I'm gonna be a *star*!' Nobody
could have expected that. I began getting a
little bit of fan mail after a month or so on the
show, and this was when it was still only local.

"Then, it must have been only a few weeks
after the show went national, I met Kenny Rossi
on the show. We met right there in the studio. I
think what attracted us to each other was the
fact that we looked so much alike. We were like
brother and sister. That hooked me a bit right
off, and then we found we got along together
and we danced well together, so it just went
from there. I was already a regular by then and
Kenny was new, so for a while I took him
around the studio and introduced him to everyone as my brother! It was actually a few
months before everyone found out we weren't
really related."

"Yeah, that's true," laughs Kenny Rossi, "we
did look alike. We both had that ethnic look,
dark wavy hair and all that. In fact, I think that's
an angle nobody's ever really explored about
the show's popularity back then. You had all
these regular kids dancing on the show, all
these Italian kids like me and Justine Carrelli and
Pat Molitierri . . .think about it. I think a lot of
people in the viewing audience had never really
been exposed to this kind of ethnic concept. It
was reinforced, I think, when the teen idols
came out and they were all Italian, too.

"Like many of the regulars, I went to West
Catholic High School, which was only a couple
of blocks away from the studio. So when I first
began hearing about *Bandstand*, it was no big
deal for me to go down and check it out. I liked
it right away. The second day I went, I met
Arlene. We ended up going out with each other
in real life, but that was after about six months.
Up to that time, I would dance slow dances
with Arlene, and fast dances with Pat Molitierri.
I just went there to dance, really. Everything else
happened later. I spent a year and two months

Three photos taken
by viewers from
their television
screens: Top: Frani
Giordano and partner
in a ladies' choice
dance. Center: Carole
Scaldeferri. Bottom:
Rosalie Beltrante
(Big Ro).

Dick Clark congratulates the winners of the Cha-lypso contest, 1957.

on the show from 1957 to 1958 and I got voted the most popular boy on the show. Arlene and I won a dance contest and we each got thousands and thousands of fan letters each week. We both had our own fan clubs, nationwide, as did a lot of the other regulars. I'd have my entire family—mom and dad and brothers and sisters and aunts and uncles and cousins—help out with answering the mail."

Bill Cook was another of the early regulars who lasted from the pre-network Bob Horn days through the end of the fifties. He remembers that "the relationship between the fans and the regulars was so *intense*, I can't think of anything else to compare with it, I really can't. I mean, there were all the letters we'd get, right? I got one or two shopping bags full per *day*, and I wasn't even the most popular kid on the show! I remember for a while the big thing was, they'd have fan mail call before the show and kids would take these big rubber-banded wads of envelopes and have them sticking out

of their pockets while they danced. But later they moved the fan mail call to the end of the show, because after a while there was so much fan mail it would just litter up the bleachers and the dance floor and get in everybody's way! Seriously, it became an honest-to-God physical

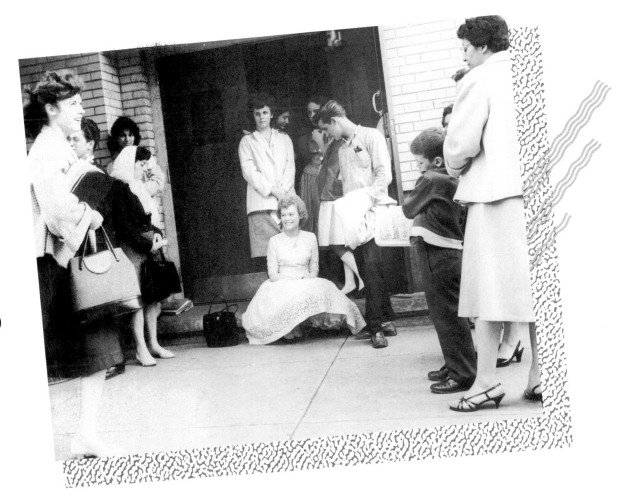

Janet Hamill (seated) waits with the rest of her friends to be admitted to the WFIL studio.

obstacle in there! Of course, in that studio, it was like maybe twenty by forty feet or something, there wasn't much room anyway.

"But beyond the fan mail, I would go down to the studio and run into these kids on the street who had come from *thousands* of miles away to try to get into the show. Whole families or school classes scheduled their vacations for Philly just so the kids could get into the show.

"I think for a lot of the people at home watching the show became like a soap opera. If so-and-so didn't happen to be dancing with his regular partner that day, a few days later there'd be thousands of letters asking what was wrong, were they ill, had they broken up? Some of the letters could just rip your heart right out, like the one I got once from a woman in Texas I think who said I reminded her of her dead son, and that's why she loved to see me on TV—I mean what can you *say* to something like that? And then there were all the unsolicited gifts . . . one time I told Dick during a roll call that I liked V-neck sweaters. *Boom*, a week later I got V-neck sweaters in the mail! One time around Christmas a huge box arrived for me at the studio. It was a complete suit, a tie, two shirts, cuff links, a watch, a tie clasp (expensive stuff, too), and this was sent to me by someone just because they happened to like the way I looked on the show. It was something. I just looked at this box of stuff and I honestly did not know what to say or do. I think I just stared at it and went 'Jesus . . .'"

As many of the onetime regulars have attested, being the idols of millions was the last thing on their minds when they started attending the show. They went to dance, to have fun, to indulge in those strange pursuits that only teenagers can really understand. A vivid example of what they were really thinking about is provided by viewing the December 2, 1957, *Bandstand*. At one point in the show, after a studio full of kids had jitterbugged furiously to Jerry Lee Lewis's "Great Balls of Fire," Dick Clark called regular Barbara Levick up to his podium.

Yvette Jimenez, Myrna Horowitz, and friends outside the studio with Dick Clark.

DICK CLARK: Lemme ask you, Barbara, you've got the Cookie Jar there—no, that's the *Courier*, pardon me, that's a high school or junior high school paper, right? And the Cookie Jar is a column inside it?

BARBARA LEVICK: It's a junior high school magazine.

DC: Are you a subscriber or a writer?

BL: Subscriber!

DC: Why don't you read this article to the folks at home—I thought they might be interested in hearing what is a dream faculty. It says, ''Wouldn't it be wonderful if we had a faculty like this?'' You read it now.

BL: Okay. ''Principal—Sal Mineo. Vice Principal—Tony Perkins. Girls' Gym Teacher—Tony Curtis. English—Ricky Nelson. Algebra—Johnny Saxon. Language—Tab Hunter. Music—Elvis Presley. Junior Business Training—Bob Cummings. History—Hugh O'Brian.

Dick could only be persuaded to dance with the girls on the holiday shows. Here he dances with Janet Hamill on a Christmas show in the late 1950s.

General Math—Frankie Avalon. Study Hall—Johnny Mathis. Art—James Darren. Faculty Advisor—Dick Clark!'' (Applause, shouts of ''yea!'' from the crowd.)

DC: Couldn't you see going to a school where Sal Mineo is the principal?

GIRLS IN STUDIO: Yeah!

DC: A lot of work would get done at that school, I have a feeling it might be a little bit distracting for some of you there. Thank you, Barbara. We've got one more ladies' choice dance this afternoon, let's make it this one, okay? Joni James with ''I Give You My Word.''

''Those were fun, innocent days,'' says Carol Scaldeferri, a *Bandstand* regular from 1957 through the early sixties. ''The world was so different then. I wonder if kids today can even begin to relate to what it was like for us. To be thrust into this limelight all of a sudden, to get all this attention focused on you, when all you wanted was to go to the show to have fun. To dance, to be with people . . . And you'd be getting thousands of letters a week telling you how much people loved you, how beautiful you were, people asking how you made yourself so beautiful, how you danced so well, how could they be more like you. . . . I was never really impressed with myself, I don't think, but I *was* impressed by the fact that other people were impressed by me. Know what I mean? You get all those letters and it has to have some sort of effect on you. People seemed to get to know me just by watching me on TV, and that fascinated me. The world became both a much bigger and a much smaller place through television. I experienced meeting teenagers and celebrities from all over the country. In fact, it was just like traveling around the country— only everyone came to *you* instead of you going to see them!

''I started going to the show in the summer of 1957 because Sal Mineo was going to be on and I had a crush on him. I never did get into that show, the lines were too long. That made me angry and I decided that one way or another I was going to get into that show. After trying and failing a few more times, I found a way to get in, through the backstage door that the stars used. To this day I wonder if Dick Clark or anyone else knew that *I* knew about that backstage door!

''In December 1957, I finally became an official regular. Before that I'd been sneaking into the show nearly every day. I became more familiar and recognizable to people during that time, and one day Arlene Sullivan came over and said hello and began talking to me. She was the first regular to talk to me. Before that I'd always be excited to get into the show, but then I'd see the regulars and sigh and wonder if I'd ever get to *their* level. . . . So Arlene started it off, and then of course Kenny Rossi came over, and it just went from there. I belonged. Then in December Tony Mammarella came over to me

The bleachers got pretty crowded when everyone sat during a performance.

and said he wanted to talk. I thought he was going to chew me out about sneaking in the back door, but instead he said, 'How would you like to be a Committee member?' I said, '*Would I? Are you kidding*?' So I got my little card that said 'Carol Ann Scaldeferri is an official member of the *American Bandstand Committee*,' and that meant that I could get in at the door ahead of everyone in the line and I just felt fantastic about that.

"In 1958 or so, though, they changed that system. They began to use tickets rather than the Committee cards, and they rationed the tickets out. That was a good idea, I thought— it was only fair, because the show was such a sensation at the time that kids were literally coming from all over the country. And it wasn't fair that only the kids from Philadelphia could get into the show ahead of everyone else. So some of us would go on Mondays or Wednesdays, and others on Tuesdays and Thursdays, or

whatever. There were between fifty and a hundred regulars by that time, so they could surely afford to spread us out like that."

Frank Brancaccio was a *Bandstand* regular at

Dick Clark at another holiday dance.

the same time with Carol. He has one of the most vivid recollections of what it was like to attend the show for the first time.

"I remember it so well, because it meant so much to me then. I remember walking through the door, and the guy at the door was Bob the Cop. And I went through the door, and walked down a hall, climbed a couple of steps, walked down another corridor, and there was a door at the end that said Studio B. And I walked in that studio door and the first thing I heard was Johnny Mathis's record 'Chances Are' and the first person I saw was this gorgeous redhead, Charlotte Russo, who'd been on the show awhile. I'd gotten a crush on her from watching her on the show. So I was faced with all this my first time. It was like instant heaven, this was what I went for, and there it all was. I could practically hear a heavenly choir in my head, like 'You have *arrived*.'

"Why did going to the show mean so much to me? It was really my only outlet as a teenager. I grew up in a very tough part of Philadelphia, Tenth and Christian streets. I thought all the kids there were growing up to be gangsters! I did go out once with some of my peers for amusement, and what they would do was

douse cats with kerosene and light them on fire and watch them streak across empty lots. I just couldn't take that kind of stuff. I knew I didn't belong with that crowd, but I didn't know what other crowd I belonged with, either. So right there in my living room I found the crowd I wanted to belong to—the *Bandstand* people. I always liked to dance, and the minute I first watched that show—back when Bob Horn and Lee Stewart were doing it locally—I fell in love with it. And then I fell in love with the regulars, like Charlotte Russo, Joanne Montecarlo, and Rosalie Beltrante. The show was starting to become my whole life. And I thought that there I could maybe find people I belonged with, because I had nobody else."

Frank did get into the show finally, and did find friends with whom he belonged. Then he found that, as a result of the show's exposure, he also belonged to the whole country:

"I always tried to keep a perspective on the fan mania, but it *was* really something. Every day outside the studio there'd be these manager and publicist types wanting to make a deal of some kind with you, make you a real star, and of course we couldn't do that, go professional, and remain on the show. That became a dilemma for some kids, having to decide if it was unreasonable not to take the money or if it was more important to them to stay on the show. I didn't get as much fan mail as a lot of other kids, I didn't have as many fan clubs, I didn't get to write my own *Bandstand* column for *16* magazine the way Pat Molitierri and Justine Carrelli and Arlene Sullivan did. So it was easier for me to keep it in perspective, I guess. But it was really something. I mean, we would even go to this one lady's house in Cleveland and spend weekends there, just because she'd seen us on the show and liked us. She came to see us in Philadelphia, then she invited me and Billy Cook to visit her."

Ed Kelly, another regular in the late fifties and early sixties, tells a similar tale: "One lady wrote me from Wisconsin to say that I looked exactly

Just one of the guys.

a lifetime thing. The craziest part of it was so many of us became these instant celebrities, yet none of us really had any *talent*. Sure, some of us were okay dancers, and some of us were cute and acted nice on camera, but is *that* a talent that deserves getting thousands and thousands of adulatory letters each week, and getting written up in *16* and *Teen* and getting your own columns in those magazines, and having your own fan clubs across the country and getting offers from recording and film studios? Gimme a break. It was all just incredible. We were just kids who lucked out, got in the right place at the right time, and found ourselves in the midst of this amazing soap opera with the rest of the country.''

One of Ed's regular dancing partners was Carmen Jimenez, one of the two look-alike Jimenez sisters. Carmen and her sister Yvette were instantly recognizable to *Bandstand* viewers for a few reasons: they were among the few, and certainly the most prominent, of the show's Hispanic regulars; they had ebullient personalities and were fine dancers; and they

like her son, who was serving with the Army in Pakistan at the time. She actually had me out to her house for a weekend. Just because I looked like her son, you know? It was strange, what happened in those days. I don't think it could ever happen that way now. That was a once in

This photo was taken on *Bandstand* in 1957.

both started a fashion trend by dyeing blonde streaks in their bangs.

"Carmen," says Ed Kelly, "was the real *Bandstand* darling in my era, which was 1959 to 1961. Boy, was she adored. I'll never forget walking down the street in Philadelphia with her one day when this little girl, who couldn't have been more than five or six years old, shouted from across the street, 'It's Carmen! It's Carmen!' Carmen was like the show's mascot in those days."

Aside from the fan mail, the *16* magazine articles, the unsolicited gifts, the trips around the country, and the rest, another aspect of being a *Bandstand* regular was Pop Singer's drugstore. Simon "Pop" Singer was a benevolent old man who ran a drugstore that was lucky enough to be located right across the street from WFIL's studios. A tiny place set up in classic "Happy Days" hangout fashion, with a fountain and stools on one side and a row of booths on the other, it became *the* place for regulars to congregate before and after the show.

Betty Romantini recalls: "Pop was a wonderful man, a really neat guy, loved by everyone. In fact, we had three incredible gentlemen associated with that show, Pop, Dick Clark and Tony Mammarella. Every one of them was just loved to death by all the kids, they were like our guiding lights. Anyway, Pop just loved the kids, he'd let us hang out there for hours after the show just sucking on a five-cent Coke or whatever, he never minded. I guess he liked the

Several dancing couples. Carmen Jimenez is at the far left and Frani Giordano is standing next to Dick Clark.

The kids anxiously await the day's performance.

47

Christmas time on
Bandstand.

youthful atmosphere or something. He did take a real interest, though, and he'd often come over to the studio and act as an unofficial chaperone backstage and in the bleachers and all.

"There were many different indications that you'd really made it as a regular on the show: when you got enough fan mail that they had to bring it to you in a box or a shopping bag. Or if on your birthday you got so many gifts in the mail that your parents and everyone else you knew had to come in a bunch of cars and pick you up to haul it all back home, then you knew you'd made it big. But the other surefire way to

know was if, for your birthday, Pop Singer brought over a big birthday cake with your name on it. That was an unwritten law among the regulars."

Adds Joanne Montecarlo, "You went to the show right from school, because a lot of us went to West Catholic High, right down the street from the studio. Then after the show you'd go over to Pop Singer's for a cheeseburger and a Coke, and we'd sit there and talk about who did what on the show that day and who was going to do what the next day, and what was up over the weekend, and who was fighting with whom, just typical teen talk, you know. We'd hang out there for a couple of hours and then beat it on home for dinner. The cheeseburger and Coke were like an appetizer for us, and we'd be able to have dinner at home, too. We were young, energetic kids, so I guess that accounted for part of it, but also we'd been dancing our little butts off for a couple of hours and, you know, we'd worked up quite an appetite. Then the big thing became,

if you were able to get out of school early enough, or if you were a certified regular and didn't have to worry about waiting in those long lines to get into the show, then you'd go to Pop's *before* the show, too. So you'd hang out there before and after the show."

If it all sounds like unending, head-spinning fun for the regulars in those days, well, for the most part it was. But there were other aspects to it. Joanne Montecarlo remembers the time Dick Clark brought two busloads of *Bandstand* regulars up to New York to be in the studio audience for one of the first installments of Dick's "Saturday Night Show":

"It was *terrifying*. We went up in a blizzard to New York, two buses of us, and by the time we got there the bus windows were so caked with snow we couldn't see out. Then we finally got to New York, outside the Little Theater on Forty-fourth Street, where they did the show. I remember a policeman came in the bus and

said, 'Under no circumstances are any of you to open the windows of this bus.' Then he told us not to do anything until he came back and told us what to do. We all looked at each other and wondered what was up. Then I think it was Arlene who opened one of the windows and peeked out. There was a horde of fans out on the street and when they got a glimpse of her we heard this incredible screaming and all of a sudden this *crash* and *thump* and the bus began rocking from side to side. The kids out there were rushing the bus! The cops finally pulled them off the bus and then they had to form a wedge to get us through the crowd into the theater. They brought us out two by two. I remember my mother, who was along as a chaperone, got her glasses smashed *inside her purse*, that's how intense it was. Kenny Rossi had the clothes ripped off his back, and this was in the middle of a blizzard! Our hair was getting pulled on the way in. It was very very scary, like Beatlemania. Dick didn't bus us up to the show again after that, and I couldn't blame him. I don't think I would have gone anyway. It

THE KIDS

The holiday spirit flourishes.

was too much for me.''

Frank Brancaccio remembers an even more unfortunate side effect of the fame that came with being a *Bandstand* regular. ''We were hated in Philadelphia. *Hated*. You walked down the street and you were 'a *Bandstand* faggot.' It was very schizoid in a way. I'd been on the bus trip up to Dick Clark's 'Saturday Night Show' in New York and been through that mob scene, and we'd all been getting the fan mail from all over the country. Everywhere outside of Philadelphia, we were loved for no particular reason. But then right there in Philly, we literally could not go to a lot of public places because there would always be mobs of people outside threatening to beat us up. Sometimes people came down to the studio like that. I remember once some guy I didn't recognize came up to me in the studio and said, 'I got some of my boys outside waiting for you.' And this glower,

and then he was gone. I didn't know what to make of it, but I'll tell you, that day after the show I didn't go to Pop Singer's, I just ran all the way home. Sometimes they had to have police escort us out of the studio or to a dance or a hop somewhere because of the threats. I never actually heard of anyone getting really, seriously beat up, but just having that animosity and jealousy against you all the time was bad enough."

Justine Carrelli elaborates another downside of sudden celebrity: "It really did a number on my head after a while. I mean we were like . . . how can I put this in terms people today would understand? We were all, all of a sudden, like a bunch of Michael Jacksons. Honest to God, that's what it was like for a while there. It was a real high, of course, but the extreme attention and notoriety made it a very abnormal adolescence, for sure. Making records, fan magazines, personal appearances . . . there were both unnatural adoration and unnatural envy from people, it was strange to be so loved and so hated by total strangers. And then when I graduated high school and had to leave the

The dancing never stops.

show, you know, my father told me, 'You can't be in Disneyland forever, little girl—it's time to rejoin the real world, you've had your fling. . . .' But I felt such a void in my life. How could I not? I mean, how can you go from being a national teenage idol to millions of kids who were always telling you how lovely you were, what a great dancer you were, how can you go from that to being, say, a Marine Corps steno typist, which I did? I lasted six months at that, hated every minute of it. It took me a while to get over *Bandstand*.''

It's a miracle that more of those kids weren't permanently affected by what happened to them on the show. In those early years, most of the regulars went simply because, to paraphrase the Cyndi Lauper song, kids just want to have fun. In many cases—like those of Joanne Montecarlo or Frank Brancaccio—the show provided a teenage social life that had never really existed in their lives before. Kenny Rossi,

who was voted the most popular boy on *Bandstand* in 1959, originally had no interest in attending the show. "My mother goaded me into it," he says, "because she wanted to see how I looked on TV." In all cases, instant stardom was the furthest thing from their minds; yet that's exactly what many of them got, simply by being there. Surely, some of them were embittered by the ultimately frustrated expectations their sudden fame must have generated. But speaking to them today, all that comes across is joy and gratitude for having been lucky enough to be a part of cultural history, and a perfectly reasonable nostalgia for those days. Justine Carrelli concludes, "All things considered, I loved every single minute of it and wished it would never, ever end. Would I do it all over again? Are you kidding? Absolutely!"

And what *did* happen to Bob and Justine and those other regulars?

Bob Clayton and Justine Carrelli tried their hands at a show-biz career and made a few records, none of which were successful. Bob went into business for himself and is now the happy, prospering manager of a chain of shoe stores in Delaware. Justine married bandleader Paul Dino, who had a hit record with "Ginnie Bell" in 1961 (it reached 68, and yes, it was played on *Bandstand*). She sang with her husband's band at the Frontier Hotel in Las Vegas for a time, then they left show biz for real estate. They had a couple of kids and got divorced; now Justine is still in Las Vegas, remarried to a psychologist.

Arlene Sullivan has been married and divorced, works in a Philadelphia hotel, and lives in New Jersey. Kenny Rossi entered the music business after leaving *Bandstand,* released three records that scraped the bottom of the charts, then became a talent agent in Philadelphia before moving into book publishing; he's been married, divorced, and remarried.

Joanne Montecarlo lives in south New Jersey, works for Bamberger's department stores, and may open a business of her own on the Jersey Shore. Betty Romantini is married and living in Philadelphia; she has three children and is a social worker at Albert Einstein Hospital there. Carol Scaldoferri is married, has a daughter every bit as beautiful as she, who is in fact a fashion model; Carol divides her time these days between helping her beautician husband run a salon in Philadelphia and doing social work with emotionally disturbed children.

Bill Cook is married and works for the city of Philadelphia. Frank Brancaccio lives in New York City, where he works in publicity and promotion; he's also done some acting on TV and in the theater, and worked for a time in the record business. The Jimenez sisters opened a beauty salon in New York City; Carmen now lives in Philadelphia, Yvette in Florida. Ed Kelly works for a New York City law firm. Pat Molitierri, one of the most vivacious and best loved of all the fifties regulars, died in the mid-seventies at the age of thirty-three of a sudden stroke that came while she was hanging clothes out to dry on the wash line outside her Philadelphia home.

Dottie Horner and Frank Spagnuola celebrate their Chalypso contest win.

'50s THE DANCING

Dancing was, is, and always will be at the heart of *American Bandstand*. In the fifties and early sixties numerous dance trends were started on the show, and all across the country the various *Bandstand*-originated dances became classified under the general heading of Philly-style dancing.

Basically, there have been two types of dancing on the show: fast and slow. When the show first went network the dominant fast dance was the Jitterbug, a frenetic leftover of the swing-era ballroom days that was only slightly less acrobatic than the Lindy. In the Lindy, the man would literally throw his partner in the air, twirl her in midair, and often catch her upside down as she came down on his back. In the Jitterbug, the couple simply executed incredibly fast and furious footwork more or less within the traditional two-step arrangement of the fox-trot. Every few beats or measures of a song, the partners would sway back apart from each other, each holding one of the other's hands, and with the joined hands held aloft, the male partner would spin the female. In the crowded *Bandstand* studio, anything more athletic than the Jitterbug would probably have been dangerous, if not physically impossible.

In the early days the standard slow dance was the basic fox-trot. Slow dances gave the viewers at home a great opportunity to focus on particular kids and who they were dancing with—and *how* they were dancing with each other, whether or not they really seemed to like each other or were just performing for the camera, etc. And the fast dances? You have to see a kinescope of a fifties show to appreciate an extended closeup being held for, say, ten full seconds on a few pairs of feet moving like lightning through the

54

intricate steps of the Jitterbug. This was serious, exhausting *work*, and the way Ed Yates and his camera crew caught it made the show a literal (and valuable) at-home dance class, five afternoons a week.

Probably the first two new dances to come along and be popularized on *Bandstand* were the Bop and the Bunny Hop. The latter was, to Dick Clark's recollection, the only teen dance craze ever started by an adult's record rather than by the kids themselves. It was sparked by bandleader Ray Anthony's record of the same name, and the dance simply consisted of as many kids as possible in a long conga line, with each kid holding the hips of the kid in front of them, putting out the left foot, then the right, then hopping forward, back, and then forward three times in a row.

The Bop was very important because it was the first dance to lean toward those sixties dances where partners usually did not touch. Instead, they gyrated athletically a few paces apart from each other. In the Bop, the partners faced each other and jumped up and down in place, grinding their heels back and forth each time they landed. It was a physically demanding dance so holding hands was virtually impossible for more than a few moments into it. The dancers needed to direct their energy to the pogo-style movements involved; usually hand-holding just got in the way. The Bop first started in Southern California, but was popularized on *Bandstand* when some California kids happened to drop by the show while on vacation in Philadelphia. Dick Clark recalls in *Rock, Roll and Remember* that he caught the Californians doing the new dance at the far end of the studio, asked them what it was, and then asked them to show the dance steps to some *Bandstand*

The Jitterbug was one of the most popular dances on the show. It was demanding—but it was *fun!* Here our three couples demonstrate some variations in the complex steps.

55

A dance that *Bandstand* made popular: the Bunny Hop. A seemingly endless line of kids, hopping across the floor, each trying *very* hard not to step on the heels of the person in front of them!

regulars. Pat Molitierri, Bill Cook, Bob Clayton, Justine Carrelli, and a few others went into Studio A with the Californians and came back a half hour later exhausted but well versed. While the Californians had begun doing the Bop to Gene Vincent's rockabilly classic "Be-Bop-a-Lula," on *Bandstand* it was more often done to a later Vincent hit, "Dance to the Bop," or to such upbeat numbers as Danny and the Juniors' "At the Hop."

A typical afternoon on *American Bandstand.* Number One on the Top Tunes list in the background is "Love Is Strange," by Mickey & Sylvia —if the kids are dancing to it, they're doing the Cha-lypso.

The Stroll was the next big dance craze, appearing just after *Bandstand* went network. A slow dance with a difference, the Stroll was a line dance—a hip update of the old Virginia reel. Males and females formed two lines opposite each other and performed a series of slow "walk" steps while one couple sashayed in their coolest, most low-down fashion between the two lines; when they reached the end, they would separate and rejoin their respective lines as the next couple began to "stroll" down the lane. R&B singer Chuck Willis, known for a time as "King of the Stroll," kicked off the dance in black communities with his record "C.C. Rider." In *American Graffiti* there's a scene where the Stroll is danced to the song of the same name by the Canadian doo-woppers the Diamonds (who also had a huge hit in "Little Darlin'"). The Diamonds appeared on *Bandstand* in late 1957 to do a minor hit called "Silhouettes" (a cover record of the Rays' classic). The Stroll was just catching on at the time, and the group's manager remarked about it to Dick Clark. Dick told him there was no song for this particular dance yet, and within a month, the Diamonds had recorded "The Stroll"—a classic with a rhythm and arrangement as low-down and ominous in its own way as Link Wray's downright-scary "Rumble."

Then came such self-descriptive but relatively minor dance fads like the Walk (sparked by

Jimmy McCracklin's record of the same name) and the Shake, which was essentially a stripped-down version of the Bop and another true forebear of the wilder sixties dances. The cha-cha and calypso were both popular dances on the show, and then in 1958 they were merged into the "cha-lypso."

"One of the biggest dances on the show in my day," recalls Joanne Montecarlo, "was what we used to call the Circle Dance. This was something that was totally originated by the kids on the show. It was like an alternate version of a square dance or the line dances we sometimes did: About six or eight regulars would form a circle and dance around the back of someone and take their hand and go to the next one, and so on. Say, a girl would start, and she would turn around and take the arm of a guy and dance around the back of the circle, outside of it, making hand contact with everyone, and then she would end up in line and the next person would go. And it was all done in a circular fashion."

Betty Romantini recalls a dance called "the Slop—can you believe that? I have no idea how it got that name, but it probably had to do with the fact that the moves were a sort of sloppy version of the Bop."

According to Ed Kelly, "Just after the Bunny Hop began to decline in popularity, Pat Molitierri reinvented it by combining it with the Bop and she called it the Hop. She took it in a whole new direction and a lot of people picked up on it, but nobody could do the Hop like Pat. Then right at the end of the fifties the Pony came in. That was basically a lot of skipping and jumping and very little touching or hand contact. It was a takeoff from the Bop and one of the very first of those freestyle dances that really caught on in the sixties."

And Justine Carrelli mentions "the Chicken, the Monkey . . . all these animal dances, right around the time of the Pony, and all of them basically took off from the Bop, in the sense that they were freestyle and athletic rather than

based on the old touch-dance, couples style. I loved 'em all, but the Jitterbug was probably my favorite. Bob and I won the first *Bandstand* dance contest doing the Jitterbug. We each won a jukebox filled with two hundred records. That was great—but then the next year Kenny and Arlene won, and they each got a car of their own. Boy, were Bob and I angry over *that* for a while!"

Justine also recalls that "we would often make personal appearances at record hops and functions like that around the country, and I always noticed that we were way ahead of the other kids around the country in terms of being up on the latest dances. It seemed that once the show became as hot as it did, there was this sort of pipeline for the latest dances to come to us first. We'd go to other places in the East or Midwest and do some new dance, and we'd look up and see the other kids *not* dancing —they'd just be there watching, picking up the steps from us. Afterward they'd always tell us how they learned dances from watching us on the television."

Two dances nobody could have learned from watching *Bandstand* were the Dog and the Alligator. They were both banned from the show as too risqué—the only dances ever to be forbidden from Bandstand.

do-it-yourself department

Try it yourself, and you'll agree . . .

It's the latest, the greatest, you ever did see . . .

It just takes a little rhythm . .

The dance rage of the Delaware Valley is Cha-lypso! It all began because somebody had to find a way to dance to all the calypso tunes. The BANDSTANDERS tried a Cha-Cha, but not quite a Cha-Cha; almost calypso, but not quite. So—they found a new name for it: Cha-lypso!

It caught on fast, and when Billy Duke visited the show, he decided to write a new tune about the dance—a mighty popular record called (natch) "Cha-lypso" with Billy Duke and the Dukes.

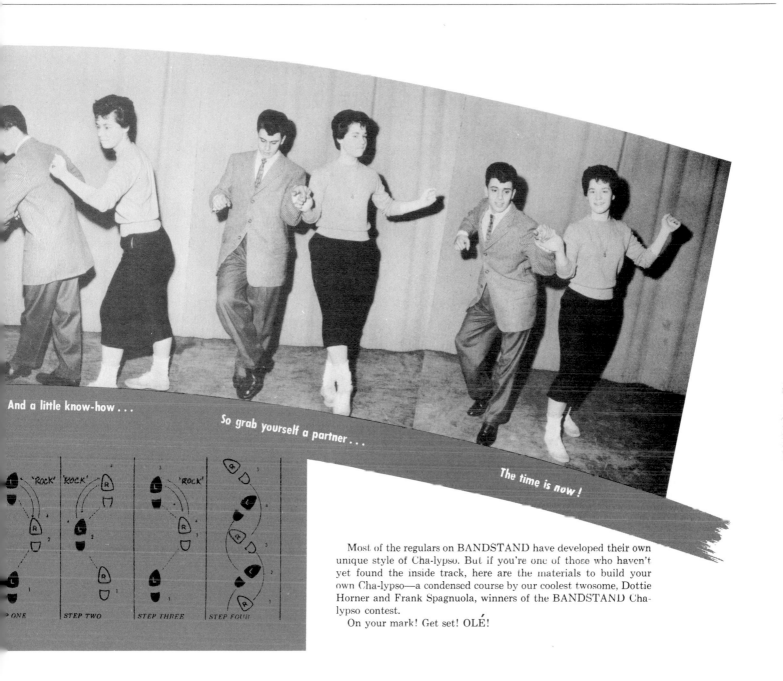

And a little know-how . . .

So grab yourself a partner . . .

The time is now !

'ROCK' 'ROCK' 'ROCK'

STEP ONE | STEP TWO | STEP THREE | STEP FOUR

Most of the regulars on BANDSTAND have developed their own unique style of Cha-lypso. But if you're one of those who haven't yet found the inside track, here are the materials to build your own Cha-lypso—a condensed course by our coolest twosome, Dottie Horner and Frank Spagnuola, winners of the BANDSTAND Cha-lypso contest.

On your mark! Get set! OLÉ!

Getting ready for the show in the ladies' room.

This was the fifties, after all. You already know there was a dress code in effect on *Bandstand* to set a good example for the viewing audience, so you would not have seen kids on *Bandstand* looking like James Dean in *Rebel Without a Cause* or, heaven forbid, Marlon Brando in *The Wild One* or even like Elvis Presley. But within the restrictions of the dress code there was plenty of variation, especially on the distaff side, and you can bet that the show's millions of viewers caught it all and copied it all across the nation.

The guys wore suits, or sports jackets with dress slacks. Ties were mandatory, and no open-necked shirts were allowed until much later. Frequently, though, guys would add a V-neck or crewneck sweater to their outfit. The shirts were almost always white, as were the socks. Ties were conservative—not too narrow, not too wide and not too loud. The suits or sports coats were often in conservative gray flannel, but just as frequently they were big-shouldered,

Straight skirts and flats were the order of the day.

Coats and ties, short back and sides.

beautiful confetti tweeds, or intricate cross-hatched tweed patterns fading into deep navy or black, or box-back nubby wool sports coats, or even shiny sharkskins. They were, in other words, the original editions of the very same items sold at high prices today in the hippest antique-clothing boutiques on both coasts. And they don't make 'em like that anymore! On certain occasions you might also see something more formal—a pastel-colored, shawl-collared dinner jacket with black trim on the lapels, or a plaid coat with black lapels. The pants were inevitably baggy and pleated, carryovers from the zoot suit look of the swing era, just as the Jitterbug was to the dancing. The shoes were either conventional wing tips or oxfords, or

penny loafers. White bucks and hush puppies made their appearances, too, but would be seen even more in the early sixties.

Back then the guys wore their hair short. Short back and sides, leave a little on top—as the barbershop saying went. In fact, it probably still goes that way today, since all of the styles of that era seem to keep coming back again and again. While the back and sides would be cut short, out-and-out crew cuts were something of a rarity. More common by far were the slicked-back DA and the Brylcreemed pompadour in front.

The ladies wore their hair short and pixieish, or teased up into a sort of proto-bouffant (actual bouffants wouldn't really come into

THE FASHIONS

This page and following—the range of fashions on *American Bandstand*.

THE FASHIONS

Getting ready for a big show.

Crew cuts and narrow ties...

vogue until the early sixties), or with little flips (which also would get much bigger within a few years), or in braids, ponytails, or pigtails. Of course, barrettes and bobby pins were in abundance. In fact, Dick Clark and Tony Mammarella carried loads of hairpins in their pockets, just to be sure of averting the many catastrophes that seemed to be forever on the verge of happening to any number of the regular girls on the show.

Carol Scaldeferri pioneered headbands. "I always loved bows and headbands in my hair," she says, "but I was using ribbons to tie my hair up a few years before the headbands were even invented."

Sweaters and collars were probably the two biggest sartorial items for girls on the show. The sweaters were angora wool or cotton blend or one of the new synthetics; cardigans or crewnecks or even V-necks with something on underneath; solid or patterned. But they almost always had fur collars, especially rabbit fur. Velvet, satin, and leopard—often with corresponding belts—were also big as far as trim

Ponytails were very popular.

went. About the only thing as popular as the rabbit-fur-collared sweaters were outfits with Peter Pan collars and bibs.

And then there was the "Philadelphia collar." Joanne Montecarlo explains: "A lot of us went to parochial school, and you'd better believe the schools hated the idea of us being on *Bandstand*. But if they couldn't stop us from going, at least they could threaten us with suspension if they ever saw us wearing the school uniforms on the show. That was like a venial sin to them or something! But most of us had to run right over to the show from school, right? So what you'd do is bring a sweater or a full change of clothes in a bag with you to school that morning, and depending on how much time you had to spare when you got to the show, you'd either change in the ladies' room or you'd leave the uniform on and put a sweater on over it. You'd whip on a cardigan and button it all the way up, or you'd throw on a crewneck, and then you'd take the uniform collar—which was this white, sort of abbreviated Peter Pan collar—and have that sticking up over the top of the sweater. So some of us did that, and the school never seemed to catch on. But after a week or so, we all began getting these letters from people saying, 'Hey, where can I get myself one of those Philadelphia collars?' I guess it just proves the old saying, that necessity is the mother of invention."

Betty Romantini describes the typical skirts worn in those days: "They were long, down at least around the midcalf or lower. There were A-lines—some widely flared and some not so widely flared —and they could be in dark or light solids or patterns like the dark green and blue plaids, or the big black-and-white window-pane plaids. Then there were the tight, pencil-thin skirts, usually in gray or something, and then there were the big felt circle skirts with all the crinolines underneath."

Such outfits were most often accessorized with strings of pearls, brooches, circle pins, fanciful wearable "toys" like mink dogs. The footwear: bobby sox with saddle shoes, of

Party clothes for the holiday show.

loafers, ballerina pumps, or moccasins. High heels and pointy shoes were a rarity. Here again, Carol Scaldeferri was something of a fashion innovator: ''I never wore saddle shoes and bobby sox. I thought they were ugly and unfeminine. I would wear Capezio-type ballerina shoes, sometimes the kind that laced up the ankle and calf with the ribbons, and a lot of the time I would wear pointy pumps with a *slight* heel—I actually found the short heel more comfortable for dancing than the flats. And for stockings I always liked opaque hosiery.''

Most kids wore flats because, as Justine Carrelli puts it, ''the dancing was *serious*, and if you wore high heels you felt you might break an ankle or something. Which is why it amazes me when I catch *Bandstand* nowadays and see how some of those girls dance in high, high heels. I just don't know how they do it.''

And why were the saddle shoes so often worn with the bobby sox doubled up—as in two socks on each foot?

''Don't ask *me!*'' laughs Carol Scaldeferri. ''I guess it was just crazy kids doing something to

course. Not the world's most feminine look, no, but it had a certain style of its own. While the bobby sox were almost *de rigueur* for every *Bandstand* female, for variety's sake the saddle shoes might be alternated with, say, penny

"Diamond" tiaras were *very* popular as evidenced by the photos on this page.

be different," shrugs Justine Carrelli. "I think," says Joanne Montecarlo, "that the saddle shoes themselves were so ugly and ungainly that the bobby sox were worn like that just to take attention away from the shoes. It was just the look that was in back then, you know? We did some crazy things in those days. We used to put things like little bells and pom-poms on the thick part of the bobby sox. To be *really* dressed up on the show, you'd wear hose and a pair of flat ballerina shoes. Unless it was one of the Christmas party shows, where we'd all be in pretty fancy ball gowns with our nicest stockings and high-heeled pumps and all."

Yes, it was an innocent age. So it's all the more ironic that subsequent, more enlightened, and less innocent generations have kept returning to those very clothes that were constantly showcased in the early years of *Bandstand*. Even before groups like the Stray Cats made the rockabilly revival official in the late seventies and early eighties, both tulle party dresses padded with multiple crinoline petticoats underneath and those short-waisted, sharply cut, tweed-patterned rockabilly boys' coats were back in vogue, strongly influencing contemporary fashion design. Those very same oversized black, white, and gray windowpane checks so frequently favored by fifties *Bandstand* regulars made a huge comeback in the eighties via British pop impresario Malcolm McLaren's "Buffalo Gals" movement. And need it be mentioned how much those recent short-back-and-sides, full-on-top haircuts for guys *and* girls owe to what were borderline-civil haircuts on those same regulars way back when?

However one interprets the incestuous recycling of trends and nostalgia that constitutes so much of fashion's "progression" as time goes by, the fact remains that *Bandstand* is probably the only thing in the broadcast medium that's been around long enough to be able to capture that entire span, from inception to revival and back again.

If you wanted to give your feet a fighting chance, you wore sneakers.

They sent in letters by the thousands each week. They sent in all manner of gifts: toys, stuffed animals, clothing both casual and formal, kicky and sophisticated, cheap and expensive. They sent in jewelry and household items. They sent in food. Many of them set up fan clubs for the regulars they watched every day, wrote to, emulated, adored. Some of them traveled to the show numerous times to meet and greet in person those to whom they'd grown attracted

and attached through a miracle of modern technology. And some of them even invited the regulars out to *their* homes.

There were millions of them back in the fifties, those *Bandstand* fans, and their mania for the show was *serious*. As the regulars tell it, their fans saw the show as a soap opera. "Think about it," says Arlene Sullivan, who, like dozens of other regulars through the years, and especially in the fifties, had her minions by the millions and multiple national fan clubs, "you had all those teenagers, *and* their mothers in a lot of cases, all getting into this show in a big way. They all felt like they knew us, because we were in their living rooms for over an hour a day, five days a week." As some other regulars have already noted, in some cases viewers *really* felt they knew the kids they saw on TV— because they resembled friends or relatives, often those who were then far away or gone forever. There were letters to *Bandstand* that

Dick Clark and Frani Giordano beside a mountain of fan mail.

could make grown men weep, though mostly the mail was typical of teenage mania. This was really the first such large-scale and concentrated example of the kind of exuberant adolescent media-worship we've grown used to since rock was born.

But let some of the fans themselves tell their own stories.

Lydia Beban was a fourteen-year-old high school student in Fall River, Massachusetts, when she first encountered *American Bandstand* in 1958. She subsequently became president of Kenny Rossi's fan club.

"I had this one girlfriend I walked to school with every day. One day she began talking about this television program. Believe it or not, I'd never really been that familiar with it before. But she kept going on and on about *American Bandstand*, and especially about this one guy. She said, 'Oh, there's this *handsome* guy on this show, you gotta see him!' Then she said, 'Tell you what—you go home after school and put on the TV and when he comes on I'm gonna call you.' Which she did, and I saw Kenny and I said, 'Oh *yeah*, you were right, he is *something*!'

Waiting in line outside the studio —an integral part of the *Bandstand* experience.

A group of kids take a bus trip to New York for Dick Clark's Saturday Night Show; their legion of fans were there to greet them.

71

The measure of fame: magazine articles, a Dick Clark doll . . .

THE BANDSTAND REGULARS TELL...

"ALL ABOUT US"

ARLENE SULLIVAN   CARMEN JIMENEZ   MARY BELTRANTE   FRANI GIORDANO   KENNY ROSSI   SUE BELTRANTE
CAROLE SCALDEFERRI   MIKE BALARA
BARBARA LEVICK
BILL COOK
IVETTE JIMENEZ   PAT MOLITTIERI   BUNNY GIBSON   BETTY ROMANTINI
JUSTINE CARRELLI
JANET HAMILL
ARLENE DI PIETRO
RONNIE VERBIT

ANOTHER 16 EXCLUSIVE

He was a real dreamboat, as we used to say. But I really fell in love with the whole show just as much as him. I always loved dancing and just watching that show was such an amazing dancing lesson, right there in your own living room. I'd watch it and copy steps, practice in front of the TV, clear the furniture away. You'd pretend you were them, and dance like them and dress like them, everything—wear your hair like the girls and wish you could date the guys on the show.

"Very soon after I started watching the show, I'd be running home from school every day to catch it. If it was preempted for any reason, or if somehow I missed it, I'd be very upset. Kenny and Arlene and Bob and Justine were just *it* for me back then. I became so involved in it I decided I wanted to go down to the show. So I wrote a letter to Kenny, and ironically his mom picked up my letter—his entire family helped him answer all his fan mail, you know—and she read it and I guess she thought I seemed like a nice girl. So she answered my letter and from there I made arrangements to get down to Philly. My father drove me down. It took six or seven hours. Kenny met me outside the studio, and then we went over to Pop Singer's to hang out before the show and I met all the regulars, Arlene and Bob and Justine and Carol Scaldeferri, and Bill Cook and Joanne Montecarlo and Frank Brancaccio and so many others—it was just one big blur of excitement. After the show, my dad and I got to meet Kenny's father and mother, who were simply wonderful. Was I excited? Beyond that. I was beside myself. Kenny took me down to the cellar and we danced to records. Oh Lord, was it incredible—I don't know how I didn't faint! After that I made my father drive me down about a dozen more times over the next year or two.

"So then I began the Kenny Rossi fan club, and we had many thousands of members all across the country. It was a big operation—I mean I wasn't the only person running it, there were chapters in different parts of the country. But I think my chapter may have kept going longer than most others. We kept getting letters for Kenny for several years after he left the show, even after he'd tried making a few records that didn't really go anywhere. Would you believe I *still* get letters for him? I really do. And I've kept every letter he ever sent me, and I have all the fan letters I ever got for him up in my attic. And I still have lots of copies of the autographed photos and letters and stuff that I used to send back to all those fans of his.

"Meeting Kenny and his family back then was more than just fulfilling a dream. It was the beginning of a long, great friendship, too, and I don't know how often that worked out between *Bandstand* regulars and their fans. We still keep in touch all the time these days, we went to each other's weddings and all. All I can say as I reflect back on those days is how lucky I was to have been a part of it. There never will be anything comparable to those days, I don't think."

For several years Dave Frees has been running the American Bandstand Fan Club out of his home in Pennsylvania (Box 131, Adamstown, Pennsylvania, 19501). As often as he can, he

publishes the *Bandstand Boogie* newsletter — full of vintage and current photos, updates, trivia, and nostalgia on all the regulars from the show's Philadelphia days—and mails it to the club's several hundred members. He may have even collected more *Bandstand* memorabilia than Dick Clark himself. Which is not bad for a guy who, though he grew up about fifty miles outside of Philadelphia in the fifties, never actually got to attend the show himself!

"Back when I was around nine or ten years old," Dave recalls, "and I was living in Green Hills, fifty or sixty miles outside of Philadelphia, we used to get *Bandstand* when Bob Horn had

...a profile of
Carole Scaldeferri in
16 Magazine.

73

HOW TO GET **HIM** TO LIKE **YOU**

by Georgia Winters

and realized that *everyone* was reading all these magazines about these kids. And everyone felt the same way about those kids that I did.

"Here's something really crazy. That show was really a private dance lesson as much as anything else. Especially back then, now *that* was dancing. I'd have the show on, and my father and mother would both be out working, and I would use the *refrigerator door* as a dance partner while I watched the show! It was great—it was just the right weight, not too heavy but not as light and flimsy-feeling as, say, a broomstick, and it had this nice smooth motion on its hinges, and you could pull it out and let it swing back and almost close and then catch it, like you were spinning your partner in a jitterbug. And you could pretend it was Carmen or Justine or Frani or Carol or Arlene. I'd actually use the handle of that door and swing the thing open and shut to the music, and practice my dance steps that way. I would never have told anyone back then that I did that, but *now* I

it as a local thing. I remember by the time I was ten I was watching it and learning to dance from it. When Dick Clark took over as host —*that's* when everyone at school started jabbering about it, and it was always like 'Get out of my way, I gotta get home to catch *Bandstand*!'

"It got to the point where everyone at school would be talking about who was dancing with who, who was gonna sing on the show that day, and to us it was like a whole other collection of friends we had when we got home from school. Then I happened to see a copy of *Teen* magazine, which I would never have looked at twice but there was Frani Giordano on the cover. *That* sure caught my eye! When I realized there were *magazines* writing about these people, I began buying them all—*16*, *Photoplay*, *Teen Screen*, all of 'em. That was it for me, because when I read about them I felt *more* like I knew them, and then I got *more* interested in them. And then one day I looked up at school

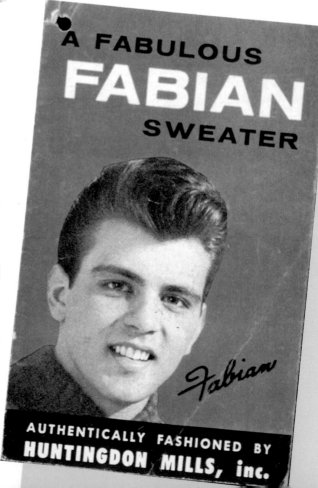

A FABULOUS **FABIAN** SWEATER

Fabian

AUTHENTICALLY FASHIONED BY **HUNTINGDON MILLS, inc.**

keep running into people who sort of sheepishly confess to *me* that they used to do it, too, and when they tell me I give them this look and it's classic, you know, like 'Yeah? *Me too!*'

"So that's how the whole thing really started, with the refrigerator door. Then when I had a baby-sitter who was only a few years older than me we'd practice dancing with each other while the show was on. After doing that for a couple of years (by the time I was in sixth grade, I think), a friend and I dragged a couple of twelve-year-old girls in heavy makeup to a high school dance, and we got in! And we danced like crazy. Then I had a cousin who went to West Catholic High with a lot of the regulars, so I used to get some *Bandstand* gossip that way.

"So given all that, and what I do now with the fan club, it *is* pretty absurd that I never actually got to go to the show myself. Believe me, I know! It's a really tragic story. My father was never that crazy about the idea of the show, or me going into Philadelphia to see it, but he'd just say, 'When you're old enough to drive, you can drive yourself in, I'll never have time to take you.' Though at times he promised to, something always came up. Then one time I got some tickets to the show from Sandy Short, who was a regular in the early sixties. I used to write to her and she was always very nice in writing back. We struck up a little pen pal thing, and she invited me to come on the show and dance with her. Wow! Fantastic, right? Oh, she wrote, 'Come as long as you're *tall*—I'm the tallest girl on the show and I can never find a partner.' And I was tall for my age, right? So she sent me these tickets and everyone at school was so jealous of me, and then I get home that day and my mom says, 'No, you're not going.

Barbara Levick tells on BILL COOK!

Two of your top

THERE MUST BE thousands of girls and guys out there in the broad expanse of TV-land who would really like to know the lowdown on that dashing, dancing *Bandstand* idol, Bill Cook. Since I know Billy pretty well and have had many, many opportunities to talk with him — I feel that maybe I'm the person to spill the beans and tell *all* on our boy, Bill Cook.

Here goes:

His real name is William John Cook, Jr. and he turned 18 on August 25. He is 5'10" tall and weighs 143 pounds. He lives at home with his parents and a younger sister, Peggy.

Bill attended Bishop Newmann High School for boys in Philadelphia, and now he is dreaming of the day when he will go to New York and study dancing and eventually become a top dancer and choreographer for Broadway and movie musicals. In fact, it is little known, but this dream is really the most important thing in Bill's life. Knowing his talent and determination, I feel very sure that he will make it straight to the top!

Bill's lighter side includes a deep-seated love for all Italian food. In tough straits he'll settle for a vanilla soda and potato chips — but he still longs for lasange and the whole works!

Bill loves to double-date and usually does so with a *Bandstand* couple — and takes along his favorite date, lovely Aggie Poller, also of Philly. For informal dates, Bill digs going to a drive-in movie or a drive-in restaurant (preferably both), or just lounging around somebody's house listening to records and practicing new dance steps.

However, when "Romeo" decides to do the town up orange, he really loves to go about it in the right way. Bill dolls up in a dark Continental-cut suit with a narrow tie and crisp white shirt. He likes his dates to wear bouffant and very faminine dresses. First, they will go to a really fine restaurant, and then to a play or a musical comedy. Later, they hit a nice supper club and dance and listen to a good combo.

Sounds groovey — doesn't it, girls?

Bill loves to vacation at the beach and has just learned water-skiing. He longs to fly his own plane one day and plans to take flying lessons. Bill loves traveling and meeting new friends. Since he likes long trips best of all, he naturally wants to visit Hawaii and the West Coast one day. Like all of us, he is deeply interested in meeting young people in show business. Incidentally, Johnny Tillotson is one of Bill's best friends.

Bill hates Chinese food, show-offs, and people who break promises. He considers dancing one of the greatest "releases" and exercises in life, and recommends that everyone try it — and not to worry about being good. Just get up there and DANCE!

If you'd like to know more about this dancing 'teen idol, send a self-addressed stamped envelope to his national fan club, DeeDee Sturtevant, Box 2282, Philadelphia 3, Pa.

favorites on BANDSTAND reveal each other's top secrets!

WELL, WELL, WELL — now it's my turn! But does anyone here to introduce the ever-popular and well-known Barbara Levick? For those of you who have been stranded on Mars for the past year or so — here is a little info:

Barbara Levick lives with her brother, Mom and Dad in a Philly suburb. She was 17 on August 2 and has brown hair and brown eyes. She stands 5'3" tall and goes to Kensington High School.

Her closest friends are Arlene Sullivan, Betty Romantini and Steve Brandt, though she has many, many other friends. Right now (at this very minute, that is) she gets a hazy look at the mention of Mike Balara's name, but knowing my little friend — that can change with the weather.

Barbara is a truly superb dancer with a built-in sense of timing and rythm that won the *Fast Dance* crown this year. Aside from dancing, she loves Italian food, the color violet, and going on wild rides at amusement parks. She usually dresses casually in button-down shirts with a bulky sweater, and Bermudas or Capri slacks.

Barb is a great one for gabbing on the phone. Another favorite pastime is listening to LPs. She prefers Paul Anka, Annette, Sinatra and Johnny Mathis. Right now, her favorite song is *A Million To One*. For movies, Barb picks Tony Curtis for her idol. Recently, she was crestfallen (as we all were) when her favorite TV show, *The Saturday Night Dick Clark Show*, was cancelled. But we all (and that includes you) are writing letters to ABC-TV, 7 West 66th Street, New York City, about that!

If one of Barbara's main dreams ever comes true, she'll be driving her own big white convertible one of these days. And if she ever gets to travel, there'll be no stopping Barb. She wants to visit Paris and to spend a long vacation in Italy. Barb also plans to learn to speak Italian fluently.

Our girl has a zany sense of humor and is great for pulling practical jokes — but she can take them, too! She loves to entertain at informal parties at home and invariably dances to every record played. She eats like it was going out of style, but can't gain any weight. Every time she sees a thin girl, she yells, "Look, there's someone thinner than I am!"

Barbara hates Chinese food, the color orange, doing dishes, having to get up in the morning, and two-faced people. Her favorite sport is swimming — and she's a whiz at it.

If any of you cats want to learn more about Barbara Levick, send a self-addressed stamped envelope to Maureen Kilheaney, 11011 South Perry Avenue, Chicago, Illinois.

And for those of you who really want a wonderful and swinging surprise — *PLEASE TURN THE PAGE!*

Bill Cook tells on BARBARA LEVICK!

Another *16 Magazine* feature.

A popular comic feature from *16 Magazine*.

That television show is located in a bad part of Philadelphia.' Which it sort of was, it was known as a kind of a rough part of town, but the thing that I didn't know and my mother didn't know at the time was the subway actually let you off right in front of the studio, practically. So it would've most likely been okay anyway. But she nixed that, can you believe it? I mean, I don't hold a lifelong grudge against my mom for that or anything, but . . . I had a helluva time lying to the kids in school who hadn't seen me on camera that day.

"The final thing is that when I finally reached the age of sixteen and I was old enough to drive, what do you think happened? The show moved out to California!''

Despite these crushing ironies, Dave Frees has remained a fan of *Bandstand*, as steadfast in his ardor as the show's format itself. And he's been rewarded with more than the supercolossal collection of *Bandstand* memorabilia and photos he's managed to compile in twenty years. (That collection was lost at one time. After Dave had been in the Army a couple of years, he returned home, went to his attic to gaze fondly at his *Bandstand* lore, and found that a leaky roof had ruined it all; he redoubled his efforts, in order to replace everything, and not only succeeded but located even more teen-mag articles and photo spreads, photos fans took of the show off the TV, *Bandstand* buttons and tie clasps and pins and yearbooks and records, and even a Dick Clark doll—things he'd never seen before.)

"In the Army," says Dave, "I broke my legs in a parachute jump. I could not believe my luck. I was dying to come home and *dance*, watch *Bandstand* and all, and instead I'm in a cast. But through some administrative snafu I finally got a break. They put me in a Navy hospital in Philadelphia instead of an Army hospital in Virginia or Ohio or wherever. When I found out I was going there, I wrote to one of my favorite ex-regulars from the show, Doris Olsen, and told her I'd be at this hospital. And she was kind enough to come and visit me and wish me well and spend some time, with her husband and all, even though she *hates* hospitals.

"Then I got to meet Pop Singer in Philadelphia and see his store. As it turned out, I got to do that just before he died and the store was closed. Boy, what a wonderful, wonderful guy. Just so nice, the minute you met him you felt you'd known him all your life, you know? He let us hang out till all hours and take pictures, and we talked about this and that and he told us all these stories, it was like a dream come true. And I've gotten to meet Carmen and Yvette Jimenez, and now we're all good buddies —they are two of the absolutely nicest people you could ever want to meet.

"So now I've got this trove of *Bandstand* stuff here, it must be worth a fortune by now. I must have every magazine article ever done anywhere on the show. I have a *Bandstand* T-shirt that Dick Clark was kind enough to autograph and send me. I have the paperbacks Dick wrote in the fifties for teenagers, *To Goof or Not to Goof*—what a title, eh?—and *Your Happiest Years*. They're not bad, actually. I have all the records all the regulars ever made: 'Drive In Movie' by Bob and Justine, 'I'll Never Smile Again,' 'But I Do,' and 'She Loves Me, She Loves Me Not' by Kenny Rossi, and 'Do the USA' by Pat Molitierri. I've got a Christmas record by

Dick Clark and his first wife Barbara, and all it says on the label is 'Merry Xmas, Dick and Barbara Clark.' It's Dick and Barbara saying they don't know how to wish you all happy holidays, and wondering how the stars would wish you happy holidays, and then they have someone impersonating Elvis and Little Richard and Chuck Berry and whoever else singing 'Merry Christmas' and stuff. Then I have this incredible thing Dick Clark did in the late sixties. Remember that record 'An Open Letter to My Teenage Son' by Victor Lundberg, the one about how 'If you burn your draft card you are not my son'? Well, Dick Clark made an answer record to that, called 'An Open Letter to the Older Generation.' He really is America's Oldest Living Teenager!''

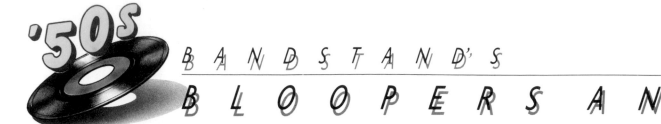

With so many performers lip-synching to records on *American Bandstand*, you'd guess there must have been some rather embarrassing technical miscues in the show's lengthy history. Of course, you'd be right. During the show's very first week on the ABC network, guest Paul Anka was lip synching his first hit, "Diana," when the needle got stuck in the grooves of the 45. It happened right in the middle of the chorus, as Paul's voice was launching into that long, heartfelt "Oh" that precedes "Please stay with me, Diana." Seeing Paul try to hold that unnaturally long note for a few seconds, then finally detecting the soft skipping sound of the needle stuck in the groove, then cracking up with laughter as his recorded voice seemed to hold the note forever is something nobody who saw it would ever forget.

Original *Bandstand* lighting director Bill Russell remembers other similar occurrences. "One time we had the country singer Jimmy Dean come on, and we set it up with a low-angle camera shot of him in the darkness, snapping his fingers as the music started. Then the camera pulled out slowly as the lights came up and he stepped to the mike to start singing—and then, another voice began to croon! Someone had put the wrong record on. Well, Jimmy Dean, bless him, he was as much of a trouper as Dick Clark I guess, because without batting an eyelash and even before Dick could apologize, Jimmy just drawled, 'Could we hear that there girl's record one more time?' Everybody on the crew was dying." (The high-pitched voice on the record belonged to a very talented *male* singer, Dee Clark.)

"Another time, Dick was a guest on a Perry Como special for NBC. Now, what would a guy like Dick do on a show like that? The guy doesn't sing. He doesn't act. He's never done skit comedy. He doesn't dance. They decided to teach him to sing, and he sang 'Bye Bye Blackbird,' and he held his own alright. But

there's that one line in the song about love and understanding, right? Okay. Director Ed Yates and I decided to have a soundman friend of ours dub a tape of Dick singing that on TV onto an acetate and make a record out of it. Then we kept that record handy in the studio—and decided to cue it up to that line, so that if and when Dick ever got really flustered or angry about anything, we'd be ready. Well, it was a long wait, naturally—the guy was such a darned pro, and this was on a live TV show that never even had rehearsal. But we knew it would happen one day, and it finally did. One little thing kept going wrong one day, and finally Dick couldn't take it and he slammed his microphone down on his podium and we could see him holding back a scream. So we cued up that record, and at the right moment I said, 'Now!' and Ed let it go, and the voice of Dick Clark crooning came blasting out over the studio. Dick stopped cold, stood bolt upright, wide-eyed, frozen, at a loss for words for the first and only time I think I'd ever seen him. Finally, after a minute or so, he just looked in our general direction, shook his head, and said, 'You guys really got me.'"

When Dick was in Philadelphia in 1983 to appear on WPVI's "A.M. Philadelphia," Russell dropped by the control booth and let that record go again. "I have the only copy of that record in the world," Russell chuckles, "and Dick knows that, so he knew what was going on right away. But we still got a good laugh out of it. He's been trying every trick in the book to get that record from me. And you know what? He never will!"

Also in the way of practical jokes, fifties regular Bill Cook remembers when "Dick decided, as a gag, to get ratings during some sort of sweeps week or something, to have me get a haircut on the show. They told me they'd get a professional barber, it'd be great, the works. I said, 'Fine.' I get into the chair in the studio and this guy comes in and right away I knew they must've pulled this guy in off the street and that he'd probably never given anyone a haircut in his life. Well, the guy gave me this hideous crew cut—I mean I could hardly even *look* at myself. You'd better believe I got a lot of ribbing in school for that one! It was all in good fun, of course, and it was no real big deal for me, but it did take about eight or nine weeks to grow back in—and my mother wouldn't even talk to me that whole time!"

Dick Clark remembers some of his own bloopers well indeed: "Once I was in the bleachers interviewing some kids, filling time before a commercial, and I was flanked by two girls, both wearing unusual-looking pins, so of course I asked about them. One girl I asked about this thing she had around her neck, and she said, 'Oh, it's a Tiki God, I got it from a mail-order catalog.' I turned to the other girl and said, 'So what's that *you're* wearing?' She mumbled something indistinct. I leaned closer and said, 'I'm sorry, I couldn't make that out—what is it again?' And she gave me this how-could-you look and stammered, 'It's a, a, virgin pin!' I thought I would keel over and die right there. But somehow I just turned to the camera and said, 'That's nice. We'll be right back after this.' I apologized as profusely as I could, but I don't think anyone ever really ended up catching it.

"Another time, Connie Francis came on the show after she'd become a big star, and she had her hair dyed *red*. Of course the show was black-and-white, so nobody at home could probably catch it, but I was just so stunned to see her come on like that I just went, 'Connie! What have you *done* to yourself?!?' I then became extremely embarrassed—and so did she, of course—and I hemmed and hawed and played it down and made a joke out of it and all. But the funny thing was, viewers wrote in to her by the millions and she ended up going back to black hair in a few weeks. She even came back on the show and told me 'thanks' for helping her correct her 'mistake.'"

A series of occasional blunders came from the Rate-a-Record segments. Anyone who knows *Bandstand* knows how Rate-a-Record works. Back in the fifties, the segment came on at 3:15 every day (the show is still paced so consistently that former seventies regular Deb-E Chaffin says she can set her watch by the show's segments), with Dick Clark selecting four kids from the studio audience to judge two different records. Three kids would judge, one would keep score (occasionally, Dick would have to help them with their math). This, of course, is the part of the show that gave birth to the best-known *Bandstand*-related saying, "It's got a good beat and you can dance to it. I'll give it an 85." Actually, the Rate-a-Record ratings must fall between 35 and 98—based on Dick Clark's admirably rational theory that no record can be absolutely terrible or absolutely perfect.

Rate-a-Record bloopers most often involved low scores being given to records that would soon go on to become huge hits. The one case that everyone seems to remember concerns one of the few records ever to get a 35. It happened in the first week of December 1958, to "The Chipmunk Song," by Alvin and the Chipmunks—alias David Seville, alias Ross Bagdasarian, who sang all the chipmunk voices and then played them back at various speeds to get the high-pitched, nasal effect. Within two weeks, the song had hit number one on the pop charts. By the end of the year, it was a million-seller.

Rate-a-Record wasn't wrong all that often. But when it was—look out! There's one other all-time unforgettable Rate-a-Record gaffe, but we'll get to that one in the next chapter.

NOTE: For all appendices, where *Bandstand* dates are missing from the listings, it's for one of three reasons: information for that particular day's show is simply not available; it so happened that no charting tune was performed on the show that date; or the show was preempted (which happened most often with ABC's Saturday afternoon college football).

Joel Whitburn's *Pop Annual 1955 through 1982* used for research. Copyright © 1983 by Joel Whitburn and published by Record Research Inc., P.O. Box 200, Menominee Falls, Wisconsin 53051.

All chart data compiled from *Billboard* magazine and copyrighted 1955 through 1985 by Billboard Publications, Inc. No part of the *Billboard* chart data may be reproduced, stored in a retrieval system, transmitted in any form or by any means, electronic, mechanical, photocopying, recording, or otherwise, without the prior written permission of the copyright proprietor.

TOP 100 CHART SONGS PERFORMED AND OTHER IMPORTANT APPEARANCES ON *AMERICAN BANDSTAND*, 1950s.

1·9·5·7

BANDSTAND APPEARANCE	AB/TV DEBUT	ARTIST	SONG(S) PERFORMED	DATE APPEARED ON CHART	PEAK CHART POSITION	WEEKS ON CHART
8/5 (M.)	AB	Billy Williams	"I'm Gonna Sit Right Down and Write Myself a Letter"	6/3	#3	23
8/5 (M.)	AB	Chordettes	"Just Between You and Me"	9/9	#8	15
8/6 (Tu.)	AB/TV	Dale Hawkins	"Susie Q"✔	6/10	#27	19
8/6 (Tu.)	AB	Don Rondo	"White Silver Sands"	7/15	#7	19
8/7 (W.)	AB/TV	Paul Anka	"Diana"✔	7/15	#1	29
8/9 (F.)	AB	Lee Andrews & the Hearts	"Long Lonely Nights"✔	8/12	#45	10
8/12 (M.)	AB/TV	Gene Vincent & His Blue Caps	"Lotta Lovin'" / "Wear My Ring"	8/19 / 8/19	#13 / #26	19 / 7
8/12 (M.)	AB	Four Coins	"Shangri-La"	5/27	#11	21
8/13 (Tu.)	AB/TV	Jodi Sands	"With All My Heart"✔	5/27	#15	18
8/13 (Tu.)	AB	Sal Mineo	"Start Movin'"✔ / "Lasting Love"	5/20 / 9/9	#9 / #27	19 / 10
8/16 (F.)	AB/TV	Ted Newman	"Plaything"*	9/30	#45	9
8/19 (M.)	AB/TV	Jerry Lee Lewis	"Whole Lotta Shakin' Going' On"✔	6/24	#3	29
8/19 (M.)	AB/TV	Jimmy Bowen & the Rhythm Orchids	"Warm Up to Me Baby"	5/20	#57	7
8/21 (W.)	AB	Randy Starr	"A Dance, a Kiss, a Promise"	8/26	#97	2
8/26 (M.)	AB/TV	Buddy Holly & the Crickets	"That'll Be the Day"✔	8/12	#1	22
8/26 (M.)	AB/TV	Doc Bagby	"Dumplins"*	9/30	#69	4
8/27 (Tu.)	AB/TV	Johnny Nash	"A Very Special Love"✔	12/30	#23	10
9/2 (M.)	AB	Andy Williams	"Lips of Wine"	9/23	#17	13
9/2 (M.)	AB/TV	Bobbettes	"Mr. Lee"✔	8/5	#6	24
9/3 (Tu.)		Mello-Kings	"Tonite, Tonite"*	8/19	#77	10
9/9 (M.)	AB/TV	Diamonds	"Zip Zip" / "Little Darlin'"	8/26 / 8/16	#16 / #2	11 / 26
9/10 (Tu.)	AB/TV	Jimmie Rodgers	"Honeycomb"✔	8/12	#1	28
9/11 (W.)	AB/TV	Webb Pierce	"Holiday for Love" / "Don't Do It"	NOTE: neither tune charted pop but both were country hits.		
9/12 (Th.)	AB/TV	Nick Noble	"Moonlight Swim"♦	9/9	#37	8
9/12 (Th.)	AB/TV	Tune Weavers	"Happy Happy Birthday to You"*	9/16	#5	19
9/13 (F.)	AB/TV	Everly Brothers	"Wake Up Little Susie"	9/30	#1	26
9/18 (W.)	AB/TV	Frankie Avalon		(no hits until 1958)		
9/20 (F.)		Don Rondo	"There's Only You"♦	10/28	#77	2
9/25 (W.)	AB	Eileen Rodgers	"Third Finger, Left Hand"	9/16	#82	2
9/26 (Th.)	AB/TV	The Rays	"Silhouettes"✔	10/14	#3	20
9/30 (M.)	AB	Sonny James	"Uh-Huh-Mm"	12/30	#92	1

BANDSTAND APPEARANCE	AB/TV DEBUT	ARTIST	SONG(S) PERFORMED	DATE APPEARED ON CHART	PEAK CHART POSITION	WEEKS ON CHART
10/3 (Th.)	AB	Marvin Rainwater	"Gonna Find Me a Bluebird"✔	5/20	#18	22
10/4 (F.)	AB/TV	Jackie Wilson	"Reet Petite (The Prettiest Girl You Ever Wanna Meet)"✔	11/4	#62	10
10/9 (W.)	AB/TV	Johnny Mathis	"Chances Are"	9/16	#1	28
10/10 (Th.)	AB/TV	Thurston Harris	"Little Bitty Pretty One"✔	10/21	#6	17
10/11 (F.)	AB	Del-Vikings	"Come and Go with Me"✔ / "Whispering Bells" / "Cool Shake"	2/18 / 7/8 / 7/15	#4 / #9 / #12	31 / 18 / 16
10/14 (M.)		Four Coins	"My One Sin"	9/23	#28	15
10/15 (Tu.)	AB/TV	Carol Jarvis	"Rebel"*	9/2	#48	16
10/21 (M.)	AB	Five Satins	"To the Aisle"	7/22	#25	17
10/23 (W.)	AB	Georgia Gibbs	"Walkin' the Floor over You"	6/3	#92	1
10/29 (Tu.)	AB/TV	Bonnie Guitar	"Dark Moon"✔ / "Mr. Fire Eyes"	4/15 / 10/28	#6 / #71	22 / 8
11/1 (F.)	AB	Four Esquires	"Love Me Forever"	11/18	#25	10
11/4 (M.)		Jerry Lee Lewis	"Great Balls of Fire"	11/18	#2	21
11/5 (Tu.)	AB	Sparkletones	"Black Slacks"	8/26	#17	19
11/6 (W.)	AB/TV	Jerry Reed		(no hits until 1962)		
11/8 (F.)	AB/TV	Chuck Berry	"Rock 'n' Roll Music"	11/11	#8	19
11/12 (Tu.)	AB	Joni James	"Summer Love"	7/15	#97	1
11/13 (W.)	AB/TV	Janice Harper	"Bon Voyage"✔ / "That's Why I Was Born"	9/2 / 12/16	#46 / #84	14 / 4
11/22 (F.)	AB/TV	Tom & Jerry (Paul Simon and Art Garfunkel)	"Hey Schoolgirl"*	12/23	#49	9
11/27 (W.)	AB	Bill Haley & the Comets	"You Hit the Wrong Note, Billygoat"	6/10	#60	7
12/2 (M.)	AB/TV	Danny & the Juniors	"At the Hop"✔	12/9	#1	28
12/2 (M.)	AB/TV	Jimmy Dee & the Off-Beats	"Henrietta"	1/6/58	#47	10
12/12 (Th.)		Frankie Avalon	"De De Dinah"✔	1/20/58	#7	15
12/16 (M.)		Gene Vincent & His Blue Caps	"Dance to the Bop"♦	12/9	#23	9
12/17 (Tu.)	AB/TV	Bobby Darin		(no hits until 1958)		
12/19 (Th.)	AB	Jerry Vale	"Pretend You Don't See Her"	11/25	#45	15
12/25 (W.)	AB/TV	Mike Pedicin Quartet	"Shake a Hand"*	2/10/58	#71	2

✔First hit by a performer   *Only hit by a performer   ♦Last hit by a performer

Bandstand Appearance	AB/TV Debut	Artist	Song(s) Performed	Date Appeared on Chart	Peak Chart Position	Weeks on Chart
1/7 (Tu.)	AB/TV	Buddy Knox	"Hula Love"	9/2/57	#9	23
			"Swingin' Daddy"	2/10	#80	6
1/7 (Tu.)	AB/TV	Hollywood Flames	"Buzz-Buzz-Buzz"*	11/25/57	#11	17
1/10 (F.)	AB	George Hamilton IV	"Why Don't They Understand"	12/2/57	#10	19
1/10 (F.)		Sal Mineo	"Party Time"	11/11/57	#45	8
			"Little Pigeon"	1/27	#45	8
1/13 (M.)	AB/TV	Dickie Doo & The Don'ts	"Click-Clack"✔	2/10	#28	14
1/14 (Tu.)	AB/TV	Sam Cooke	"I Love You for Sentimental Reasons"	12/30/57	#17	11
			"Desire Me"	12/30/57	#47	12
1/20 (M.)	AB/TV	Dale Wright & the Rock-Its	"She's Neat"✔	1/13	#38	13
1/21 (Tu.)	AB/TV	Johnny Cash	"Ballad of a Teenage Queen"	2/3	#14	19
1/23 (Th.)	AB/TV	Connie Francis	"Who's Sorry Now"✔	2/24	#4	22
1/24 (F.)	AB	Frankie Lymon & the Teenagers	"Goody Goody"♦	7/22/57	#20	17
1/29 (W.)	AB/TV	Eddie Cochran	"Jeannie Jeannie Jeannie"	3/10	#94	1
2/3 (M.)	AB	Ames Brothers	"Little Gypsy"	2/24	#67	2
2/4 (Tu.)	AB/TV	Royal Teens	Short Shorts"✔	1/27	#3	16
2/13 (Th.)	AB/TV	Lou Monte	"Lazy Mary/Luna Mezzo Mare"✔	3/10	#12	18
2/14 (F.)	AB/TV	Ersel Hickey	"Bluebirds over the Mountain"*	4/28	#75	6
2/26 (W.)		Jackie Wilson	"To Be Loved"	4/14	#22	16
2/28 (F.)	AB	Tommy Sands	"Sing Boy Sing"	2/17	#24	11
3/3 (M.)	AB/TV	Larry Hovis		(Never had a hit record; Hovis starred as "Carter" in TV series "Hogan's Heroes.")		
3/5 (W.)		Andy Williams	"Are You Sincere?"	2/17	#3	17
3/11 (Tu.)	AB/TV	Jack Jones		(no hits until 1962)		
3/11 (Tu.)	AB	Four Lads	"Put a Light in the Window"	12/9/57	#8	14
3/12 (W.)	AB/TV	Merv Griffin		(no hits until 1961)		
3/17 (M.)	AB	Four Voices	"Dancing with my Shadow"♦	3/24	#50	6
3/18 (Tu.)		Jerry Lee Lewis	"You Win Again"	2/17	#95	1
			"Breathless"	3/3	#7	15
3/24 (M.)	AB/TV	Billie & Lillie	"La-Dee-Dah"✔	1/6	#9	13
3/26 (W.)	AB/TV	Don Gibson	"Oh Lonesome Me"	3/10	#7	21
3/28 (F.)		Frankie Avalon	"You Excite Me"	4/14	#49	9
4/7 (M.)	AB/TV	Jim Reeves	"Anna Marie"	2/3	#93	1
4/10 (Th.)	AB/TV	Barbara McNair		(never had a charting record)		
4/15 (Tu.)		Ames Brothers	"A Very Precious Love"	3/31	#23	11
4/16 (W.)	AB/TV	Dion & the Belmonts	"I Wonder Why"✔	5/19	#22	13
4/18 (F.)	AB/TV	Huey Smith & the Clowns	"Don't You Just Know It"	3/24	#9	13
4/23 (W.)	AB/TV	Laurie London	"He's Got the Whole World in His Hands"	3/24	#1	19
4/29 (Tu.)	AB/TV	Buddy Greco		(no hits until 1962)		
5/1 (Th.)	AB	Roy Hamilton	"Don't Let Go"	1/13	#13	16
5/7 (W.)	AB/TV	The Champs	"Tequila"✔	5/24	#1	19
			"El Rancho Rock"	5/26	#30	10
5/7 (W.)	AB	The Playboys	"Over the Weekend"*	8/25	#62	6
5/9 (F.)	AB/TV	Jody Reynolds	"Endless Sleep"✔	5/19	#5	17
5/12 (M.)	AB/TB	Mickey & Sylvia	"Bewildered"	6/16	#57	5
5/16 (F.)	AB/TV	Jack Scott	"Leroy"✔	6/9	#25	13
			"My True Love"	6/30	#3	19
5/22 (Th.)	AB	Four Aces	"Rock 'n' Roll Rhapsody"	3/24	#63	4
5/23 (F.)	AB	Julius LaRosa	"Torrero"♦	6/16	#21	1
6/4 (W.)		Danny & the Juniors	"Rock 'n' Roll Is Here to Stay"	3/3	#19	11
			"Dotty"	6/23	#39	6
6/10 (Tu.)	AB/TV	Leslie Uggams		(no hits until 1959)		
6/11 (W.)	AB/TV	Jimmy Clanton	"Just a Dream"✔	7/14	#4	10
6/19 (Th.)	AB/TV	Fabian		(no hits until 1959)		
7/21 (M.)		Dale Hawkins	"La-Do-Da-Da"	8/25	#32	12
7/24 (Th.)	AB/TV	Duane Eddy	"Moovin' and Groovin'"	3/17	#72	3
			"Rebel Rouser"	6/30	#6	14
8/5 (Tu.)	AB/TV	The Coasters	"Yakety Yak"	6/2	#1	16
8/6 (W.)		Jackie Wilson	"We Have Love"	9/22	#93	2
8/6 (W.)		Royal Teens	"Harvey's Got a Girlfriend"	8/11	#78	2
8/7 (Th.)	AB/TV	Poni-Tails	"Born Too Late"✔	7/21	#7	16
8/7 (Th.)		Dion & the Belmonts	"No One Knows"	8/25	#19	16
8/11 (M.)	AB/TV	Bobby Freeman	"Betty Lou Got a New Pair of Shoes"	8/4	#37	9
			"Do You Wanna Dance"✔	5/12	#5	17
8/14 (W.)		Kingsmen (Comets sans Bill Haley)	"Week End"*	8/25	#35	3
8/20 (W.)	AB/TV	Kirby Stone Four	"Baubles, Bangles, and Beads"*	7/28	#25	3
8/22 (F.)	AB/TV	Tommy Edwards	"It's All in the Game"✔	8/18	#1	22
8/26 (Tu.)		Eddie Cochran	"Summertime Blues"	8/4	#8	16

✔First hit by a performer   *Only hit by a performer   ♦Last hit by a performer

BANDSTAND APPEARANCE	AB/TV DEBUT	ARTIST	SONG(S) PERFORMED	DATE APPEARED ON CHART	PEAK CHART POSITION	WEEKS ON CHART
9/1 (M.)	AB/TV	Frankie Ford		(no hits until 1959)		
9/4 (Th.)	AB/TV	Jerry Butler & the Impressions	"For Your Precious Love"✔	6/16	#11	12
9/10 (W.)	AB/TV	Little Anthony & the Imperials	"Tears on My Pillow"✔	8/11	#4	19
9/11 (Th.)		Dickie Doo & the Don'ts	"Nee Nee Na Na Na Na Na Nu Nu" "Flip-Top Box"	5/5 6/9	#40 #61	8 8
9/18 (Th.)	AB/TV	Arlene Smith & the Chantels	"I Love You So"	6/16	#42	8
9/24 (W.)	AB/TV	Johnny Tillotson	"Well I'm Your Man"✔ "Dreamy Eyes"	10/6 11/3	#87 #63	3 9
10/9 (Th.)		Duane Eddy	"Ramrod"	8/25	#27	8
10/17 (F.)		Roy Hamilton	"Pledging My Love"	11/17	#45	12
10/28 (Tu.)		Buddy Holly & the Crickets	"Think It Over" "Fool's Paradise" "Heartbeat"	7/21 8/4 12/29	#27 #58 #82	9 1 4
10/29 (W.)	AB/TV	Phil Spector (with the Teddy Bears)	"To Know Him Is To Love Him"✔	9/22	#1	23

BANDSTAND APPEARANCE	AB/TV DEBUT	ARTIST	SONG(S) PERFORMED	DATE APPEARED ON CHART	PEAK CHART POSITION	WEEKS ON CHART
11/5 (W.)	AB/TV	Earl Grant	"The End"✔	9/15	#7	19
11/7 (F.)	AB	The Cadillacs	"Peek-a-Boo"♦	12/8	#20	10
11/10 (M.)		Four Aces	"The World Outside"	11/24	#63	4
11/14 (F.)		Eddie Cochran	"C'mon Everybody"	11/24	#35	12
11/19 (W.)		Duane Eddy	"Cannonball"	11/3	#15	12
11/28 (F.)	AB	Bobby Helms	"The Fool and the Angel" "Jingle Bell Rock"	12/8 12/22	#75 #35	6 4
12/12 (F.)		Fabian	"I'm a Man"✔	1/12/59	#31	10
12/15 (M.)		Four Coins	"The World Outside" (same as Four Aces tune!)	11/10	#21	11
12/18 (Th.)	AB/TV	Bobby Day	"Rockin' Robin" "The Bluebird, the Buzzard and the Oriole"	8/4 12/29	#2 #54	21 6

1 • 9 • 5 • 9

BANDSTAND APPEARANCE	AB/TV DEBUT	ARTIST	SONG(S) PERFORMED	DATE APPEARED ON CHART	PEAK CHART POSITION	WEEKS ON CHART
1/9 (F.)		Dion & the Belmonts	"Don't Pity Me"	12/22/58	#40	12
1/15 (Th.)		Duane Eddy	"The Lonely One"	1/19	#23	13
1/20 (Tu.)		Jim Reeves	"Billy Bayou"	12/8/58	#95	1
1/23 (F.)	AB/TV	Little Willie John	"You're a Sweetheart"	8/11/58	#66	4
1/26 (M.)		Georgia Gibbs	"The Hula Hoop Song"♦	10/6/58	#32	5
2/6 (F.)		Poni-Tails	"Seven Minutes in Heaven"	12/1/58	#85	3
2/10 (Tu.)	AB/TV	Link Wray & His Wraymen	"Rawhide"	1/26	#23	13
2/13 (F.)	AB/TV	Skyliners	"Since I Don't Have You"✔	2/16	#12	19
2/16 (M.)		Little Anthony & the Imperials	"So Much" "Wishful Thinking"	12/22/58 3/23	#87 #79	2 2
2/17 (Tu.)	AB	Rivieras	"Moonlight Serenade"	2/9	#47	11
2/18 (W.)		Roy Hamilton	"I Need Your Lovin'"	4/20	#62	5
2/20 (F.)	AB/TV	Platters	"Smoke Gets in Your Eyes" "Enchanted"	11/17/58 3/23	#1 #12	19 15

BANDSTAND APPEARANCE	AB/TV DEBUT	ARTIST	SONG(S) PERFORMED	DATE APPEARED ON CHART	PEAK CHART POSITION	WEEKS ON CHART
3/5 (Th.)		Chuck Berry	"Anthony Boy" "Almost Grown"	2/16 3/30	#60 #32	5 13
3/6 (F.)	AB/TV	Fats Domino	"Telling Lies" "When the Saints Go Marching In"	2/16 2/16	#50 #50	9 9
3/12 (Th.)		Fabian	"Turn Me Loose"	3/30	#9	13
3/20 (F.)	AB/TV	Bobby Rydell		(no hits until later in year)		
3/23 (M.)		Frankie Ford	"Sea Cruise"✔	2/9	#14	17
3/25 (W.)	AB/TV	Flamingos	"Lovers Never Say Goodbye"✔	1/19	#52	10
3/27 (F.)	AB/TV	Annette (Funicello)	"Tall Paul"✔ "Ju-Jo the Dog-Fared Boy"	1/5 4/13	#17 #73	15 4
4/3 (F.)	AB/TV	Neil Sedaka	"I Go Ape" "The Diary"✔	3/9 12/8/58	#42 #54	8 14
4/21 (Tu.)	AB/TV	Jesse Belvin	"Guess Who?"♦	3/30	#31	13
4/22 (W.)		Johnny Nash	"As Time Goes By"	3/16	#43	11
4/24 (F.)		Teddy Bears	"I Don't Need You Anymore" "Oh Why"♦	2/16 3/9	#98 #91	1 2
4/28 (Tu.)	AB/TV	Rockin' R's	"The Beat"	3/23	#57	8

BANDSTAND APPEARANCE	AB/TV DEBUT	ARTIST	SONG(S) PERFORMED	DATE APPEARED ON CHART	PEAK CHART POSITION	WEEKS ON CHART
4/29 (W.)	AB/TV	Chubby Checker	"The Class"✔	5/18	#38	7
4/30 (Th.)	AB/TV	Dee Clark	"Just Keep It Up"	5/4	#18	15
5/1 (F.)	AB/TV	Freddy Cannon	"Tallahassee Lassie"✔	5/11	#6	15
5/4 (M.)	AB/TV	Martin Denny	"Quiet Village"✔	4/13	#4	16
5/5 (Tu.)	AB/TV	The Crests	"Six Nights a Week"	3/23	#28	13
			"Flowers of Love"	6/8	#79	6
5/13 (W.)	AB/TV	The Falcons (featuring Wilson Pickett)	"You're So Fine"✔	4/20	#17	20
5/15 (F.)	AB/TV	Dave "Baby" Cortez	"The Happy Organ"	3/16	#1	17
5/18 (M.)	AB/TV	Jesse Lee Turner	"The Little Space Girl"*	1/5	#20	12
5/26 (Tu.)		Four Lads	"Fountain of Youth"	5/4	#90	2
6/1 (M.)		Dion & the Belmonts	"A Teenager in Love"	4/20	#5	15
6/3 (W.)	AB/TV	Preston Epps	"Bongo Rock"✔	5/18	#14	13
6/4 (Th.)	AB/TV	Johnny & the Hurricanes	"Crossfire"✔	4/27	#23	14
			"Red River Rock"	8/3	#5	17
6/12 (F.)	AB	Anita Bryant	"Till There Was You"	6/29	#30	13
6/18 (Th.)		Bobby Freeman	"Mary Ann Thomas"	6/1	#90	2
6/29 (M.)		Sam Cooke	"Everybody Likes to Cha-Cha"	3/9	#31	11
			"Only 16"	6/8	#28	10
6/30 (Tu.)	AB/TV	Drifters	"There Goes My Baby"	6/1	#2	19
7/1 (W.)		Jimmy Clanton	"My Own True Love"	8/3	#33	12
7/3 (F.)		Ray Peterson	"The Wonder of You"	5/18	#25	16
7/7 (Tu.)	AB/TV	Tradewinds**	"Furry Murray"♦	8/10	#91	2
7/15 (W.)		Duane Eddy	"40 Miles of Bad Road"	6/15	#9	15
			"The Quiet Three"	6/29	#46	8
7/29 (W.)		Frankie Ford	"Alimony"	8/3	#97	2
8/4 (Tu.)		Bobby Rydell	"Kissin' Time"✔	6/29	#11	17
8/4 (Tu.)	AB/TV	Carl Smith	"10,000 Drums"♦	7/6	#43	9
8/5 (W.)		Annette (Funicello)	"Lonely Guitar"	7/6	#50	11
8/6 (Th.)	AB/TV	Eugene Church & the Fellows	"Miami"♦	8/3	#67	5
8/7 (F.)	AB/TV	Skip & Flip	"It Was I"✔	6/22	#11	16
8/7 (F.)		Dave "Baby" Cortez	"The Whistling Organ"	6/8	#61	8
8/11 (Tu.)		Johnny Tillotson	"True, True Happiness"	8/24	#54	9
8/12 (W.)	AB	LaVern Baker	"So Hi, So Lo"	7/27	#52	10
			"If You Love Me"	8/17	#79	2
8/17 (M.)	AB/TV	Ronnie Hawkins & the Hawks	"Forty Days"✔	6/8	#45	8
			"Mary Lou"	8/17	#26	16
8/18 (Tu.)	AB	Edd "Kookie" Byrnes	"Like I Love You"	8/10	#42	9
8/19 (W.)		Leslie Uggams	"One More Sunrise"	9/14	#98	1
9/15 (Tu.)		Duane Eddy	"Some Kinda Earthquake"	9/28	#37	8
			"First Love, First Tears"	9/28	#59	9
9/16 (W.)	AB/TV	Barry Mann	(no hits until 1961)			
9/23 (W.)	AB	Clovers	"Love Potion #9"♦	9/14	#23	17
9/25 (F.)	AB/TV	Rock-a-Teens	"Woo-Hoo"*	10/5	#16	12
10/1 (Th.)		Poni-Tails	"I'll Be Seeing You"♦	10/26	#87	3
10/12 (M.)	AB/TV	Tempos	"See You in September"*	6/29	#23	14
10/16 (F.)	AB/TV	Revels	"Midnight Stroll"*	10/19	#35	10
10/26 (M.)	AB/TV	Marv Johnson	"You Got What It Takes"	11/2	#10	22
10/27 (Tu.)	AB/TV	Stonewall Jackson	"Waterloo"✔	5/25	#4	16
11/6 (F.)		Freddy Cannon	"Okeee-fun-okee"	8/24	#43	9
			"Way Down Yonder in New Orleans"	11/23	#3	15
11/9 (M.)		Annette (Funicello)	"First Name, Initial"	10/26	#20	18
			"My Heart Became of Age"	10/26	#74	3
11/10 (Tu.)		Fats Domino	"Be My Guest"	10/26	#8	14
			"I've Been Around"	10/26	#33	9
11/24 (Tu.)		Tommy Edwards	"Honestly and Truly"	11/2	#65	8
			"The Ways of Love"	11/16	#47	9
11/26 (Th.)		Coasters	"What About Us"	12/7	#47	10
12/3 (Th.)		Drifters	"Dance with Me"	10/12	#15	15
			"True Love, True Love"	11/2	#33	11
12/7 (M.)	AB	Kitty Kallen	"If I Give My Heart to You"	10/5	#34	12
12/11 (F.)		Johnny Tillotson	"Why Do I Love You So"	1/18/60	#42	14
12/16 (W.)	AB/TV	Mark Dinning	"Teen Angel"✔	12/21	#1	18
12/22 (Tu.)		Duane Eddy	"Bonnie Came Back"	12/28	#26	9

✔First hit by a performer   *Only hit by a performer   ♦Last hit by a performer

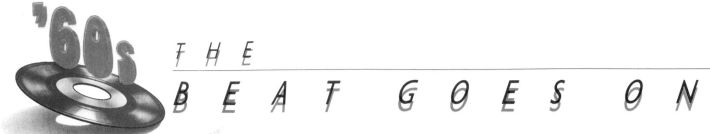

Congratulations

DICK CLARK
&
AMERICAN
BANDSTAND

Celebrating Five Years on ABC-TV
AUGUST 10, 1962

Philadelphia's only regularly scheduled Network origination.

50 minutes daily, produced for ABC at WFIL-TV, leader in Philadelphia television for more than five years.

The sixties: a decade of upheaval and change, and, to many, *the* most tumultuous decade of this century. The sixties—the generation gap, the sexual revolution, the hippies, peace and free love, racial unrest, and the coming of self-consciousness and political awareness to the huge population that resulted from the postwar baby boom. How did *Bandstand* handle it all?

In a way, the show's tremendous influence on the music business was responsible, in part, for the fact that what we know as the "tumultuous Sixties" actually didn't start till almost midway through the decade. Through 1964, the sixties were virtually indistinguishable from the fifties. On the surface, at any rate, that same aura of innocence prevailed. Until the hideous assassination of President John F. Kennedy, the early sixties were the age of Camelot and the New Frontier, when the country felt powerful, self-confident, young, and good-looking. When Kennedy was killed, an era ended. The time was ripe for the upheaval that followed, a period of change that, at its outset, paralleled the cultural revolution that was the British Invasion of 1964.

But before all that change, *Bandstand* continued to reign supreme. John Oates noted earlier that in the fifties *Bandstand* drew such numbers of people to the WFIL studios that he didn't even bother trying to get into the show. Joe Bonsall, of the hugely popular country band the Oak Ridge Boys, grew up in North Philadelphia during the sixties half of the great *Bandstand* era. His recollections of the show are markedly similar to John's. But Joe managed to get into the show.

"I grew up in a section of North Philly called K and A," says Joe, "for Kensington and Allegheny. Around 1960, '61, '62, I was in junior high, and there was this girl named Cathy who was a *Bandstand* freak. She'd go down to the studio every day. And she couldn't always find someone else to go with her, so sometimes she'd ask me, like once a week. So we'd get on the El [subway] stop right near school and we'd go all the way to Forty-sixth Street, where the studio was. The El let you off right in front of WFIL. We'd get off the El and get in line. It was a *looooong* line. Some days we got in, most days we didn't. The days we didn't, we stopped at Pop Singer's corner drugstore right by the studio, had a milkshake, and then took the El right back home to catch *Bandstand* on TV.

"Some days, though, we'd get there early enough and be far enough up in line that we'd get in. I saw the Shirelles sing there once, and I saw Chubby Checker at the height of Twistmania. I remember I even wore my red and black Twister shoes, got 'em at Thom McAn.

Remember them?

"What I remember most vividly is the size of the studio. On TV it looked practically like a ballroom. In person you were struck by how tiny and crowded it was. I'd sit up there in the bleachers and not believe they could even *fit* the bleachers in, plus Dick Clark's podium, the Rate-a-Record stand, the autograph table, and the stage and dance areas. It was a really tiny setup. And they had all these kids and these three big cameras. I'll never forget watching the way the kids who were dancing would all respond when the red lights on the cameras changed. When the red light's on, it means that camera's on. You had to be there to see these kids shifting direction en masse in the middle of the Twist or the Pony or whatever. One camera's red light would go on, they'd all shuffle over there. Another would go on, they'd shuffle back the other way. Guys dragging their girls. Girls dragging their guys.

"But I was always excited about going down to the studio because that show was all about getting close to what was happening in music, in teenage life in general. The dancing, the clothes, the music, the excitement, everything.

That show was the *source* for all that was happening for us. I always loved music, loved rock 'n' roll, loved Elvis—you know, I wanted to be Elvis just like everyone else. And this was the show that brought all that into my living room every day. I didn't even think about the show being national. I just was so taken by the fact that it came from the other side of *my town*, and that I could either go there in person or at least catch it on TV at home, five days a week.

"I still watch the show today whenever I get a chance. That format, with the kids picking the records, and the dancing, and all that, you just can't beat it. The fact that the show has endured the way it has is a remarkable thing. It's just magic. It was magic back then when I used to go in Philly, and it's still out there today. So it must have something right. It kills me how little the show's really changed. That kind of timeless appeal, that's the magic of it. And I give Dick Clark full credit for that. The man just knows

They're *still* standing in line . . .

how to reach the heart of American youth.''

But beneath the placid surface of the early sixties, big changes were a-brewing. Motown had gotten itself established at the very tail end of the fifties and would soon become an enormously important musical/cultural force by crossing black music over to the mass pop market as never before. In fact, one factor in Motown's revolutionary success lay in an assimilative tactic not unlike *Bandstand*'s own dressing up of its audience—that is, the famous Motown Finishing School set up by label chief Berry Gordy, Jr. (last seen writing Jackie Wilson's first solo hit single, ''Reet Petite''), who believed that proper grooming, appearance, and behavior were just as crucial to success as raw musical talent.

Other changes in the music scene that were documented on *Bandstand* included the emergence of California surf music, which manifested itself in both the vocal music of the Beach Boys and Jan and Dean (the latter appeared many times on the show) and the guitar-

American Bandstand goes "on location" for the first time. WFIL's press release announced this special show to the world.

TRIANGLE STATION

WFIL-TV 46th & Market Streets / Philadelphia 39, Penna.

NEWS

For Immediate Release   7/22/60

"AMERICAN BANDSTAND SPLASH PARTY" FROM DREXEL HILL
ON WFIL-TV AND ABC-TV NETWORK JULY 29

PHILADELPHIA, July 22:-- For the first time in its three years on the coast-to-coast ABC-TV Network, "American Bandstand" on WFIL-TV travels outdoors for a "Splash Party" complete with music, dancing, guest stars and swimming and diving exhibitions Friday, July 29, from 3:30 to 5:30 p.m.

The Drexelbrook Swimming and Tennis Club in Drexel Hill, Pa., is the scene of the two hour aquatic outing with Dick Clark and stars from the worlds of popular music and water sports. The poolside program will be telecast on Channel 6 and 145 stations in the U.S. and Hawaii.

Among the guests for the show are the Brothers Four, whose recording of "Greenfields" has been one of the nation's best-sellers for the past few months.

The "American Bandstand Splash Party" will also feature water safety demonstrations as well as water ballets and both comic and fancy diving exhibitions.

Former Olympic swimming champion Joe Verdeur, heads the water carnival performers along with Chris Ames, Dave Detwiler, and Chris Keller all champion divers from Delaware Valley.

(more)

dominated instrumentals of bands like the Ventures (who also became *Bandstand* staples during those years) and Dick Dale and His Del-tones. Then there was Phil Spector, the "first tycoon of teen," who became a revolutionary music producer with his patented Wall of Sound, the first modern pop production technique to make full use of a studio's possibilities for sonic layering through multiple overdubs (Phil started with the Teddy Bears, who appeared on *Bandstand* in October 1958). Especially through his stable of girl groups like the Ronettes and the Crystals (both of whom, like many other Spector artists, were also frequent *Bandstand* guests), Spector crafted some of the most glorious and enduring music ever in rock 'n' roll, and his cache of classics alone belies those critics who dismiss the early, pre-Beatle sixties as fallow years for great rock music.

Also in the early sixties, such British teen-idol Elvis-clones as Cliff Richard appeared on the show. Though none of these protean British rockers (others included Tommy Steele, who went on to greater glory as a Broadway star in the hit show *Half a Sixpence*, Billy Fury, and Adam Faith) ever had any real hits in the United States (Richard finally did, but not until over a decade later), their very presence on the scene was a subtle harbinger of big things to come.

Bandstand itself went through some changes, too. On January 31, 1962, when "The Mickey Mouse Club" finally left the airwaves, the show moved back to a 4:30 P.M. starting time and continued to 5:30 P.M. Not long after that, *Bandstand* began taping its episodes for the first time. On September 9, 1967, *Bandstand* finally went color, one of the last network TV shows to do so. "In the early years, we had a studio that had always been lighted for black-and-white," Dick Clark explains. "In the late fifties, we had to go from three black-and-white cameras to just one color camera. It was *horrible*. Imagine doing the show with just one camera. The thing was these color cameras were new, and they were huge, big as a couch,

Dick Clark about to present a Gold Record to The Grass Roots, 1968.

CALLING ALL KIDS! SAN FRANCISCO STARS ON DICK CLARK'S "AMERICAN BANDSTAND"

Today, two Bay Area high school students take you on an exciting teen tour of San Francisco!

4:00 KGO-TV 7

As *American Bandstand* became even more popular, so did Dick Clark himself. Here's a typical magazine cover of the day.

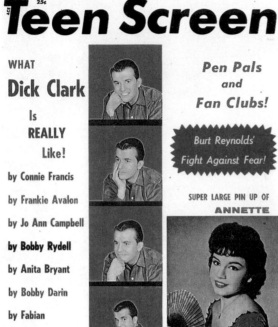

Dodie Stevens' Secret Classroom Loves!

25¢

Teen Screen

WHAT

Dick Clark

Is

REALLY

Like!

by Connie Francis

by Frankie Avalon

by Jo Ann Campbell

by Bobby Rydell

by Anita Bryant

by Bobby Darin

by Fabian

by Dion

Pen Pals
and
Fan Clubs!

Burt Reynolds'
Fight Against Fear!

SUPER LARGE PIN UP OF
ANNETTE

and immobile. And I had to go to the station executives and explain that if we didn't go back to black-and-white cameras, at least we had to get color cameras that were more manageable, or else it'd kill the show. Of course, the show was very profitable for them, so we went back to black-and-white. And we stayed that way until 1967, when ABC decided to make us the last show to go to color.''

But the biggest changes in *Bandstand*'s history came in 1963 and 1964. Just as summer turned to fall and the school year began, *TV Guide*'s *Bandstand* listing for Friday, August 30, 1963, read ''last show of series.'' Alarmed *Bandstand* watchers were calmed the next day when they saw their new *TV Guide*—and then were taken aback again by what they saw for the *Bandstand* listing. The show was still on, alright, but now it was listed on *Saturday*, September 7, at 1:30 P.M. The show had moved

to once-a-week broadcasting. Then on February 8, 1964, viewers opened their *TV Guides* and read, ''*Bandstand* begins broadcasting from Hollywood, as Dick Clark welcomes Jackie DeShannon and Dick and DeeDee.'' The look of the show was changed: a roomier studio with a sleeker, more spartan look dominated by bright white—a perfect symbol of the differences between Eastern, urban Philadelphia and wide-open, sunlit, fun-and-health-happy California. But the basic setup in the studio was not that different from the earlier days, and in form *Bandstand* remained consistent.

With the move west and the schedule change from five days a week to once a weekend, *Bandstand*'s status and influence were changed forever. The show simply became that much less of a fixture in the lives of its viewers, and that much less of an influence on the music business. It may or may not be purely coincidental that the show's greatest period of influence came to an end just as the era of the teen idols was making way for the British Invasion.

There was another big change involved here: The regulars were gone—forever, as it turned out. While the show would go on to have numerous regular dancers, they would never be featured as prominently, or adored so intensely by the viewers, as they had been back in Philadelphia. Why? Dick Clark has the answer: ''It was just simple, natural evolution, the way it worked out. When the show went to once a week from five times a week, it was just that much harder to maintain the continuity of identity that we once had. It was due more to going once a week than moving to California. We never had a problem attracting kids to the show in California, and we did have our share of regulars since the move, but you weren't seeing them five days a week. The fan mail level dropped off, the following changed. There were people who were recognizable, who got followings of their own. For instance, we had our first regular black couple on the show in the mid-sixties, Famous Hooks and June Strode. But

TV SCOUT®
ENTERTAINMENT NEWS AND FEATURES

Meet Dick Clark

He Thinks His Show Can Run for 30 Years

By JOAN CROSBY

PHILADELPHIA—Among critics of television, this past week has seen a raised eyebrow or two caused by the fact that Dick Clark's American Bandstand has just celebrated its fifth anniversary on the ABC network. The show, they had figured, wouldn't last.

However, they could have saved themselves the trouble of predicting an early demise if they had just consulted Clark himself.

"I think it can run for 30 years," he said, adding, "if the people at the network think enough of it to handle it properly. It has a Breakfast Club kind of longevity. Nothing really changes, except, like people, it adds lines in the face, gains weight, loses hair. It's a program that can adjust itself to the times, the music of the day and the tastes of the teens .... rs
....delphia, and ...

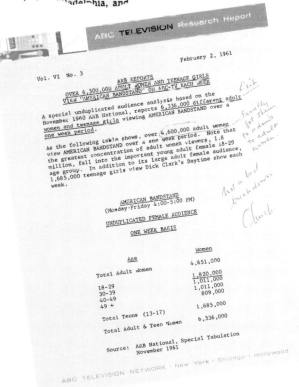

Press coverage increased tremendously; there were even statistical analyses done once people realized how wide the audience actually was.

THE BEAT GOES ON

The famous Hong Kong show. Below, Dong Kingman being interviewed by Dick Clark.

it was not anything like what we had going in Philadelphia—that was a very special, once-in-a-lifetime phenomenon. I don't think anything like that will ever happen again.''

Why did the show make the move? Dick Clark explains:

''The times were changing in the music business, and since it was the business of myself and the show to stay on top of trends in the music business, we were well aware of it. The early Philadelphia music scene was fading. Frankie Avalon, Fabian, and Bobby Rydell had moved out to California to make it in Hollywood. Deke Heyward, who had produced my ''Saturday Night Show'' in New York starting in 1958, moved to Hollywood to do the beach-blanket movies with Frankie and Annette after the "Saturday Night Show" ended. The surf music thing was starting out there. Everywhere we looked things said, 'California definitely *is* happening.' California truly looked like the 'promised land' back then, just like that old Chuck Berry song says. Meanwhile, I had already developed ties to Hollywood through making movies like *Because They're Young* and *The Young Doctors*. It just didn't make sense to stay in Philadelphia. And California just kept looking better and better. So—we went."

One thing the move to California ensured was that there could never be a repeat of what had happened on a 1962 *Bandstand* that many still talk about. It was winter, there was a terrible blizzard in Philadelphia that day, and a transit strike was on to boot, which meant that hardly anyone was able to get to the studio. "We had to keep vamping for time until more people got to the studio," Dick Clark recalls, "so what we did out of desperation was open up the big sliding doors that made up the studio's back wall, and we went out into the station parking lot and played in the snow, had snowball fights, that sort of thing. We got phone calls and letters from people in Arizona and Florida, who'd never seen such a thing and couldn't believe it. To them, seeing real live snow falling was like seeing the man in the moon or something, I guess."

Any dip in the show's influence and popularity as a result of its move and schedule change was insignificant, however—*Bandstand* continued to fulfill its function of chronicling the seemingly constant changes in the pop scene that took place in that decade. While the show was still in Philadelphia, the start of the sixties saw the all-time peak of the dance crazes it has always had a sizable hand in instigating. There were the Twist, Swim, Mashed Potato, Locomotion, Watusi, and so many others, all of them introduced and popularized by *Bandstand*. There were the sweeping changes in teen fashions, from the more buttoned-down fifties styles

through the more casual look of the early sixties to the ultraliberated hippie era. Psychedelia and theatrically inclined rock bands made their debuts this decade, and they too were on the show. Indeed, despite the shock that much of the show's audience may have received from the reduction to one broadcast a week and the change of venue, as the sixties went on and the times seemed to change more and more rapidly, the show's dependably consistent format became something to truly cherish.

And, as has always been the wont of TV programmers, the *Bandstand* premise was also something to imitate, or at least be inspired by. The sixties were the decade that saw the Establishment finally, fully, and irrevocably recognize rock and its culture; one of the best indicators of that recognition was the flood of rock shows that began showing up on television. Dick Clark had his own "Where The Action Is," a daytime show that ran five days a week, Monday through Friday. During prime time at night, we had "Shindig," "Hullabaloo," and "The Music Scene" —shows that were all a little more wide-open in format and self-consciously hip in their selection of acts than *Bandstand*. But there can be no argument that by making rock 'n' roll safe for America (and vice versa), *AB* paved the way for them. (It's interesting to note that many of these shows capitalized on the notion of "regulars"—only they used professional go-go dancers instead of ordinary kids. Remember Layda Edmund, Jr., from "Hullabaloo," and Carol Shelyne with the huge owl glasses from "Shindig"?)

"The Lloyd Thaxton Show" and Clay Cole's "Disk-o-tek" were blatant *Bandstand* clones that were wilder and woolier than their forebear. They, too, found their audiences, if only temporarily. But neither of them lasted very long. *Bandstand* is still going strong, while the rest are but memories.

For whatever reasons, the original is still the greatest—first, last, and only.

THE MUSIC

Dick Clark and Mary Wells, 1962.

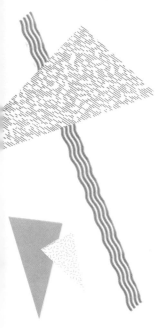

Remember that "Merry Christmas" record from the Clarks that *Bandstand* fan Dave Frees mentioned where someone did imitations of various rock stars giving their season's greetings? That someone was none other than Chubby Checker, Mr. Twist himself and another star who owed much of his career to *Bandstand* exposure.

It all started shortly before Christmas 1958. When Dick had this idea to send his friends a Christmas record rather than a Christmas card, his music business acquaintance Bernie Lowe, of the Philadelphia label Cameo Records, offered the services of his latest discovery, a portly hometown teenager named Ernest Evans, fresh from a Philadelphia high school where one of his classmates had been *Bandstand* regular Frank Brancaccio. In the studio, Evans did his impressions of Elvis Presley and Fats Domino for the disc. Watching him, Dick's first wife, Barbara, remarked, "He's cute. He looks like a little Fats Domino—like a chubby checker." Bernie Lowe did a double take and said, "Aha!" The name stuck and history was made—again.

Chubby made his *Bandstand* debut on Wednesday, April 29, 1959, singing his first hit single under his new name, "The Class," which *just* made the Top 40. Some nine months later, Dick Clark spotted some kids in the *Bandstand* audience gyrating to the music in a rather peculiar way—as if they were spinning invisible hula hoops or something. When he approached the kids during a station break and asked what they were doing, they replied, "A new dance—it's called the Twist." The dance had been inspired by an obscure B side of a single by the veteran R&B vocal group Hank Ballard and the Midnighters. (In the late summer of 1959, they'd had a minor hit with "Teardrops on Your Letter.") The B side of that single was "The Twist," but since the A side hadn't made much impact, it slipped right by most people. But such was the growing mania for dances in those days that an obscure song

Dion & the Belmonts, 1963.

was able to start a trend, even before the song itself became a hit! Dick Clark later called Bernie Lowe and mentioned the new dance, as he always did when there was a dance craze brewing with no record to go with it. Bernie had Chubby Checker cover "The Twist" and in the summer of 1960, it became a monumental smash hit, the biggest-ever of all the many dance-craze records.

The Twist not only irrevocably changed popular dancing styles—changes that had been signaled first by the Bop and then by the Pony—but also started an enormous trend in records. There were a host of spin-off records, many of which became hits mainly on the strength of their association with the name and beat of "The Twist." There were the Isley Brothers' "Twist and Shout" (later, of course, a smash for the Beatles), Sam Cooke's "Twistin' the Night Away," Joey Dee and the Starlighters' "Peppermint Twist," Gary U.S. Bonds's "Dear Lady Twist," and Santo and Johnny's Christmas instrumental "Twistin' Bells," a bouncy, steel-guitar remake of "Jingle Bells." Chubby Checker's "The Twist" hit number one *twice*, and in between Chubby hit again with —what else? —"Let's Twist Again." The Twist became the first dance craze to cross over from the teen world itself (at that time still very foreign territory to adults), to the mainstream of society: Newspapers and magazines like *Time* and *Newsweek*, as well as non—pop music TV shows, all featured demonstrations and instructions on how to twist.

In the fall of 1960, Jerry Lewis, who was then at the peak of his popularity, appeared on *Bandstand* with singer Jo Ann Campbell. She tried to teach him to twist, but she needn't have

The Righteous Brothers, 1966.

Jackie DeShannon, 1966.

97

"Little" Stevie
Wonder, 1963.

The Mamas & the
Papas, 1966.

bothered. Not only did Jerry never calm down
long enough to attempt a proper step, but his
own maniacally spastic gyrations actually made
the Twist look rather square by comparison!
Those who saw it remember it as one of
Bandstand's funniest afternoons ever.

In the late 1970s, the B-52's had a hit record
called "Dance This Mess Around," a tribute to
the dance crazes that flourished in the sixties
(the singers reeled off the names, like the Hippy
Shake, the Boogaloo, etc.) and some they *wished*
had been around (the Aqua Velva and Shy Tuna
for instance). Their title came from that of a
1960 hit by Bobby Freeman, "(Do the) Mess
Around." Though Chubby Checker had the
bigger hit, Bobby Freeman was perhaps the real
king of the dance-craze records, with several
different ones to his credit: "I Do the Shimmy
Shimmy," "C'mon and Swim," and "S-W-I-M"

and "Battle of New Orleans," Frankie Lymon was on the show in July 1960, singing the last hit of his brief but bright career, a version of Thurston Harris's earlier hit "Little Bitty Pretty One." The venerable "nonsense song" genre saw one of its first classics appearing on *Bandstand* in June 1960, as Dante and the Evergreens performed "Alley Oop" (later a hit once more for the Hollywood Argyles). Maurice Williams and the Zodiacs performed what would become something of an elegy for the dying Doo-Wop movement, the number-one "Stay," in December 1960 (it would be a hit all over again nearly twenty years later for Jackson Browne). Teen idols continued to appear on the show—some of them familiar, and some of them newer, like Brian Hyland, who at age sixteen appeared on *Bandstand* in the summer of 1960 to sing his first hit, the number-one "Itsy Bitsy Teenie Weenie Yellow Polka Dot Bikini." He'd go on to have many more hits through the decade and into the seventies.

And of course, new styles were introduced

among them. Fittingly, his career was kicked off with the 1958 classic "Do You Wanna Dance." Bobby made dozens of *Bandstand* appearances through the sixties.

As already mentioned, the styles that had been established in the previous decade still held sway, too. *Bandstand* presented performers like the Drifters with the immortal "Save the Last Dance for Me"; seminal rock instrumentalists like Duane Eddy with an endless string of hits and Johnny and the Hurricanes with "Down Yonder" and "Rocking Goose"; organist Dave "Baby" Cortez with "The Happy Organ" and "Rinky Tink"—early instances of the one-finger style of portable-organ playing that would fully flower in the mid-sixties with such garage-rock classics as ? and the Mysterians' "96 Tears"; and Preston Epps with the exotically funky "Bongo Bongo Bongo." Just as Johnny Horton was beginning his career with such historical-Americana pop ballads as "Johnny Freedom"

The Shirelles, 1962.

99

regularly, as they broke. On August 3, 1960, Jan and Dean made their *Bandstand* debut with one of their first hits, "We Go Together," which introduced the world to California surf rock. The guitar/instrumental surf-rock genre was kicked off on *AB* by the Duals, with "Stick Shift," in October 1961. The girl group sound, which would flourish over the next few years, was introduced in October 1960, when the Shirelles lip-synched "Tonight's the Night." In one remarkable case of the foresight that was a fringe benefit of the show's eclecticism, the blues revival that would come with the mid-to-late-sixties "back to the roots" movement was foreshadowed on Wednesday, July 5, 1961. That day, authentic Delta blues giant Slim Harpo appeared on the show performing one of his hits, "Rainin' In My Heart," which became a Top 40 smash. (Harpo's last hit was the 1966 top-twenty tune "Baby Scratch My Back," and he was the composer of the blues standard "I'm a King Bee," later covered by such respected blues interpreters as the Rolling Stones and Captain Beefheart.)

Some further evidence of that remarkable foresight: On November 4, 1960, Bobby Rydell

appeared on the show and performed "Sway," which would hit number 14 on the charts, *and* a tune that would reach number 70 called "Groovy Tonight." *Groovy* would not become popular teen slang for another six or seven years. On May 4, 1961, a band from Washington State, Paul Revere and the Raiders, made the first of their many *Bandstand* appearances with their very first hit, the number 38 "Like, Long Hair." While the use of *like* was already considered typical of the teenage way of destroying the King's English, the concept of long hair would remain totally foreign to males for another three or four years. Indeed, the Raiders themselves would not have any more hits for several

The Beach Boys,
1964.

100

years—not until long hair, like their own Revolutionary War-inspired coifs with ribbon-tied pigtails, had become okay for guys. Back in the early sixties, the term *long hair* was used in reference to *classical* music, and then usually only by trade magazines like *Billboard. This* is what the Raiders' song referred to.

Meanwhile, Motown made its *Bandstand* debut on December 27, 1960, as Smokey Robinson and the Miracles performed their second hit, "Shop Around," which reached number 2 (and was later just as big a hit for the Captain and Tennille). Mary Wells made her *Bandstand* debut on July 7, 1961, with her second hit, the number 33 "I Don't Want to Take a Chance" (her biggest hit, "My Guy," would come in 1964).

Ike and Tina Turner made their first appearance on the show on October 3, 1960, with the first of their twenty hits through 1975, "A Fool in Love" (it hit number 27). James Brown made the first of his dozens of *Bandstand* appearances on October 19, 1961, with "I Don't Mind" and "Baby, You're Right," his seventh and eighth hits with the Famous Flames. James would go on to have an amazing *ninety-one* hits through the early eighties. Memphis gospel/soul giant Solomon Burke debuted on the show March 20, 1962, with the second of his twenty-six hits, "Cry to Me," later covered by the Rolling Stones.

As the decade progressed, the musically inspired dance crazes kept coming. Dee Dee Sharp (who later married Philadelphia soul producer Kenny Gamble) introduced "Mashed Potato Time" on the show on March 15, 1962. Three months later she sang that she needed "Gravy (For My Mashed Potatoes)." A month after that, Little Eva (Eva Boyd—who worked as a babysitter for Carole King, a Brill Building songwriter, and later highly successful solo singer) performed "The Locomotion" on the show (it became a top hit again in the seventies, for Grand Funk Railroad). Interestingly enough, Carole King had written the song.

Shelley Fabares and Paul Peterson of TV's "Donna Reed Show" came on the show in

? & the Mysterians, 1966.

1962 to lip-synch their hits, "Johnny Angel" and "My Dad" respectively. At the other end of the musical spectrum, Queen of Soul Aretha Franklin made her *Bandstand* debut on August 2, 1962, with her fifth and sixth hits, "Don't Cry Baby" and "Try a Little Tenderness," neither of which got any higher than number 92 on the

Dick with Martha Reeves & the Vandellas, 1965.

A special interview with Bobby Rydell, 1960.

The Supremes, 1967.

charts. Bubblegum king Tommy Roe, who made many a *Bandstand* appearance, debuted with his first hit, ''Sheila,'' on August 13, 1962. The following week Jerry Lee Lewis, still trying to get his career back in gear after his marital scandal, appeared and lip-synched ''Sweet Little 16,'' which only reached number 95 for him. At the end of that month, the inimitable Rod McKuen came on to lip-synch ''I Dig Her Wig'' on a show that also featured wig-care tips from hairdressers. The song failed to chart, and in

fact Rod's only hit would be the number 76 ''Oliver Twist'' in 1962. In September 1962, Bobby ''Boris'' Pickett and His Crypt Kickers premiered their classic Halloween novelty, ''Monster Mash,'' which hit number one just in time for Halloween and which hit the top ten again eleven years later. And a month later Marvin Gaye made his TV debut with *his* first hit, ''Stubborn Kind of Fellow.''

In May 1963, Peter, Paul and Mary marked the emergence of the folk boom by presenting their number 2 hit, ''Puff the Magic Dragon.'' One week later Darlene Love appeared with one of Phil Spector's greatest, ''Today I Met the Boy I'm Gonna Marry,'' a song that one critic later called ''the most innocent rock song of all time.'' A couple of weeks later Lesley Gore came on the show to lip-synch her masterpiece, ''It's My Party,'' which hit number one while she was still sixteen (it was produced and arranged by none other than Quincy Jones). In September, the Ronettes delivered the immortal ''Be My Baby,'' which made number 2 (not number one, as many erroneously recall), and a month later the Chiffons came on the show with "He's So Fine."

In the late fall of 1963, another of Dick Clark's music business friends, who'd been doing some business in London, brought Dick a record that was burning up the British charts. So Dick agreed to give it a spin on *Bandstand*'s Rate-a-Record. Dick announced, "This record is 'She Loves You' by the Beatles." Some of the kids in the audience snickered at the group's name. When the record was over, the first reviewer said, "It's all right, sort of Chuck Berry and the Everly Brothers mixed together. I give it a 77." The second grumbled, "It's not that easy to dance to—I give it a 65." The third said, "It doesn't seem to have anything special, but it is kind of catchy. The best I can give it is a 70." The average score: a 71. Score another miss for Rate-A-Record!

By February 15, 1964, just a week after the Beatles were on "The Ed Sullivan Show," Beatlemania had struck with full force, and *Bandstand* was on the case immediately with a Beatles tribute show. On April 18, 1964, the Fab Four phoned into *Bandstand*, which was as close as they ever got to a personal appearance on the show (not unlike Elvis Presley, who never appeared on *Bandstand* in person but did phone in August 1958 to congratulate Dick on the show's first network anniversary).

Dick Clark with Connie Stevens and Troy Donahue, 1962.

Dick Clark with the legendary Jackie Wilson and his Gold Records, c. 1961.

The Chiffons, 1963.

Even with the British Invasion, previous trends continued apace. The Pyramids performed their surf-rock instrumental classic, "Penetration," on the show in March 1964. A month later the Beach Boys appeared to sing "Fun Fun Fun" (number 5) and "I Get Around" (number one). In May 1964, British songbird Dusty Springfield made her American TV debut on the show with her second hit, "Stay Awhile." In August 1964, that marvelous era of the one-hit wonders was officially kicked off, when the Premieres appeared and lip-synched their hit, the number 19 "Farmer John," which had a wonderfully heavy beat that would resurface in similar form on the McCoys' "Hang On Sloopy," which also debuted on the show. (The Premieres were Mexican-Americans from California, and thus also initiators of the "Pachuco" garage-rock subgenre.) Later that same month another group of garage-rock greats, the Standells, made their TV debut with "Help Yourself," which failed to chart. In fact, the Standells would not have a hit until "Dirty Water" in the spring of 1967. And when that one came out, they did it on *Bandstand*

With some friends: Fabian (behind Dick), Neil Sedaka, Freddy Cannon, Bobby Rydell, and Chubby Checker, 1960.

A special interview
with Fabian, 1960.

Lenny Kaye. It has continued with the release of
dozens of similar compilations, and with hundreds of bands across America and in Europe
bringing back those simple beat-combo sounds.

From roughly 1966 to 1968, when garage
rock flourished all over the charts, nearly all of
these one-hit bands made appearances on
Bandstand: ? and the Mysterians had one of
the greatest hits of them all, "96 Tears"; the
Count Five, garbed in mysterioso capes and
robes, with "Psychotic Reaction," a specific
response to the rave-up guitar sounds of the
Yardbirds; the Knickerbockers, with the remarkable Beatle-soundalike "Lies"; instrumentalists
the T-Bones, whose only hit, "Whatever Shape
Your Stomach's In," started its life as the theme
of a famous Alka Seltzer commercial; the Blues
Magoos with "We Ain't Got Nothin' Yet"; the
Gentrys with "Keep On Dancing"; the Shad-
ows of Knight (named after their manager Terry
Knight, who would later go on to work with
Grand Funk Railroad) with their cover of the
British band Them's "Gloria"; the Buckinghams
with "Kind of a Drag"; the Syndicate of Sound

(incidentally, though "Dirty Water" extols Bos-
ton as the singer's home, the band was actually
from San Jose, California; and the singer was
Larry Tamblyn, brother of actor/dancer Russ).

Garage rock was a grass-roots American
response to the British Invasion. Regular kids by
the thousands all across America took the un-
toward popularity of those limey moptops as
something of a challenge. They grew moptops
of their own, bought the cheapest instruments
they could find—Danelectro or Mosrite or Supro
guitars, Farfisa or Vox organs—and proceeded
to take the country by storm with a seemingly
endless succession of sullenly stomping or bounc-
ily catchy classics. Nearly all of the garage
rockers had one and only one hit, and then
each of them faded back into oblivion—which,
in retrospect, is part of their charm. After the
classic sounds of fifties rock, mid-sixties garage
rock has been revived more often than any
other classic rock sound. The renewed interest
in the garage-rock one-hit wonders was sparked
by the early seventies release of *Nuggets*, the
double-album set by rock critic and musician

Gary "U.S." Bonds,
1961.

105

with "Little Girl"; the Music Machine (whose bassist was Keith Olsen, later a big-time record producer for Fleetwood Mac and others) with "Talk Talk"; the Music Explosion with "Little Bit O' Soul," which marked the crossover from garage rock to bubblegum pop with style, a crossover begun earlier by the Monkees (yes, they were on *AB*, too); and so many more. All of them came and went like *that*, but left an extraordinary legacy behind. If pop music is largely defined by ephemerality, then the garage-rock era embodied one of modern pop's ultimate periods of greatness.

Even Don Grady, of TV's "My Three Sons," got into the one-hit-wonder act, forming a garage-folk-rock band called Yellow Balloon who lip-synched their only hit, 1967's number 25 "Yellow Balloon," on the show. However, not every band that helped define those classic sounds faded away after one hit. Paul Revere and the Raiders, for instance, came back after a four-year hiatus with a string of mid-sixties

classics like "Steppin' Out," "Just Like Me," and "Kicks," all of which helped make their three-cornered-hats, ponytails, and colonial soldier suits as familiar a sight to *Bandstand* viewers as Dick Clark himself, or, say, such well-known and long-running *Bandstand* sponsors as Dentyne gum and Clearasil (and need it even be mentioned just how crucial *Bandstand* was to the fortunes of the Clearasil company?).

In 1967, things suddenly began to change. Hippies. Psychedelia. Flower power. Exotic Eastern mysticism. Peace and love and antiwar protests. And drugs. *Bandstand* was never big on drugs or political protest, but psychedelic rock got its airtime on the show, just like any other contemporary pop phenomenon. On January 21, 1967, Otis Redding was joined on the show by the Buffalo Springfield, whose membership included Neil Young, Stephen Stills, Richie Furay (later to form Poco), and Jim Messina

Smokey Robinson & the Miracles, 1960.

106

(later of Loggins and). They performed their protest-rock classic "For What It's Worth," and afterward Neil Young—in marked contrast to the distant,spaced-out persona he's usually projected in his rare TV appearances—was downright friendly and outgoing with Dick Clark, constantly smiling and saying thank you.

The very next week, the Standells performed their one really big hit (they did have a few other minor ones), "Dirty Water." They also performed "Try It," a song that was banned due to its sexually suggestive title, and never made the charts.

On March 11, 1967, Dick Clark introduced two of the first music videos, the Beatles' films of "Strawberry Fields Forever" and "Penny Lane," and then quizzed the kids in the studio audience for their generally mystified reactions to those bizarre, special-effects-laden pieces. It seemed that the kids in the bleachers had a little trouble with the mystical symbolism!

On June 3, 1967, the Jefferson Airplane lip-synched their first two hits, "White Rabbit" and

"Somebody to Love," both of which went top ten. Over fifteen years later, Airplane chanteuse Grace Slick reappeared on the show with the revamped Jefferson Starship, and claimed to not even remember her first appearance on the show. But she admitted, with typical candor, that she was probably under the influence of something or other back in 'sixty-seven.

On July 22, 1967, Dick Clark showed another seminal music video, for the Bee Gees' first hit,"New York Mining Disaster 1941." Then he counted up the Teen Top Ten, which read thus:

10. The Buckinghams—"Mercy Mercy"
 9. Petula Clark—"Don't Sleep in the Subway"
 8. Stevie Wonder—"I Was Made to Love Her"
 7. Herman's Hermits—"Don't Go Out in the Rain"
 6. Four Seasons—"Come On Marianne"
 5. Nancy Sinatra and Lee Hazelwood—"Jackson"
 4. The Fifth Dimension—"Up, Up and Away"
 3. Jefferson Airplane—"White Rabbit"
 2. The Doors—"Light My Fire"
 1. Procol Harum—"A Whiter Shade of Pale"

Janis Joplin, 1967.

107

Then Dick, seated in the audience, turned to a young man next to him and said, ''You were just saying something about your favorite tune by our next guests, the Doors. What is it?'' ''Uh, 'Crystal Ship,''' the kid replied. ''That's exactly what they're going to do for us right now,'' said

Dick, ''so that makes a nice intro. Ladies and gentlemen, the Doors!''

And there they were, led by the Lizard King himself, Jim Morrison, who leaned into his microphone and lip-synched the opening line of that tune (which was never a hit, though it did serve as the name of a late-seventies, New York–based Doors revival band), ''Before you slip into unconsciousness, I'd like to have another kiss.'' After the tune, Dick Clark did his customary band-interview segment, and when he spoke with Morrison, who was nowhere near as spaced-out as he always seems to have been in typical footage of the period, this exchange took place:

DICK CLARK: A lot of people think you come from San Francisco. Is that true?
JIM MORRISON: No, we actually got together in L.A. We do play in San Francisco a lot, though.
DC: Why is so much happening in San Francisco these days, have you figured that out?
JM: Uh . . . the West is the best, I guess!
DC (*laughter*): ''The West is the best . . .'' Alright, fair enough.

The Doors then lip-synched ''Light My Fire'' for a screaming studio audience. By the way, that line of Morrison's, ''The West is the best,'' came from ''The End,'' the eleven-minute Oedipal opus that brought their classic debut album to a shatteringly theatrical conclusion.

Jim Morrison, 1967.

Jan & Dean, 1963.

In the wake of the Beatles and the Rolling Stones, the Doors were one of the few bands to straddle the gulf between critical respect as "heavy," "meaningful" musical messengers, and overwhelmingly popular teen idols. With the growing self-consciousness of the rock generation in this decade and the trend away from singles to albums in terms of sales dominance, that gap widened. And there was a growing awareness on the part of the people making many of the records of the day: Where the garage rock of the mid-sixties was a widespread, spontaneous response to the British Invasion by scruffy American kids who wanted a piece of the action, in the late sixties there came bubblegum pop, a music that was somehow calculated to approximate the innocent simplicity and melodic and rhythmic directness of popular teen music, but was frequently made by studiobound, prefabricated groups. Where garage rock had a sullen, nasty edge and attitude, bubblegum was bright and bouncy and sweet. While the seemingly endless hordes of garage rockers came and went quickly, usually with one hit apiece, bubblegum was a deliberate

celebration and exploitation of teen pop's essential innocence. As the teen idols before them had been, bubblegum groups were groomed for easier, quicker, and wider mass acceptance than the take-us-or-leave-us-as-we-are garage rockers.

Bubblegum could soak up anything and make it come out as instantly appealing, disposable transistor-radio music. The Sandpipers even did the impossible on *Bandstand* once, transforming the ultimate garage-rock party anthem, "Louie Louie" by the Kingsmen, into soothing middle-of-the-road Muzak (as Dick Clark said after the group had performed, "It's hard to even recognize 'Louie Louie' in there"). The Monkees were the prime bubblegum variant on the Merseybeat sound of the Beatles and other Liverpool groups, and they too were on *Bandstand* (as well as their own popular prime-time series). The Grass Roots smoothed out the organ-based garage-rock bands like Paul Revere and the Raiders—who were already close to the

A special salute to The Beatles on *American Bandstand* in October 1965. Even though they never made a personal appearance on the show, their presence was always felt.

A special interview with Connie Francis.

with "I Had Too Much to Dream Last Night," and then the Strawberry Alarm Clock completely settled the issue with their flower-power smash "Incense and Peppermints." A frequent *Bandstand* guest like Tommy Roe, with such classics as "Sweet Pea" and "Dizzy," illustrated the sheer joy in craft that accounted for so much of the best bubblegum music.

And yet, with the explosion in the rock audience's size and diversity, nearly every subgenre of the vast spectrum of teen pop had its moments, and all of them were seen on *Bandstand*. Even a "pure" psychedelic band like Britain's Pink Floyd made it onto the show in 1967; though they'd just had two big hit singles back home, "Arnold Layne" and "See Emily Play," they would not have an American hit until radically changing their style in 1973 with "Money." When they appeared on *Bandstand*, singer and guitarist Syd Barrett adamantly refused to move his lips to the playback of their two British hits; he just stood there, immobile, while the rest of the band sheepishly mimed along behind him.

garage/pure-pop border themselves—and made as many appearances on *Bandstand* as the Raiders. The Electric Prunes proved that psychedelia could edge toward disposable bubblegum

One of television's most colorful impresarios, John Zacherley, came to *Bandstand* to host a Halloween show.

Peggy
my fav
show
the cro
the sh
turn th
first tir
lines a
just go
early e
that da
make i
in back
in L.A.
She to
show b
One of
get int
there v
line to
to fill t
"Sp
was al
about

Speaking of the real thing, throughout the decade there was soul music: the joyous, inspired and inspiring, super-danceable sound of black America. Through the first half of the decade, there was Motown's brilliantly bouncy, well-groomed meld of gospel, rock, and pop, and there was James Brown's gutsier, early gospel soul and later his epochal, driving, super-syncopated soul-funk. In the mid- and late sixties came the Stax-Volt soul sound, named after the label that tried to outdo Motown by introducing a meaner, "lean and hungry" sound, like Sam and Dave's immortal "Soul Man" (which, of course, they did on *Bandstand*). There were more variants on the harder soul sound, like the Fantastic Johnny C. with "Boogaloo Down Broadway," and poppier, more mainstream examples, like Brenton Wood's "Gimme Little Sign" and Clarence Carter's "Slip Away." And, in perhaps the best example of the uniquely Utopian spirit of the sixties, the mass audience ate up soul in all its varieties as much as rock.

Need it be reiterated that *Bandstand* was always there to cover the spectrum?

As the decade drew to a close, another of those rare and exceptional bands made several *Bandstand* appearances: Creedence Clearwater Revival, who crafted a remarkable string of hits from the late sixties through the early seventies. Creedence emerged from San Francisco in 1967, yet they were nothing like their psychedelic counterparts. With a hard-driving, keep-it-simple rhythm section and the beautifully coarse voice and low-down guitar of leader John Fogerty, Creedence echoed such obscure-for-the-time rock styles as rockabilly, country, and swampy Bayou soul-rock (i.e., Tony Joe White's "Polk Salad Annie") and ended up with a sound completely their own. And while their mass appeal was consistently outstanding, critics loved them too for their tough, roots-oriented sound, unwavering rhythmic attack, and unvarnished working-class sensibility.

Unlike the formatted, fragmented seventies, the sixties saw a mass pop music audience that reveled in diversity: Motown and Merseybeat, surf and psychedelic, garage rock and bubble-gum pop . . . despite their differences they were all tributaries of the same river. *Bandstand*, like the Top 40 radio of the era, presented it all side by side. But when, in the seventies, severe categorization would lead radio into its present segregation-by-format of the music, *Bandstand* would continue to cover anything popular, whatever its particular style.

Dick with Bobby Vinton, 1963.

changing back there. But I'd always get the strangest looks from the bus driver when I got off, because he'd seen me come on in my uniform and then I'd get off in full makeup and totally different clothes. Then in Philly I'd take the subway to the studio.

"Those were incredible days. I have a copy of *16* magazine with Edd 'Kookie' Byrnes on the cover and right below him it says, 'Inside: Meet Bunny Gibson.' Each month those magazines would do features on one or more of us. And there were the fan clubs all over the country, and all the fan mail and the gifts we got in the mail. But the price we paid for that fame was that we were hated by strangers in Philadelphia. I'd go out dancing seven days a week, it was my life, and every time we went out we'd be in constant fear that someone was going to make good on their threat and beat us up or something. Even gangs of girls at the Catholic school would threaten me. But it was funny, whenever we were out at a dance and some kids would gather round us glowering and making threats, it was always the black kids who would help us out of a jam. I guess they appreciated the fact that we were good dancers, and they could really relate to that schizoid thing, where people loved you and hated you at the same time. I mean, rock 'n' roll was their music, really, yet they weren't allowed to make good on it themselves for the longest time. So we developed a bit of a bond, and I owe a lot to those black kids back then."

Bunny is one of the very few *Bandstand* regulars whose exposure on the show led to an actual show-biz career. She's a model and actress who's been in many TV commercials, including one popular spot for Minute Rice where she's the one student in a cooking school whose rice always comes out wrong. She now lives on the West Coast and hopes to get into movies. The only other regular to get into show biz and still be at it is Joe Wissert, who is now a highly successful music producer in Los Angeles.

Katy K (she prefers not to reveal her real last name), now a Manhattan fashion designer and scenemaker, grew up on the North Side of Philadelphia in the late fifties and early sixties. "*Bandstand* was like my surrogate teenage life," she says, "I was a good little girl from a good home in a good neighborhood. I went to

Another location show, September, 1960.

a *very* straight school where we all had to wear uniforms, the whole bit. I had this one other girlfriend who was cool, or who like me *wanted* to be cool. Every weekday, she and I would run home after school to watch *Bandstand*. We were never able to dress like the kids on the show, not during the weekdays anyway. My school was so *square* we could hardly even *think* about trying to be cool.

"But on weekends my girlfriend and I would go down to South Philly. For me, it was like going to Paris or Rome, the ultimate in dangerous exotica. Just being there, and seeing these kids on the street who you recognized as *Bandstand* regulars, made you feel more adult, less like a teenager, and cooler, all at the same time. I know these kids had to observe a dress code for the show itself, but in 'real life,' on the street, they were *tough*. And tough was *cool*.

"At that time," Katy continues, "the looks for girls were changing radically. The fifties was all about a sweet, innocent, romantic look, with a very full, sort of padded-out shape to clothes —the poodle skirts, the A-line skirts, the heavy, looser sweaters and stuff. In the early sixties, looking *tough* was the thing: looking *sexy*. *Tight* clothes; self-consciously trashy. Those were the days, alright."

Katy K also encountered the *Bandstand* kids in more "intimate" surroundings. "I used to run into them at local sock hops and dances all the time," she laughs, "in the ladies room, there they'd all be, Carol Scaldeferri and Frani Giordano and all my other idols. The hairspray was flying thick and fast. It was like those gum-snapping dialogs in records like 'Leader of the Pack' and 'Give Him a Great Big Kiss,' for real."

Katy K also managed to get into the studio once for *Bandstand*. "I'll never forget it," she recalls, "I didn't mingle with anyone. I was just frozen in the bleachers, with my head in my hands and my lower jaw on the floor, just going 'Oh my *God*, I'm really here and *they're* all here . . .' And Sam Cooke was the guest, miming 'You Send Me.' It sent *me*, alright!"

More pictures from the home viewers Top: Janet Hamill's birthday, April, 1960. Center, Carole Scaldeferri, 1961. Bottom: A set of twins, April, 1960.

THE DANCING

The wide range of dances: from the Frug to a basic Slow Dance...

One reason the Twist and similar dances caught on was that they were comparatively simple, requiring little in the way of intricate steps and moves. As Chubby describes the dance: "It's like putting out a cigarette with both of your feet and coming out of a shower and wiping your bottom with a towel to the beat of the music. It's just that simple."

Of course, the Twist was an athletic, comparatively uninhibited dance, which made it that much more youth-oriented. And which made it

The decade began with the Twist leading the way to dance craze after dance craze. But even as the Twist was catching on like wildfire, the 1960 *Bandstand* dance contest found more traditional touch-dancing carrying the day with the new couple Jimmy Petrose and Joan Buck, she of the trend-setting platinum pixie hairdo. Ed Kelly recalls, "They came on and totally revolutionized slow, couples-dancing. They did a new dance they had the patent on: the Strand, which was like a slow, Jitterbug/waltz sort of thing. They just did it so gracefully, they knocked everybody out, and especially because they were a new couple on the scene and they came right in and swept the whole contest with no problem."

But the Strand (immortalized in song more than ten years later by British band Roxy Music's "Do the Strand") would be the last gasp for traditional touch-dancing. Chubby Checker himself explains the revolution the Twist inspired: "Before the Twist came, everyone danced together. I'm the guy that started people dancing apart. You know, I taught the world how to dance as they know it today. I'm almost like Einstein creating atomic power. Whatever dances came after the Twist, it all started here."

that much more controversial: the dance was banned all over America and in Europe, China, South Africa, and the Soviet Union; there was even a national scandal around the dance when, in 1961, newspapers reported that First Lady Jacqueline Kennedy had been spotted doing the Twist at a White House party. JFK's press secretary Pierre Salinger was forced to deny it!

The dances that followed the Twist were in the same vein: simple, athletic, with self-descriptive names and songs to go with them. There were, in no particular order: the Mashed Potato; the Locomotion; the Watusi (popularized by the Orlons' "Wah-Watusi"); the Boogaloo, an all-purpose variant with perhaps the least specified moves; the Bristol Stomp, a rocking heel-and-toe movement sparked by the song of the same name by the Dovells; the Hitchhike (in which one boogalooed while making rhythmic hitching gestures with each arm, the thumb stuck up of course); the Monkey; the Pony, one of the few dances that started in the fifties and continued to grow in popularity in the sixties; the Shing-a-ling; the Limbo and Limbo-rock, (certainly among the more strenuously athletic dances, as you know if you've ever tried them!); the Jerk, popularized by the Capitols' often-covered "Cool Jerk," and definitely *not* recommended for anyone with a back problem, since the dance involves snapping your upper body forward with a jerking motion while the lower portion remains relatively stationary; the Hully

. . . to the Hully Gully.

The more traditional Slow Dance of the early 1960s.

Swim, popularized by Bobby Freeman's swim songs, in which one frugged and/or boogalooed while dipping the body and making wavy underwater movements with the arms as one dipped, or held one's nose as if submerging while dipping.

These dances were easy and fun and physical, and as such represented a challenge to the older generation. Sheer tenacity carried the day, as more new dances just kept coming throughout the decade. In the eyes of the older generation they may have represented the death of *real* dancing, but again, there was no arguing with success. Ironically, on this subject Dick Clark notes, ''One thing that always cracks me up is that as we hear from different regulars over the years, they always talk about the kids currently dancing on the show and express shock and mystification at the dances they do—just as *their* parents were appalled by *their* dancing. Some things never change.''

But the sixties, a dance-crazy decade if ever there was one, radically altered dance styles on

Gully (perhaps the only genuine ''line dance'' to make it in the sixties, a sort of successor to the Stroll and Bunny Hop); that staple of the mid-sixties and psychedelic eras, the Frug; and the

The Twist.

120

a widespread basis. Once again, *American Band-stand* led the way. And while adults may have deplored the Twist at first, they soon fell under its sway. Newspaper and magazine gossip columns told tales of the carriage trade and high society stopping off at New York's Pepper-mint Lounge to twist. *TV Guide* ran an item on January 6, 1962, that started,

> As anyone knows who has seen a maga-zine or newspaper or television set lately, there is a dance craze rampant in the nation called the Twist. And in New York, especially, is the craze, the rage. Recently, in Manhattan's posh Four Seasons restaurant, 250 prominent New Yorkers twisted them-selves silly at a benefit "Twist Party." Among the guests: grocery heir Huntington Hartford, Porfirio Rubirosa, and Henry Ford's debutante daughter Charlotte. The guest of honor: Chubby Checker, the stocky singer and swinger who is the acknowl-edged King of all the Twisters. Actually, as happens more often than most so-called sophisticated New Yorkers would care to admit, the Big Town has been a bit behind the rest of the country with the Twist —about two years behind. In fact, it was that long ago that Dick Clark, major-domo of ABC's *American Bandstand* —the Ameri-can teenager's TV tea dansant which origi-nates at Philadelphia's WFIL-TV—first began popularizing the spine-torturing, dervishlike tribal rite. For if Chubby Checker is the King of the Twisters, then Dick Clark is their prime minister. He is the man who rates most of the credit—or blame—for making the Twist what it is today.

Not even Chubby Checker himself argues with that: "I may have started the nation twisting, but I couldn't have done it without Dick Clark and *American Bandstand*. What can I say? That show was just *it* in those days. You couldn't make it without it. Once you got on *Bandstand*, you *knew* you'd made it!"

121

THE FASHIONS

The "English Look," 1965.

Just as the radical changes in dancing mirrored the social changes we all went through, so did the changes in clothes and hair. Again, they were all on prominent display on *American Bandstand*.

By 1962, while guys were still wearing suits and ties with the occasional sweater tossed in for variety, their ties and lapels were getting narrower and shorter—sleeker, more youthful, and different from adult clothes, as prominent demarcation from the oldsters began to be more important. Patent leather shoes had come in for guys and girls. In another signal of the body consciousness that would rise to such prominence, girls' clothing became more stream-lined and form-fitting and casual: stretch pants with stirrups originally intended for leisure activi-ties like skiing or skating became *de rigueur Bandstand* attire, and in warmer weather there were culottes and clam diggers and pedal pushers. The tailored look of blouses with Peter

Girls with bouffant hairdos surround Pop Singer, 1960.

Pan collars gradually gave way to simple sweaters and straight one-piece dresses that could be pulled on over the head rather than buttoned.

Girls' hair was evolving as well. The teasing and "ratting" of the late fifties had grown in sophistication to the bouffants, flips, and beehives that were dominant through the mid-sixties. Bouffants and French twists emphasized height at the top of the head, and were often adorned with little bows, ribbons, or headbands. Beehives took the height effect to outrageous extremes, with the hair piled and teased and sprayed and sprayed and sprayed up and up and up to skyscraping proportions. Beehives were considered "bad girl" hairdos for the longest time: Schoolteachers complained that girls in beehives blocked kids sitting behind them from seeing blackboards! Folkloric jokes

got started that some girls had sprayed so much lacquer onto their beehives that they ceased to be living hair anymore.

On the other hand, flips pointed the way to the more casual styles that would take hold in the near future, in which the hair hung straight down and was simply parted in the middle. The flip, a winglike upturn in the bottom hair framing the face, was geometrically symmetrical. It was a high time for the hair-roller industry.

By 1964, flips and bouffants had scaled down, and girls wore their hair long and straight with barrettes or headbands. Their clothes evolved to shell tops of helenka, a synthetic stretch material, ribbed at the top with little zippers in the back. There were sling-belt dresses, some blousons, and sling-back pumps, a definite progression from the clunkier bobby sox and saddle shoes

the heavy eye makeup made popular by Mary Quant. All of the Beatles' girlfriends, like Jane Asher and Patti Boyd, wore this style, and it became a *must* for any fashion-conscious young lady. Jumpsuits also came in, as did one of the greatest fashion revolutions of the century— panty hose, which were not only more convenient than stockings-with-garters arrangements, but also solved the problem of wearing ever-shorter hemlines and *not* having your thighs show over the tops of the stockings when you sat down. There were tops with oversize Pilgrim collars, and long dresses with bell sleeves, the start of the granny look that would be so big from the mid-sixties through the early seventies. Girls began wearing falls (partial wigs that gave *everyone* the opportunity to have long straight hair, regardless of what their hair was like naturally) in mid- and late 1965. Dickies were everywhere on guys, as were striped V-neck sweaters over turtleneck tops, sweater-vests with ties, and wide-lapeled double-breasted jackets with a Mod look that were harbingers of the Edwardian look that came in big at the end of 1965.

In early 1966, the full flowering of the now classic sixties look took place. Girls sported op-art print mini dresses, granny glasses, white frosted lipstick, go-go boots, huge hoop earrings, even some Mondrian-print outfits, and their hair was long and straight and parted in the middle with bangs in front and maybe the hint of a twist, in emulation of the first fashion-model superstar, Jean Shrimpton. Long, floral-print peasant dresses came in as well, completing the granny look. There were ribbed poor-boy tops with low U-necklines, and there were the first empire-waist dresses (in this century at least; Napoleon's Josephine had done it before!). Gladiator sandals became the rage in footwear right along with white vinyl Courrèges go-go boots. For guys, the look was Edwardian: double-breasted, high-collared, velvet-lapeled jackets. There were polka-dot ties and shirts, suede desert boots and hush puppies, and the hair s-l-o-w-l-y got a little longer still.

fifties look. Sailor tops and sailor dresses made their debuts.

Boys began wearing a more casual look for the first time: hair got a *little* longer in tribute to the Beatles; there were buttoned cardigan sweaters with shirts and ties, pullover crewneck or even turtleneck sweaters, open-necked oxford shirts with turtleneck dickies, pointy black shoes or even Beatle boots, and casual slacks rather than formal suits. Lapelless jackets made their first appearance, also in tribute to the Beatles.

In 1965, there was a new look for the girls that also began in England: long, straight hair parted in the middle, with *very* long bangs and

Later in 1966, girls began wearing U-neck tops, jumpers over poor-boy tops, floral-printed suits, and paisley. And there were swingy A-line dresses with short hems, leather halter mini-dresses, cut-out halter dresses, and the first Sassoon hairstyles—short, cleanly sculpted, asymmetrically rounded. Guys wore Mod double-breasted blazers with open-necked shirts and little ascot scarves threaded through metal-ring holders. Occasionally, a *really* hip guy would wear something like a short-cut epaulet jacket —which really caught on in 1967, after the Beatles' *Sgt. Pepper* look.

The year 1967 was all straight, long, "organic" hair on girls, and minis with patterned panty hose; Mondrian dresses and paisley and other baroque psychedelic-era prints were everywhere. There's one *Bandstand* tape from December 9, 1967, in which Dick Clark wears a wide paisley tie. On that same show, the Music Machine appeared in matching black CPO jackets. Then there were belted-back man-tailored suits for girls, and the "English schoolgirl" look with wide-lapeled jackets and big scarf-ties. The collars on the guys' shirts got very long and pointy, and they wore more and more stream-lined neo-Edwardian double-breasted polyester suits.

By 1968 and 1969, culottes and shorts became regular attire for many girls, along with minis and halters and short A-line dresses over shorts with pockets on the dresses matching the print on the shorts. Paraphernalia dresses with deep, pointy white lapels over bright pastel colors began to dominate for girls, as did peasant-sleeve dresses. Guys wore long hair, genuinely long hair, bandannas over sweatshirts, and safari jackets. And when the Strawberry Alarm Clock appeared in late 1968 and early 1969, they wore Indian muslin drawstring pants to match their Indian "khurds."

Through it all, the older generation clucked their tongues, and Dick Clark and *American Bandstand* fearlessly showcased it every single week—even instituting occasional "fashion show" segments in the middle of shows to demonstrate and give advice on the newest trends. Right at the end of 1969, there was even a demonstration of how to achieve the latest look—tie-dyeing.

TOP 100 CHART SONGS PERFORMED AND OTHER IMPORTANT
APPEARANCES ON *AMERICAN BANDSTAND*, 1960s.

1 · 9 · 6 · 0

BANDSTAND APPEARANCE	AB/TV DEBUT	ARTIST	SONG(S) PERFORMED	DATE APPEARED ON CHART	PEAK CHART POSITION	WEEKS ON CHART
1/4 (M.)	AB/TV	Fireballs	"Bulldog"	1/11	#24	12
1/19 (Tu.)	AB/TV	Ray Smith	"Rockin' Little Angel" ✔	1/4	#22	16
1/21 (Th.)		Frankie Ford	"Time After Time"	1/18	#75	6
2/4 (Th.)	AB/TV	Johnny Burnette		(no hits until later in year)		
2/10 (W.)		Champs	"Too Much Tequila"	1/18	#30	11
2/16 (Tu.)		Annette (Funicello)	"O Dio Mio"	2/22	#10	12
2/18 (Th.)	AB/TV	Johnnie & Joe	"Over the Mountain—Across the Sea" *	5/13/57 9/26	#8 #89	22 2
				(re-entered chart)		
2/23 (Tu.)	AB/TV	Bobby Comstock & the Counts	"Jambalaya"	2/7	#90	4
2/26 (F.)	AB/TV	Lenny Welch	"You Don't Know Me" ✔	2/29	#45	13
2/29 (M.)	AB/TV	Revels	"Midnight Stroll" *	10/19/59	#35	10
3/2 (W.)		Jack Scott	"What in the World's Come over You"	1/11	#5	16
			"Burning Bridges"	4/18	#3	17
3/7 (M.)	AB/TV	Jackie DeShannon		(no hits until 1963)		
3/9 (W.)	AB/TV	Mystics	"Hushabye"	5/25/59	#20	15
			"Don't Take the Stars"	10/19/59	#98	2
3/22 (Tu.)		Playmates	"Beep Beep"	11/3/58	#4	15
3/25 (F.)	AB/TV	Temptations (not the Motown group, but a white one)	"Barbra" *	4/18	#29	10
3/30 (W.)	AB	Olympics	"Baby Hully Gully"	2/1	#72	7
			"Big Boy Pete"	5/23	#50	14
4/13 (W.)		Johnny Tillotson	"Earth Angel"	4/11	#57	7
			"Pleading My Love"	4/11	#63	6
4/15 (F.)		Freddy Cannon	"Jump Over"	5/9	#28	10
			"The Urge"	5/16	#60	3
5/3 (Tu.)	AB/TV	Charlie Rich	"Lonely Weekends" ✔	3/14	#22	21
5/12 (Th.)		Duane Eddy	"Shazam!"	3/21	#45	7
			"Because They're Young"	5/23	#4	15
5/26 (Th.)	AB	Bobby Vee	"What Do You Want?"	4/4	#93	2
5/31 (Tu.)		Johnny & the Hurricanes	"Down Yonder"	5/30	#48	9
5/31 (Tu.)		Preston Epps	"Bongo, Bongo, Bongo" ♦	8/15	#78	3
6/1 (W.)		Flamingos	"Nobody Loves Me Like You Do"	4/18	#30	10
6/10 (F.)		Crests	"Trouble in Paradise"	6/13	#29	13
6/13 (M.)	AB/TV	Johnny Horton	"Johnny Freedom"	7/4	#69	4
6/14 (Tu.)	AB/TV	Dante & the Evergreens	"Alley Oop" ✔	5/30	#15	13
6/22 (W.)	AB/TV	Hank Ballard & the Midnighters	"Finger Poppin' Time"	5/16	#7	26
7/4 (M.)	AB/TV	Jimmy Charles & the Revelettes	"A Million to One" ✔	8/22	#5	15
7/12 (Tu.)		Frankie Lymon	"Little Bitty Pretty One" *	8/8	#58	4
7/13 (W.)		Freddy Cannon	"Happy Shades of Blue"	7/25	#83	5
7/19 (Tu.)	AB/TV	Brian Hyland	"Itsy Bitsy Teenie Weenie Yellow Polka Dot Bikini" ✔	7/4	#1	15
7/28 (Th.)		Dee Clark	"You're Looking Good"	8/15	#43	10
8/3 (W.)	AB	Jan & Dean	"We Go Together"	8/1	#53	7
8/9 (Tu.)	AB/TV	Jo ann Campbell	"A Kookie Little Paradise" ✔	8/15	#61	9
8/19 (F.)		Bobby Vee	"Devil or Angel"	8/1	#6	19
			"Since I Met You Baby"	9/12	#81	1
8/22 (M.)	AB/TV	Bobby Peterson Quintet	"Irresistible You" ♦	10/31	#96	1
8/23 (Tu.)		Flamingos	"Mio Amore"	1/18	#74	6
8/25 (Th.)	AB/TV	Etta & Harvey (Harvey Fuqua of the Moonglows with Etta James)	"If I Can't Have You" ✔	8/1	#52	12
8/30 (Tu.)	AB	Ferrante & Teicher	"Theme from The Apartment" ✔	7/25	#10	20
9/6 (Tu.)		Johnny & the Hurricanes	"Rocking Goose"	8/29	#60	6
			"When the Saints Go Marching In"	8/29	#97	5
9/7 (W.)	AB	Della Reese	"And Now"	9/5	#69	5
9/8 (Th.)		Drifters	"Save the Last Dance for Me"	9/5	#1	18
9/9 (F.)		Bobby Freeman	"(I Do) The Shimmy Shimmy"	8/15	#37	13
9/12 (M.)	AB/TV	Larry Verne	"Mr. Custer" ✔	8/29	#1	13
9/21 (W.)	AB/TV	Dorsey Burnette	"Hey Little One"	6/6	#48	11
9/22 (Th.)		Johnny Tillotson	"Poetry in Motion"	10/10	#2	15

✔ First hit by a performer   * Only hit by a performer   ♦ Last hit by a performer

BANDSTAND APPEARANCE	AB/TV DEBUT	ARTIST	SONG(S) PERFORMED	DATE APPEARED ON CHART	PEAK CHART POSITION	WEEKS ON CHART
9/29 (Th.)		Chubby Checker	"The Twist"	8/1	#1	18
10/3 (M.)	AB/TV	Ike & Tina Turner	"A Fool in Love"✔	8/29	#27	13
10/10 (M.)	AB/TV	Joe Jones	"You Talk Too Much"✔	9/9	#3	13
10/12 (W.)		Jack Scott	"Patsy"	10/17	#65	4
10/19 (W.)	AB/TV	Shirelles	"Tonight's the Night"	9/12	#39	4
10/25 (Tu.)		Fats Domino	"Walkin' to New Orleans"	6/20	#6	14
			"My Girl Josephine"	10/24	#14	15
10/31 (M.)		Duane Eddy	"Kommotion"	8/22	#78	6
			"Peter Gunn"	10/10	#27	9
11/1 (Tu.)		Jerry Butler	"He Will Break Your Heart"✔	10/31	#7	15
11/2 (W.)	AB/TV	Damita Jo	"I Will Save the Last Dance for You"✔	10/24	#22	12
11/3 (Th.)		Johnny Burnette	"You're 16"	10/31	#8	15
11/4 (F.)		Bobby Rydell	"Sway"	11/7	#14	11
			"Groovy Tonight"	12/5	#70	2
11/9 (W.)		Duane Eddy	"Pepe"	12/19	#18	12
11/9 (W.)		Joni James	"My Last Date (With You)"	12/19	#38	7
11/11 (F.)	AB/TV	Santo & Johnny	"Twistin' Bells"	12/19	#49	3
11/14 (M.)	AB/TV	Wanda Jackson	"Let's Have a Party"✔	8/29	#37	10
11/18 (F.)		Mark Dinning	"The Lovin' Touch"	8/22	#84	6

BANDSTAND APPEARANCE	AB/TV DEBUT	ARTIST	SONG(S) PERFORMED	DATE APPEARED ON CHART	PEAK CHART POSITION	WEEKS ON CHART
11/21 (M.)		Neil Sedaka	"Calendar Girl"	12/19	#4	15
11/22 (Tu.)	AB/TV	Conway Twitty	"Whole Lotta Shakin' Goin' On"	10/31	#55	5
			"C'est Si Bon"	10/31	#22	10
11/28 (M.)		Bobby Vee	"Rubber Ball"	11/28	#6	14
11/28 (M.)		Ferrante & Teicher	"Exodus"	11/14	#2	21
11/29 (Tu.)		Dion	"Lonely Teenager"✔	10/17	#12	16
			"Little Miss Blue"	12/5	#96	1
11/30 (W.)	AB/TV	Chimes	"Once in a While"✔	10/31	#11	18
12/5 (M.)	AB/TV	Ronnie Love	"Chills and Fever"*	1/9/61	#72	4
12/7 (W.)		Annette (Funicello)	"Talk to Me Baby"	12/26	#92	2
12/8 (Th.)		Danny & the Juniors	"Twistin' USA"	9/19	#27	9
12/12 (M.)		Dante & the Evergreens	"Time Machine"♦	9/12	#73	6
12/14 (W.)		Jimmy Clanton	"What Am I Gonna Do"	1/9/61	#50	6
12/15 (Th.)	AB/TV	Safaris	"The Girl with the Story in Her Eyes"♦	10/17	#85	3
12/16 (F.)		Fabian	"Kissin' & Twistin'"♦	10/31	#91	2
12/16 (F.)	AB/TV	Viscounts	"Wabash Blues"	12/5	#77	7
12/26 (M.)	AB/TV	Maurice Williams & the Zodiacs	"Stay"✔	10/3	#1	18
12/27 (Tu.)	AB/TV	Smokey Robinson & the Miracles	"Shop Around"	12/12	#2	16

I · 9 · 6 · I

BANDSTAND APPEARANCE	AB/TV DEBUT	ARTIST	SONG(S) PERFORMED	DATE APPEARED ON CHART	PEAK CHART POSITION	WEEKS ON CHART
1/9 (M.)	AB/TV	Linda Hopkins	(no hits except with Jackie Wilson in duets; star of Broadway show Me and Bessie)			
1/10 (Tu.)	AB/TV	Buzz Clifford	"Baby Sittin' Boogie"*	1/9	#6	14
1/11 (W.)		Brian Hyland	"That's How Much"	10/24/60	#74	4
1/16 (M.)		Mickey & Sylvia	"What Would I Do"	12/26/60	#46	9
1/18 (W.)		Johnny Tillotson	"Jimmy's Girl"	1/9	#25	11
1/19 (Th.)	AB	Skeeter Davis	"My Last Date (With You)"	12/12/60	#26	8
1/24 (Tu.)		Johnny Burnette	"Little Boy Sad"	2/6	#17	9
1/27 (F.)	AB/TV	Carla Thomas	"Gee Whiz (Look at His Eyes)"✔	1/23	#10	14
2/3 (F.)	AB/TV	Gene Pitney	"I Wanna Love My Life Away"✔	1/30	#39	8

BANDSTAND APPEARANCE	AB/TV DEBUT	ARTIST	SONG(S) PERFORMED	DATE APPEARED ON CHART	PEAK CHART POSITION	WEEKS ON CHART
2/6 (M.)		Dion	"Havin' Fun"	2/6	#42	6
2/8 (W.)	AB/TV	Ramrods	"Ghost Riders in the Sky"*	1/9	#30	9
2/21 (Tu.)		Shirelles	"Will You Love Me Tomorrow"	11/21/60	#1	19
			"Dedicated to the One I Love"	1/23	#3	16
2/22 (W.)		Roy Hamilton	"You Can Have Her"	1/30	#12	10
2/27 (M.)	AB	Bill Doggett	"Honky Tonk Part 2"♦	1/30	#57	10
3/6 (M.)		Fats Domino	"What a Price"	1/23	#22	9
			"Ain't That Just Like a Woman"	1/23	#33	8
3/10 (F.)		Paul Anka	"The Story of My Love"	1/16	#16	8
3/13 (M.)	AB/TV	Capris	"There's a Moon Out Tonight"✔	12/26/60	#3	14
			"Where I Fell in Love"	3/27	#74	4
3/14 (Tu.)		Jerry Butler	"Find Another Girl"	3/6	#27	10

✔ First hit by a performer　　　　* Only hit by a performer　　　　♦ Last hit by a performer

BANDSTAND APPEARANCE	AB/TV DEBUT	ARTIST	SONG(S) PERFORMED	DATE APPEARED ON CHART	PEAK CHART POSITION	WEEKS ON CHART
3/15 (W.)	AB/TV	Gene McDaniels	"A Hundred Pounds of Clay"✔	3/20	#3	15
3/16 (Th.)	AB/TV	Echoes	"Baby Blue"✔	3/6	#12	12
3/29 (W.)	AB/TV	Bobby "Blue" Bland	"I Pity the Fool"	2/20	#46	7
3/30 (Th.)		Joe Jones	"California Sun"♦	4/3	#89	3
3/30 (Th.)	AB/TV	Rose (of the Originals)	"Lonely Blue Nights"	3/13	#66	4
3/31 (F.)	AB/TV	Clarence "Frogman" Henry	"(I Don't Know Why) But I Do" / "Ain't Got No Home"	2/20 / 12/17/56	#4 / #20	16 / 16
4/5 (W.)	AB/TV	Paris Sisters	"Be My Boy"✔	4/17	#56	5
4/10 (M.)	AB/TV	Del Shannon	"Runaway"✔	3/6	#1	17
4/12 (W.)		Freddy Cannon	"Buzz-Buzz a-Diddle-It"	5/15	#3	15
4/19 (W.)	AB/TV/	Frogmen	"Underwater"*	4/3	#44	8
4/21 (F.)	AB/TV	Shep & the Limelites	"Daddy's Home"✔	3/27	#2	14
4/25 (Tu.)	AB/TV	Johnny Maestro	"Model Girl"✔ / "What a Surprise"	2/6 / 4/24	#20 / #33	12 / 9
4/25 (Tu.)	AB	Faron Young	"Hello Walls"	4/10	#12	15
4/26 (W.)		Bobby Rydell	"That Old Black Magic" / "Cherie"	5/1 / 2/13	#21 / #54	8 / 4
5/1 (Tu.)		Neil Sedaka	"Little Devil"	5/1	#11	9
5/3 (Th.)		Dee Clark	"Raindrops"	5/1	#2	16
5/3 (Th.)	AB/TV	Bobby Bare	(no hits until 1962)			
5/4 (F.)	AB/TV	Paul Revere & the Raiders	"Like, Long Hair"	3/27	#38	6
5/8 (M.)	AB/TV	Regents	"Barbara Ann"✔	5/15	#13	10
5/15 (M.)		Gene McDaniels	"A Tear"	7/3	#31	8
5/23 (Tu.)	AB/TV	Little Caesar & the Romans	"Those Oldies but Goodies (Remind Me of You)"✔	5/1	#9	13
5/30 (Tu.)		Johnny Burnette	"Big Big World"	5/1	#58	7
6/1 (Th.)	AB/TV	Tony Orlando	"Halfway to Paradise"✔	5/1	#39	8
6/2 (F.)	AB/TV	Bobby Lewis	"Tossin' and Turnin'"✔	4/24	#1	23
		Carla Thomas	"A Love of My Own"	5/8	#56	6
6/8 (Th.)		Roy Hamilton	"You're Gonna Need Magic"♦	5/1	#80	3
6/14 (W.)	AB/TV	Cleftones	"Heart and Soul"	5/22	#18	10
6/16 (F.)	AB/TV	Gary U.S. Bonds	"Quarter to Three"	5/22	#1	15
6/23 (F.)		Fireballs	"Quite a Party"	6/26	#27	10
6/26 (M.)	AB/TV	Marcels	"Blue Moon"✔	3/6	#1	14
6/29 (Th.)		Wanda Jackson	"Right or Wrong"	6/5	#29	11
6/30 (F.)		Clarence "Frogman" Henry	"You Always Hurt the One You Love" / "Lonely Street"	5/15 / 8/7	#12 / #56	10 / 7
7/5 (W.)	AB/TV	Slim Harpo	"Rainin' in My Heart"✔	5/29	#34	8
7/6 (Th.)		Conway Twitty	"The Next Kiss (Is the Last Goodbye)"	4/3	#72	4
7/7 (F.)	AB/TV	Mary Wells	"I Don't Want to Take a Chance"	7/17	#33	9
7/11 (Tu.)	AB	Maxine Brown	"Funny"	3/27	#25	10
7/13 (Th.)		Freddy Cannon	"Transistor Sister"	7/31	#35	8
7/17 (M.)		Jack Scott	"A Little Feeling Called Love" / "My Dream Come True"	5/29 / 8/28	#91 / #83	2 / 4
7/21 (F.)		Gene Pitney	"Every Breath I Take"	8/7	#42	8
7/24 (M.)		Maurice Williams & the Zodiacs	"Come Along"♦	4/10	#83	2
7/25 (Tu.)		Dion	"Kissin' Game"	5/1	#82	3
8/7 (M.)	AB/TV	Jarmels	"A Little Bit of Soap"*	7/31	#12	10
8/8 (Tu.)		Ray Peterson	"Missing You"	7/31	#29	15
8/9 (W.)		Tony Orlando	"Bless You"	8/14	#15	12
8/9 (W.)		Barry Mann	"Who Put the Bomp (In the Bomp-Bomp-Bomp)"✔	8/7	#7	12
8/14 (M.)		Bobby "Blue" Bland	"Don't Cry No More"	8/7	#71	6
8/14 (M.)	AB/TV	Mar-Keys	"Last Night"✔	7/3	#3	14
8/16 (W.)		Shep & the Limelites	"Ready for Your Love"	7/10	#42	5
8/22 (Tu.)		Jerry Butler	"I'm a-Telling You"	7/24	#25	8
8/24 (Th.)		Neil Sedaka	"Sweet Little You"	8/28	#59	7
8/25 (F.)	AB/TV	Jive Five	"My True Story"✔	7/3	#3	19
9/5 (Tu.)	AB/TV	Brothers Four	"Frogg"	4/10	#32	5
9/19 (Tu.)	AB/TV	Troy Shondell	"This Time"✔	9/18	#6	13
9/22 (F.)	AB/TV	Lee Dorsey	"Ya Ya"♦	9/11	#7	13
9/26 (Tu.)		Dion	"Runaround Sue"	9/25	#1	14
9/27 (W.)		Chubby Checker	"The Fly"	9/25	#7	13
10/2 (M.)		Duane Eddy	"My Blue Heaven"	8/28	#50	5
10/3 (Tu.)	AB/TV	The Duals	"Stick Shift"*	9/11	#25	11
10/4 (W.)		Freddy Cannon	"For Me and My Gal"	10/16	#71	6
10/16 (M.)	AB/TV	Curtis Lee	"Pretty Little Angel Eyes"✔	7/3	#7	11
10/19 (Th.)	AB/TV	James Brown & the Famous Flames	"I Don't Mind" / "Baby, You're Right"	5/15 / 8/21	#47 / #49	8 / 4
10/23 (M.)		Fats Domino	"Let the Four Winds Blow" / "What a Party"	7/24 / 10/2	#15 / #22	11 / 8
11/20 (M.)		Clarence "Frogman" Henry	"On Bended Knees"	10/30	#64	5
11/21 (Tu.)	AB/TV	The Impressions (with Curtis Mayfield)	"Gypsy Woman"✔	10/16	#20	15
11/28 (Tu.)		Johnny Tillotson	"Dreamy Eyes"	12/4	#35	14

BANDSTAND APPEARANCE	AB/TV DEBUT	ARTIST	SONG(S) PERFORMED	DATE APPEARED ON CHART	PEAK CHART POSITION	WEEKS ON CHART
12/7 (Th.)	AB/TV	Dick Dale & His Del-Tones	"Let's Go Trippin'" ✔	11/27	#60	9
12/11 (M.)	AB/TV	Jimmy Elledge	"Funny How the Time Slips Away" ✱	11/13	#22	14
12/13 (W.)		Del Shannon	"Hey! Little Girl"	11/27	#38	8
12/15 (F.)	AB/TV	Glen Campbell	"Turn Around, Look at Me" ✔	10/30	#62	10
12/18 (M.)	AB/TV	James Ray	"If You Gotta Make a Fool of Somebody" ✔	11/20	#22	14

BANDSTAND APPEARANCE	AB/TV DEBUT	ARTIST	SONG(S) PERFORMED	DATE APPEARED ON CHART	PEAK CHART POSITION	WEEKS ON CHART
12/19 (Tu.)		Dion	"The Majestic"	12/4	#36	8
12/20 (W.)		Gary U.S. Bonds	"Dear Lady Twist"	12/11	#9	16
12/22 (F.)		Tony Orlando	"Happy Times Are Here to Stay"	11/27	#82	3
12/25 (M.)	AB	The Lettermen	"When I Fall in Love"	11/20	#7	14
12/26 (Tu.)		The Belmonts	"I Need Someone"	12/25	#75	4

1 · 9 · 6 · 2

BANDSTAND APPEARANCE	AB/TV DEBUT	ARTIST	SONG(S) PERFORMED	DATE APPEARED ON CHART	PEAK CHART POSITION	WEEKS ON CHART
1/15 (M.)		Shirelles	"Baby It's You"	12/18/61	#8	14
1/16 (Tu.)		Gene Pitney	"Town Without Pity"	10/30/61	#13	19
1/18 (Th.)		Ike & Tina Turner	"Poor Fool"	11/27/61	#38	11
1/19 (F.)		Frankie Avalon	"You Are Mine"	3/24	#26	11
1/22 (M.)	AB/TV	Gene Chandler	"Duke of Earl" ✔	1/13	#1	15
1/26 (F.)	AB/TV	Lou Rawls	(no hits until 1965)			
1/29 (M.)		Jackie Wilson	"The Greatest Hurt"	1/13	#34	9
2/1 (Th.)	AB/TV	Don & Juan	"What's Your Name" ✔	2/10	#7	13
2/6 (Tu.)	AB	Jack Jones	"Lollipops and Roses" ✔	3/3	#66	8
2/8 (Th.)	AB/TV	Angels	"Cry, Baby, Cry"	2/17	#38	11
2/9 (F.)		Jack Scott	"Steps 1 and 2" ◆	11/6/61	#86	3
2/12 (M.)	AB	Brenda Lee	"Break It to Me Gently"	1/13	#4	13
			"So Deep"	1/13	#52	4
2/13 (Tu.)		Paul Anka	"Love Me Warm and Tender"	2/24	#12	12
2/14 (W.)	AB/TV	Eddie Holland	"Jamie" ✔	1/20	#30	13
2/15 (Th.)	AB	Paul Peterson	"She Can't Find Her Keys" ✔	3/3	#19	12
2/20 (Tu.)	AB/TV	Joey Dee & the Starlighters	"Peppermint Twist" ✔	11/20/61	#1	18
			"Hey Let's Twist"	2/17	#20	6
2/22 (Th.)	AB	Patsy Cline	"She's Got You"	1/27	#14	13
3/7 (W.)	AB/TV	Clyde McPhatter	"Lover Please"	3/3	#7	14
3/9 (F.)		Brian Hyland	"Ginnie Come Lately"	3/10	#21	11
3/12 (M.)	AB/TV	Jimmy Soul	"Twistin' Matilda" ✔	3/31	#12	14
3/14 (W.)	AB/TV	Arthur Alexander	"You Better Move On" ✔	2/24	#24	12
3/15 (Th.)	AB/TV	Dee Dee Sharp	"Mashed Potato Time" ✔	3/3	#2	18
3/19 (M.)	AB/TV	Barbara George	"I Know" ✔	11/13/61	#3	19
			"You Talk About Love"	3/31	#46	6
3/20 (Tu.)	AB/TV	Solomon Burke	"Cry to Me"	1/27	#44	10

BANDSTAND APPEARANCE	AB/TV DEBUT	ARTIST	SONG(S) PERFORMED	DATE APPEARED ON CHART	PEAK CHART POSITION	WEEKS ON CHART
3/22 (Th.)	AB/TV	Al Casey Combo	"Cookin'" ✔	4/7	#92	2
3/26 (M.)	AB/TV	Ronnie & the Hi-Lites	"I Wish That We Were Married" ✱	3/31	#16	12
4/3 (Tu.)		Mary Wells	"The One Who Really Loves You"	3/24	#8	17
4/6 (F.)	AB/TV	Jay & the Americans	"She Cried" ✔	3/17	#5	14
4/13 (F.)		Neil Sedaka	"King of Clowns"	3/31	#45	9
4/20 (F.)	AB/TV	Ketty Lester	"Love Letters in the Sand" ✔	2/24	#5	14
4/23 (M.)		Duane Eddy	"Deep in the Heart of Texas"	4/21	#78	5
4/27 (F.)		Fats Domino	"You Win Again"	2/24	#22	10
			"Ida Jane"	3/3	#90	2
5/3 (Th.)	AB/TV	Yvonne & the Sensations	"Let Me In"	1/6	#4	18
			"That's My Desire" ◆	4/28	#69	6
5/9 (W.)	AB/TV	Castells	"So This Is Love"	4/14	#21	13
5/28 (M.)		Smokey Robinson & the Miracles	"I'll Try Something New"	5/12	#39	10
6/4 (M.)		Ferrante & Teicher	"Smile"	3/17	#94	3
			"Lisa"	6/16	#98	2
6/6 (W.)		Dee Dee Sharp	"Gravy (For My Mashed Potatoes)"	6/16	#9	10
6/7 (Th.)	AB/TV	Claude King	"Wolverton Mountain"	5/26	#6	16
6/8 (F.)	AB/TV	Orlons	"Wah-Watusi" ✔	6/9	#2	14
6/11 (M.)		James Brown & the Famous Flames	"Night Train"	4/14	#35	11
			"Shout and Shimmy"	7/7	#61	4
6/12 (Tu.)	AB	James Darren	"Conscience"	4/14	#11	10
			"Mary's Little Lamb"	6/30	#39	8
6/14 (Th.)		Brenda Lee	"Everybody Loves Me but You"	4/14	#6	11
			"Here Comes That Feelin'"	4/28	#89	3
6/15 (F.)		Five Satins	"Memories of Days Gone By" ◆	2/24	#71	5

✔ First hit by a performer   ✱ Only hit by a performer   ◆ Last hit by a performer

BANDSTAND APPEARANCE	AB/TV DEBUT	ARTIST	SONG(S) PERFORMED	DATE APPEARED ON CHART	PEAK CHART POSITION	WEEKS ON CHART
6/19 (Tu.)	AB	Shelley Fabares	"Johnny Angel" ✔	3/3	#1	15
6/20 (W.)	AB/TV	Bobby Curtola	"Fortune Teller" ✔	5/5	#41	14
6/21 (Th.)	AB/TV	Bobby Vinton	"Roses Are Red" ✔	6/9	#1	15
6/25 (M.)		Jerry Butler	"Make It Easy on Yourself"	7/7	#20	11
6/27 (W.)	AB/TV	Joanie Sommers	"Johnny Get Angry"	5/26	#7	14
7/2 (M.)	AB/TV	Barbara Lynn	"You'll Lose a Good Thing" ✔	6/16	#8	13
7/8 (Tu.)	AB/TV	Ruth Brown	"Shake a Hand"	6/23	#97	2
7/15 (Th.)	AB/TV	Little Eva	"The Locomotion" ✔	6/23	#1	16
7/11 (W.)		Fats Domino	"Nothing New"	6/30	#77	5
			"Dance with Mr. Domino"	7/21	#98	1
7/16 (M.)		Freddy Cannon	"Palisades Park"	5/12	#3	15
7/17 (Tu.)		Brian Hyland	"Sealed with a Kiss"	6/9	#3	14
7/19 (Th)		Duane Eddy	"Ballad of Paladin"	7/7	#33	9
7/20 (F.)		Johnny Tillotson	"It Keeps Right on a-Hurting'"	5/12	#3	14
7/24 (Tu)		Chubby Checker	"Dancin' Party"	6/23	#12	10
7/25 (W.)		Dion	"Lovers Who Wander"	4/21	#3	12
8/2 (Th.)	AB/TV	Aretha Franklin	"Don't Cry Baby"	7/21	#92	1
			"Try a Little Tenderness"	9/29	#100	1
8/8 (W)		Joe Dee & the Starlighters	"What Kind of Love Is This"	8/25	#18	10
8/13 (M.)	AB/TV	Tommy Roe	"Sheila" ✔	7/28	#1	14
8/14 (Tu.)	AB/TV	Duprees	"You Belong to Me" ✔	8/4	#7	13
8/21 (Tu.)	AB	Robert Goulet	"What Kind of Fool Am I?" ✔	10/6	#89	2
8/23 (Th.)		Jerry Lee Lewis	"Sweet Little 16"	9/15	#95	3
8/24 (F.)		Dave "Baby" Cortez	"Rinky Dink"	7/14	#10	14
8/27 (M.)		Ketty Lester	"But Not for Me"	6/23	#41	7
8/28 (Tu.)		Jimmy Clanton	"Venus in Blue Jeans"	8/18	#7	13
8/29 (W.)	AB/TV	Rod McKuen	(only hit earlier in year)			
8/30 (Th.)		Jimmie Rodgers	"No One Will Ever Know"	9/1	#43	11
9/4 (Tu.)		Johnny Cash	"Bonanza!"	9/15	#94	1
9/11 (Tu.)	AB/TV	The Majors	"Wonderful Dream" ✔	8/11	#22	11
9/12 (W.)		Freddy Cannon	"What's Gonna Happen When Summer's Done"	9/8	#45	4
9/19 (W.)		Brian Hyland	"Warmed Over Kisses (Left Over Love)"	9/22	#25	28

BANDSTAND APPEARANCE	AB/TV DEBUT	ARTIST	SONG(S) PERFORMED	DATE APPEARED ON CHART	PEAK CHART POSITION	WEEKS ON CHART
9/24 (M.)	AB/TV	Bobby "Boris" Pickett & the Crypt Kickers	"Monster Mash" ✔	9/8	#1	14
9/27 (Th.)		Mary Wells	"You Beat Me to the Punch"	8/11	#9	12
10/10 (W.)	AB/TV	Chris Montez	"Let's Dance" ✔	8/4	#4	14
10/16 (Tu.)		Neil Sedaka	"Breaking Up Is Hard to Do"	6/30	#1	14
			"Next Door to an Angel"	10/6	#5	11
10/17 (W.)	AB/TV	Frank Ifield	"I Remember You" ✔	9/8	#5	11
10/22 (M.)	AB/TV	Marvin Gaye	"Stubborn Kind of Fellow" ✔	10/20	#46	9
10/23 (Tu.)		Bobby "Blue" Bland	"Stormy Monday Blues"	9/8	#43	13
10/26 (F.)		Joey Dee & the Starlighters	"I Lost My Baby"	11/3	#61	7
11/2 (F.)		Chubby Checker	"Limbo Rock"	9/8	#2	23
11/7 (W.)	AB/TV	Trade Martin	"That Stranger Used to Be My Girl" ✔	10/20	#28	8
			"Jelly Jelly" ✱	10/27	#100	1
11/9 (F.)		Dion	"Love Came to Me"	11/10	#10	11
11/13 (Tu.)	AB/TV	Cliff Richard		(no hits since 1959 or until 1963)		
11/16 (F.)		Tommy Roe	"Susie Darlin'"	10/6	#35	8
11/19 (M.)	AB/TV	Tommy Boyce	"I'll Remember Carol" ✱	10/13	#80	3
11/23 (F.)		Bobby Vinton	"Troubles Is My Middle Name"	12/1	#33	9
			"Let's Kiss and Make Up"	12/1	#38	9
11/26 (M.)		Paul Peterson	"My Dad"	11/17/61	#6	16
11/28 (W.)		Johnny Tillotson	"I Can't Help It"	10/27	#24	9
			"I'm So Lonesome I Could Cry"	12/1	#89	1
11/29 (Th.)	AB	Mel Torme	"Comin' Home Baby" ✱	11/3	#36	11
12/7 (F.)		Brian Hyland	"I May Not Live to See Tomorrow"	11/24	#69	7
12/10 (M.)	AB/TV	"Little" Esther Phillips	"Release Me" ✔	10/27	#8	14
12/13 (Th.)		Connie Francis	"I'm Going to Be Warm This Winter"	12/15	#18	11
12/18 (Tu.)	AB/TV	Timi Yuro	"The Love of a Boy"	12/1	#44	8
12/19 (W.)	AB/TV	Bobb B. Soxx & the Blue Jeans	"Zip-a-Dee-Doo-Dah" ✔	11/17	#8	13
12/21 (Fr.)	AB/TV	Cookies	"Chains" ✔	11/10	#17	12
12/28 (Fr.)		Mary Wells	"Two Lovers"	12/1	#7	13

1 · 9 · 6 · 3

BANDSTAND APPEARANCE	AB/TV DEBUT	ARTIST	SONG(S) PERFORMED	DATE APPEARED ON CHART	PEAK CHART POSITION	WEEKS ON CHART
1/2 (W.)	AB/TV	Dionne Warwick	"Don't Make Me Over"✔	12/8/62	#21	12
1/4 (F.)	AB/TV	Johnny Thunder	"Loop de Loop"✔	12/22/62	#4	11
1/10 (Th.)		Barbara Lynn	"You're Gonna Need Me"	12/15/62	#65	6
1/11 (F.)		Freddy Cannon	"If You Were a Rock'n'Roll Record"	11/10/62	#67	5
1/17 (Th.)		Dion	"Ruby Baby"	1/19	#2	13
1/18 (F.)	AB/TV	Paul & Paula	"Hey Paula"✔	12/29/62	#1	15
1/22 (Tu.)		Barbara Lynn	"Don't Be Cruel"	2/23	#93	4
1/23 (W.)		Johnny Mathis	"What Will Mary Say"	1/26/62	#9	12
1/28 (M.)	AB/TV	Steve Alaimo	"Every Day I Have to Cry"	1/5	#46	10
1/31 (Th.)		Bobby Comstock & the Counts	"Let's Stomp"	1/19/62	#57	6
2/4 (M.)		Bobby Rydell	"Butterfly Baby"	2/9	#23	9
2/6 (W.)		James Darren	"Pin a Medal on Joey"	2/9	#54	6
2/20 (W.)	AB/TV	Lou Christie	"The Gypsy Cried"✔	1/5	#24	13
2/25 (M.)		Neil Sedaka	"Alice in Wonderland"	2/2	#17	10
2/26 (Tu.)		Johnny Tillotson	"Out of My Mind"	3/2	#24	10
3/6 (W.)		Connie Francis	"Follow the Boys"	3/2	#17	10
3/14 (Th.)		Jo ann Campbell	"Mother Please! (I'd Rather Do It Myself)"♦	4/27	#88	3
3/19 (Tu.)		Timi Yuro	"Insult to Injury"	3/2	#81	1
3/22 (F.)	AB/TV	Wayne Newton	"Heart (I Hear You Beating)"✔	4/27	#83	4
3/29 (F.)		Jan & Dean	"Linda"	2/23	#28	13
4/2 (Tu.)		Bobby Vinton	"Over the Mountain"	3/9	#29	10
4/18 (Th.)	AB	Al Martino	"I Love You Because"	4/6	#3	16
4/19 (F.)	AB/TV	Johnny Cymbal	"Mr. Bass Man"✔	2/16	#16	13
			"Teenage Heaven"	5/11	#58	6
4/25 (Th.)		Freddy Cannon	"Pretty Baby"	5/4	#65	7
5/2 (Th.)	AB	Peter, Paul & Mary	"Puff the Magic Dragon"	3/16	#2	14
5/3 (F.)		Jimmy Clanton	"Darkest Street in Town"	1/5	#77	4
5/7 (Tu.)		Neil Sedaka	"Let's Go Steady Again"	4/27	#2	9
5/8 (W.)	AB/TV	Darlene Love	"Today I Met the Boy I'm Gonna Marry"✔	4/6	#39	8
5/14 (Tu.)	AB/TV	Rockin' Rebels	"Rockin' Crickets"*	4/27	#87	4
5/24 (F.)		Skeeter Davis	"End of the World"	1/26	#2	17
			"I'm Saving My Love"	5/11	#41	7
5/30 (Th.)	AB/TV	Lesley Gore	"It's My Party"✔	5/11	#1	13
5/31 (F.)		Brian Hyland	"I'm Afraid to Go Home"	6/29	#63	8
6/10 (M.)	AB	Ray Stevens	"Harry the Ape"	6/15	#17	9
6/12 (W.)		Chubby Checker	"Black Cloud"	6/15	#98	1
6/13 (Th.)		Timi Yuro	"Make the World Go Away"	7/20	#24	11
6/14 (F.)		Bobby Vinton	"Blue on Blue"	5/18	#3	13
6/20 (Th.)	AB/TV	Bill Anderson	"Still"	4/13	#8	14
6/21 (F.)	AB/TV	Nancy Sinatra	(no hits until 1965)			
6/26 (W.)		Paul & Paula	"Our First Quarrel"	6/1	#27	8
7/4 (Th.)		Joey Dee & the Starliters	"Dance, Dance, Dance"♦	7/20	#89	3
7/5 (F.)		Dee Dee Sharp	"Rock Me in the Cradle of Love"	6/29	#43	7
7/8 (M.)	AB/TV	Stevie Wonder	"Fingertips, Part 2"✔	6/22	#1	15
7/10 (W.)		Link Wray & His Wraymen	"Jack the Ripper"	6/15	#64	8
7/17 (W.)		Freddy Cannon	"Everybody Monkey"	8/3	#52	7
7/24 (W.)	AB	Roy Orbison	"Falling"	6/8	#22	8
8/1 (Th.)	AB/TV	Dovells	"Betty in Bermudas"	8/31	#50	7
8/8 (Th.)		Wayne Newton	"Donke Schoen"	7/13	#13	12
8/13 (Tu.)	AB/TV	Roy Clark	"Tips of My Fingers"✔	6/29	#45	8
8/19 (M.)		Duane Eddy	"Lonely Boy, Lonely Guitar"	5/18	#82	5
			"Your Baby's Gone Surfing"	8/24	#93	2
8/22 (Th.)	AB/TV	Dick & DeeDee	"Where Did the Good Times Go"	10/5	#93	1
8/23 (F.)		Barbara Lynn	"(I Cried at) Laura's Wedding"	8/10	#68	8
8/29 (Th.)		Fats Domino	"Red Sails in the Sunset"	9/21	#35	8

From this time, Bandstand was on once a week. Thus all dates from this point are Saturdays.

BANDSTAND APPEARANCE	AB/TV DEBUT	ARTIST	SONG(S) PERFORMED	DATE APPEARED ON CHART	PEAK CHART POSITION	WEEKS ON CHART
9/7		Neil Sedaka	"The Dreamer"	7/27	#47	7
9/7	AB/TV	Jaynettes	"Sally Go Round the Roses"*	8/31	#2	12
9/14		Dion	"Donna the Prima Donna"	9/14	#6	11
9/14	AB/TV	Major Lance	"Monkey Time"✔	7/13	#8	15
9/21		Skeeter Davis	"I Can't Stay Mad at You"	9/7	#7	13
9/21	AB/TV	Garnett Mimms	"Cry Baby"✔	9/28	#98	2
9/28		Bobby Rydell	"Let's Make Love Tonight"	9/28	#98	2
9/28	AB/TV	Ronettes	"Be My Baby"	8/31	#2	13
10/5		Dee Dee Sharp	"Wild!"	10/5	#33	9
10/12	AB/TV	Chiffons	"He's So Fine"	2/23	#1	15
			"A Love So Fine"	9/7	#40	9
10/19	AB/TV	Little Peggy March	"I Will Follow Him"✔	3/23	#1	14
			"Hello Heartache, Goodbye Love"	9/7	#26	9
10/26	AB/TV	Busters	"Bust Out"*	9/7	#25	10

✔First hit by a performer   *Only hit by a performer   ♦Last hit by a performer

BANDSTAND APPEARANCE	AB/TV DEBUT	ARTIST	SONG(S) PERFORMED	DATE APPEARED ON CHART	PEAK CHART POSITION	WEEKS ON CHART
11/2		Wayne Newton	"Shirl Girl"	10/26	#58	7
11/2	AB/TV	Dale & Grace	"I'm Leaving It Up to You"✔	10/5	#1	15
11/9		Gene Pitney	"24 Hours from Tulsa"	10/19	#17	11
11/16		Bobby Bare	"500 Miles Away from Home"	10/5	#10	11
11/23	AB	April & Nino	"Deep Purple"	9/14	#1	15
11/23		Dick & DeeDee	"Turn Around"	11/9	#13	13

BANDSTAND APPEARANCE	AB/TV DEBUT	ARTIST	SONG(S) PERFORMED	DATE APPEARED ON CHART	PEAK CHART POSITION	WEEKS ON CHART
11/23	AB	Trini Lopez	"Kansas City"	11/16	#23	12
11/30		Chubby Checker	"Luddy Lo"	11/2	#13	13
12/21	AB/TV	Vito & the Salutations	"Unchained Melody"*	10/19	#66	6
12/21		Neil Sedaka	"Bad Girl"	11/16	#33	8

1 · 9 · 6 · 4

BANDSTAND APPEARANCE	AB/TV DEBUT	ARTIST	SONG(S) PERFORMED	DATE APPEARED ON CHART	PEAK CHART POSITION	WEEKS ON CHART
1/4	AB/TV	Shirley Ellis	"Nitty Gritty"✔	11/16/63	#8	14
1/4	AB/TV	Trashmen	"Surfin' Bird"✔	12/7/63	#4	13
1/11	AB/TV	Crystals	"Little Boy"	2/1	#92	3
1/11		Freddy Cannon	"Abigail Beecher"	2/1	#16	8
1/18		Major Lance	"Um Um Um Um Um"	1/18	#5	11
1/25		Bobby Vinton	"There! I've Said It Again"	11/30/63	#1	13
2/1		Johnny Tillotson	"Worried Guy"	2/22	#37	7
2/1		Linda Scott	"Who's Been Sleeping in My Bed?"*	1/25	#100	1
2/8		Jackie DeShannon	"When You Walk in the Room"	1/5	#99	1
2/8		Dick & DeeDee	"All My Trials"	2/22	#89	3
2/15		Bobby Vee	"Stranger in Your Arms"	1/25	#83	3
2/22	AB/TV	Jody Miller	"Walk Like a Man"✔	2/8	#66	6
3/7	AB/TV	Rip Chords	"Three Window Coupe"	4/25	#28	9
3/14		April & Nino	"Stardust"	2/22	#11	9
3/21		Betty Everett	"The Shoop Shoop Song (It's in His Kiss)"	2/29	#6	13
3/21		Trini Lopez	"Jailer Bring Me Water"	3/21	#94	2
3/28	AB/TV	Pyramids	"Penetration"*	2/1	#18	10
3/28	AB/TV	Terry Stafford	"Suspicion"✔	2/22	#3	15
4/4		Sam Cooke	"Good News"	1/25	#11	10
4/4		Bobby Rydell	"Make Me Forget"	3/28	#43	6
4/18	AB/TV	Beach Boys	"Fun Fun Fun"	2/15	#5	11
			"I Get Around"	5/23	#1	15

BANDSTAND APPEARANCE	AB/TV DEBUT	ARTIST	SONG(S) PERFORMED	DATE APPEARED ON CHART	PEAK CHART POSITION	WEEKS ON CHART
4/25		Duane Eddy	"Son of Rebel Rouser"♦	1/4	#97	2
5/2	AB/TV	Bermudas	"Donnie"*	4/18	#62	10
5/9	AB/TV	Dusty Springfield	"Stay Awhile"	3/28	#38	7
5/9	AB/TV	Round Robin	"Kick That Little Foot, Sally Ann"*	5/30	#61	8
5/16		Jan & Dean	"Dead Man's Curve"	3/7	#8	14
5/23		Marvin Gaye	"You're a Wonderful One" / "Try It Baby"	3/14 / 6/6	#15 / #15	10 / 11
5/30		April & Nino	"I'm Confessin'" / "Tea for Two"	4/25 / 5/2	#99 / #56	1 / 5
6/6	AB/TV	Brenda Holloway	"Every Little Bit Hurts"✔	5/2	#13	10
6/13		Jimmie Rodgers	"The World I Used to Know"	5/30	#51	9
6/20		Wayne Newton	"The Little White Cloud That Cried"	5/2	#99	2
6/20	AB/TV	Johnny Rivers	"Memphis"✔	5/30	#2	12
6/27		Paris Sisters	"Dream Lover"♦	6/13	#91	4
7/11	AB	Roger Miller	"Dang Me"✔	6/13	#7	11
7/18		Terry Stafford	"I'll Touch a Star"♦	5/23	#25	8
7/18		Bobby Freeman	"Come On and Swim"	7/11	#5	12
8/1	AB/TV	Premieres	"Farmer John"*	6/20	#19	9
8/1		Dale & Grace	"The Loneliest Night"♦	5/2	#65	5
8/8	AB/TV	Rene & Rene	"Angelito"	7/11	#43	8
8/8	AB	Little Richard	"Bama Lama Bamaloo"	7/18	#82	4

BANDSTAND APPEARANCE	AB/TV DEBUT	ARTIST	SONG(S) PERFORMED	DATE APPEARED ON CHART	PEAK CHART POSITION	WEEKS ON CHART
8/22		Major Lance	"Rhythm"	8/22	#24	10
8/22		Jan & Dean	"Ride the Wild Surf"	9/19	#16	8
8/29	AB/TV	Irma Thomas	"Anyone Who Knows What Love Is"	7/4	#52	6
9/5		Johnny Rivers	"Maybelline"	8/15	#12	9
9/5	AB	Jerry Wallace	"In the Misty Moonlight"	7/25	#19	11
			"It's a Cotton-Candy World"	8/15	#99	1
9/12		Brenda Holloway	"I'll Always Love You"	8/8	#60	5
9/19	AB/TV	Superbs	"Baby Baby All the Time"*	10/3	#83	5
9/26	AB	Ventures	"Slaughter on 10th Ave."	10/24	#35	10
			"Walk Don't Run '64"	7/11	#8	11
10/3	AB/TV	Newbeats	"Bread and Butter"✔	8/15	#2	12
			"Everythin's Alright"	10/24	#16	9
10/17		Jerry Lee Lewis	"High Heeled Sneakers"	11/21	#91	1
10/24	AB/TV	The Spats	"Gator Tails and Monkey Ribs"*	9/26	#96	1

BANDSTAND APPEARANCE	AB/TV DEBUT	ARTIST	SONG(S) PERFORMED	DATE APPEARED ON CHART	PEAK CHART POSITION	WEEKS ON CHART
10/24		Bobby Vinton	"Mr. Lonely"	10/31	#1	15
10/31	AB/TV	Lou Johnson	"Always Something There to Remind Me"	8/22	#49	7
11/7		Everly Brothers	"Gone Gone Gone"	10/17	#31	10
11/14		Bobby Freeman	"S-W-I-M"♦	10/31	#56	6
11/14		Dick & DeeDee	"The Mountain's High"✔	7/31/61	#2	15
			"Thou Shalt Not Steal"	11/21	#13	13
11/28	AB/TV	Chad & Jeremy	"Willow Weep for Me"	11/14	#15	13
			"A Summer Song"	8/15	#7	14
12/5	AB/TV	Mickey Lee Lane	"Shaggy Dog"	10/10	#38	9
12/12		Neil Sedaka	"Sunny"	7/25	#86	3
12/12		Freddy Cannon	"Action"	8/15	#13	9
12/26		Bobby Vee	"Every Little Bit Hurts"	12/5	#85	5

1 • 9 • 6 • 5

BANDSTAND APPEARANCE	AB/TV DEBUT	ARTIST	SONG(S) PERFORMED	DATE APPEARED ON CHART	PEAK CHART POSITION	WEEKS ON CHART
1/2		Marvin Gaye	"Hitch Hike"	1/16	#30	12
			"How Sweet It Is (To Be Loved by You)"	11/14/64	#6	14
1/2	AB/TV	Adam Faith	"It Sounds Good"✔	1/16	#31	8
1/2		Johnny Rivers	"Mountain of Love"	10/31/64	#9	11
1/9	AB	Gale Garnett	"Lovin' Place"♦	12/5/64	#54	9
1/9	AB/TV	Jumpin' Gene Simmons	"The Dodo"	11/7/64	#83	3
			"Haunted House"	8/8	#11	11
1/16		James Darren	"Goodbye Cruel World"	10/16/61	#3	17
2/13	AB/TV	Sue Thompson	"Norman"	12/4/61	#3	16
			"Paper Tiger"	1/2	#23	10
2/20		Johnny Mathis	"Listen Lonely Girl"	10/24/64	#62	8
2/20	AB	Vic Dana	"Red Roses for a Blue Lady"	2/6	#10	12
2/20	AB/TV	Beau Brummels	"Laugh Laugh"✔	1/2	#15	12
2/27		Sonny Knight	"If You Want This Love"	10/10/64	#71	9
			"Love Me as Though There Were No Tomorrow"♦	2/6	#100	1
2/27	AB/TV	Cannibal & the Headhunters	"Land of 1,000 Dances"✔	2/27	#30	14

BANDSTAND APPEARANCE	AB/TV DEBUT	ARTIST	SONG(S) PERFORMED	DATE APPEARED ON CHART	PEAK CHART POSITION	WEEKS ON CHART
3/6	AB/TV	J. Frank Wilson & the Cavaliers	"Last Kiss"✔	9/5	#2	15
			"Hey Little One"	11/28	#85	2
3/13	AB/TV	Alvin Cash & the Crawlers	"Twine Time"✔	1/2	#14	11
			"The Barracuda"♦	3/27	#59	7
3/20		Brenda Holloway	"When I'm Gone"	3/6	#29	9
3/27		Jackie Wilson	"Baby Workout"	3/9/63	#5	12
			"Danny Boy"	2/6	#94	3
3/27	AB/TV	The Uniques	"Not Too Long Ago"✔	3/20	#66	6
4/3	AB/TV	Bobbi Martin	"I Can't Stop Thinking of You"	3/13	#46	8
			"I Love You So"	5/29	#70	7
4/3	AB/TV	Four Tops	"Ask the Lonely"	2/6	#24	8
			"I Can't Help Myself"	5/15	#1	14
4/10		Gene Chandler	"Nothing Can Stop Me"	4/17	#18	12
			"You Can't Hurt Me No More"	3/6	#92	1
4/10	AB/TV	The Reflections	"Poor Man's Son"♦	3/13	#55	5
4/17	AB/TV	Dixie Cups	"Iko Iko"♦	4/3	#20	10

✔First hit by a performer   *Only hit by a performer   ♦Last hit by a performer

BANDSTAND APPEARANCE	AB/TV DEBUT	ARTIST	SONG(S) PERFORMED	DATE APPEARED ON CHART	PEAK CHART POSITION	WEEKS ON CHART
5/1	AB/TV	Ian Whitcomb	"This Sporting Life"✔	3/13	#100	1
			"You Turn Me On"	5/22	#8	13
5/1		The Ikettes	"Peaches 'n' Cream"	3/13	#36	8
			"I'm Blue (The Gong-Gong Song)"	1/13/63	#19	12
5/15		Jackie DeShannon	"What the World Needs Now is Love"	5/22	#7	13
5/15		Ronettes	"Is This What I Get for Loving You?"	5/29	#75	4
5/22	AB/TV	Tony Clarke	"The Entertainer"♦	3/27	#31	9
6/5	AB/TV	Junior Walker & the All-Stars	"Shotgun"✔	2/13	#4	14
			"Do the Boomerang"	6/5	#36	7
6/12	AB	Eddie Hodges	"New Orleans"♦	7/3	#44	9
6/12	AB/TV	Sonny & Cher	"I Got You Babe"✔	7/10	#1	14
6/26		Steve Alaimo	"Real Live Girl"	3/6	#77	2
			"Cast Your Fate to the Wind"	6/26	#89	2
6/26		Beau Brummels	"You Tell Me Why"	7/24	#38	7
7/3	AB/TV	Terry Black	"Unless You Care"*	11/21/64	#99	2
7/10		Lenny Welch	"Darling Take Me Back"	6/26	#72	6
7/24	AB/TV	Jewel Aikens	"The Birds and the Bees"✔	1/23	#3	14
8/7	AB/TV	We Five	"You Were on My Mind"✔	7/24	#3	15
8/7	AB/TV	Donovan	"Catch the Wind"	5/15	#23	10
			"Colours"	8/14	#61	7

BANDSTAND APPEARANCE	AB/TV DEBUT	ARTIST	SONG(S) PERFORMED	DATE APPEARED ON CHART	PEAK CHART POSITION	WEEKS ON CHART
8/21	AB	Bobby Goldsboro	"Voodoo Woman"	5/1	#27	11
8/28	AB/TV	Lovin' Spoonful	"Do You Believe in Magic"✔	8/21	#9	13
8/28	AB/TV	Danny Hutton	"Roses and Rainbows"*	10/16	#73	6
9/4		Del Shannon	"Keep Searchin'"	11/20	#9	14
9/11		Gene Chandler	"Good Times"	8/21	#92	3
9/25	AB/TV	Dobie Gray	"The In Crowd"	1/9	#13	9
10/2	AB/TV	Derek Martin	"You Better Go"*	7/31	#78	6
10/9	AB/TV	Barbara Mason	"Yes I'm Ready (To Learn)"✔	5/15	#5	14
10/9	AB/TV	Vejtables	"I Still Love You"*	10/23	#84	4
10/16	AB/TV	The Toys	"A Lover's Concerto"✔	9/11	#2	15
10/23	AB/TV	Mojo Men	"Dance With Me"✔	10/23	#61	6
11/6	AB/TV	Sunrays	"I Live For The Sun"✔	9/4	#51	10
11/13	AB/TV	Fontella Bass	"Rescue Me"✔	10/2	#14	13
11/20		Smokey Robinson & the Miracles	"My Girl Has Gone"	10/9	#14	10
11/27	AB/TV	Ronnie Dove	"Kiss Away"	11/6	#25	8
12/4	AB	Gary Lewis & the Playboys	"Everybody Loves a Clown"	9/25	#4	11

1 • 9 • 6 • 6

BANDSTAND APPEARANCE	AB/TV DEBUT	ARTIST	SONG(S) PERFORMED	DATE APPEARED ON CHART	PEAK CHART POSITION	WEEKS ON CHART
1/1	AB	Mel Carter	"Love Is All We Need"	1/22	#50	8
			"My Heart Sings"	10/30/65	#38	7
1/8		Lou Christie	"Lightning Strikes"	12/25/65	#1	15
1/8	AB/TV	Knickerbockers	"Lies"✔	12/4/65	#20	13
1/15		Bobby Goldsboro	"Broomstick Cowboy"	12/18/65	#53	7
			"It's Too Late"	2/19	#23	8
1/15	AB/TV	Mitch Ryder & the Detroit Wheels	"Jenny Take a Ride"✔	12/11	#10	12
			"Little Latin Lupe Lu"	3/5	#17	9
1/22	AB/TV	Joe Tex	"A Sweet Woman Like You"	12/4/65	#29	9
1/29	AB/TV	Kingsmen	"Annie Francis"	8/7/65	#47	8
1/29	AB	Peter & Gordon	"Don't Pity Me"	11/6/65	#83	4
			"Woman"	2/12	#14	12

BANDSTAND APPEARANCE	AB/TV DEBUT	ARTIST	SONG(S) PERFORMED	DATE APPEARED ON CHART	PEAK CHART POSITION	WEEKS ON CHART
2/5		Paul Revere & the Raiders	"Just Like Me"	12/4/65	#11	16
			"Kicks"	3/19	#4	14
2/12		Al Martino	"Spanish Eyes"	12/4/65	#15	12
			"Think I'll Go Somewhere and Cry Myself to Sleep"	3/12	#30	8
2/12	AB/TV	Young Rascals	"I Ain't Gonna Eat Out My Heart Anymore"	12/25/65	#52	9
			"Good Lovin'"	3/12	#1	14
2/19	AB/TV	Mamas & Papas	"California Dreamin'"✔	1/8	#4	17
2/19	AB	Bob Lind	"Elusive Butterfly"✔	1/22	#5	13
2/26	AB/TV	T-Bones	"Whatever Shape Your Stomach's In"✔	12/11/65	#3	13
			"Sippin' and Chippin'"	3/26	#62	5

BANDSTAND APPEARANCE	AB/TV DEBUT	ARTIST	SONG(S) PERFORMED	DATE APPEARED ON CHART	PEAK CHART POSITION	WEEKS ON CHART
3/5		Freddy Cannon	"Dedication Song"	2/19	#41	6
3/12		Chris Montez	"Call Me"	1/8	#22	10
3/12	AB/TV	B.J. Thomas & the Triumphs	"I'm So Lonesome I Could Cry"✔	2/19	#8	13
3/26		Sir Douglas Quintet	"She's About a Mover"✔	4/3/65	#13	12
			"The Rains Came"	1/29	#31	11
4/2		Mel Carter	"Band of Gold"	4/9	#32	8
4/2		Ventures	"Secret Agent Man"	2/26	#54	7
4/9		Beau Brummels	"One Too Many Mornings"♦	6/4	#95	3
4/16	AB	Norma Tanega	"Walkin' My Cat Named Dog"*	2/26	#22	9
4/16	AB/TV	Eddie Holman	"This Can't Be True"✔	1/15	#57	11
4/23	AB	Martha & the Vandellas	"My Baby Loves Me"	1/22	#22	11
4/30		Jackie DeShannon	"Come and Get Me"	5/28	#83	3
4/30	AB/TV	Bob Kuban & the In-Men	"The Cheater"✔	1/29	#12	11
5/7	AB/TV	Otis Redding	"Satisfaction"	3/5	#31	8
5/7	AB	Shadows of Knight	"Gloria"	3/19	#10	12
			"Oh Yeah"	6/4	#39	6
5/14		Brian Hyland	"3000 Miles"	4/16	#99	1
5/14	AB/TV	Just Us	"I Can't Grow Peaches on a Cherry Tree"*	3/12	#34	11
5/21	AB	Roy Head	"Treat Her Right"	9/4/65	#2	11
			"My Babe"	3/12	#99	1
5/21	AB	Tokens	"The Lion Sleeps Tonight"	11/13/61	#1	15
			"I Hear Trumpets Blow"	3/19	#30	8
5/28	AB	Gentrys	"Keep On Dancing"✔	9/11/65	#4	13
			"Everyday I Have to Cry"	5/14	#77	5
5/28		Olympics	"Mine Exclusively"	4/30	#99	2
6/4		Sunrays	"Andrea"	1/22	#41	8
			"Still"♦	5/7	#93	2
6/4		Roy Orbison	"Pretty Woman"	9/26/64	#1	15
			"Twinkle Toes"	4/30	#39	6
6/18	AB	Love	"My Little Red Book"✔	4/30	#52	11
6/18		Steve Alaimo	"So Much Love"	5/21	#92	2
6/25	AB/TV	Neil Diamond	"Solitary Man"✔	5/21	#55	10
7/2	AB	The Vogues	"Land of Milk and Honey"	6/4	#29	8
			"Magic Town"	2/26	#21	9
7/9	AB/TV	The Leaves	"Hey Joe"*	5/21	#31	9
7/23	AB	Turtles	"You Baby"	2/5	#20	12
7/30	AB/TV	Syndicate of Sound	"Little Girl"✔	6/4	#8	10
			"Rumors"	8/20	#55	7
8/6		James Brown	"It's a Man's Man's Man's World"	4/30	#8	9
			"Money Won't Change You"	7/30	#53	9
8/13	AB	Righteous Brothers	"Go Ahead and Cry"	8/6	#30	6
8/13	AB/TV	Joe Simon	"Teenager's Prayer"	6/18	#66	7
8/20	AB/TV	Temptations	"Ain't Too Proud to Beg"	5/28	#13	13
			"Beauty Is Only Skin Deep"	8/20	#3	12
8/20	AB/TV	Sandy Posey	"Born a Woman"	7/23	#12	14
8/27		Johnny Rivers	"Poor Side of Town"	9/17	#1	15
9/3		Lou Christie	"Rhapsody in the Rain"	3/26	#16	8
			"Painter"	6/25	#81	5
9/10		Tommy Roe	"Sweet Pea"	6/11	#8	14
			"Hooray for Hazel"	9/17	#6	13
9/10	AB	Hollies	"Bus Stop"	7/23	#5	14
			"I Can't Let Go"	3/19	#42	10
9/17		Neil Diamond	"Cherry Cherry"	8/20	#6	12
9/24		Martha & the Vandellas	"What Am I Going to Do Without Your Love"	6/11	#71	5
10/1	AB/TV	? & the Mysterians	"96 Tears"✔	9/3	#1	15
			"I Need Somebody"	11/19	#22	10
10/1		Lesley Gore	"Young Love"	3/26	#50	6
10/8		Mel Carter	"You You You"	7/16	#49	7
			"Take Good Care of Her"	10/8	#78	5
10/8		Roy Head	"To Make a Big Man Cry"	9/17	#95	2
10/15		Stevie Wonder	"Blowin' in the Wind"	7/23	#9	10
			"Nothing's Too Good for My Baby"	4/16	#20	7
10/15		Jackie DeShannon	"I Can Make It with You"	9/10	#68	6
10/22	AB	Left Banke	"Walk Away Renee"✔	9/10	#5	13
11/12	AB/TV	Count Five	"Psychotic Reaction"*	9/10	#5	12
11/12	AB/TV	Fantastic Johnny C.	"Boogaloo Down Broadway"✔	10/8	#7	8
12/3		Otis Redding	"Fa Fa Fa Fa Fa"	10/1	#29	8
12/3	AB/TV	Music Machine	"Talk Talk"✔	11/12	#15	12
			"The People in Me"♦	1/28/67	#30	7
12/17	AB/TV	Sandpipers	"Louie Louie"	10/22	#30	7
			"Guantanamera"✔	7/30	#9	11
12/17	AB	Monkees	"I'm a Believer"	12/10	#1	15
			"Steppin' Stone"	12/17	#20	8
12/24	AB/TV	Hard Times	"Fortune Teller"*	12/31	#97	2
12/31	AB	Mrs. Miller	"Downtown"✔	4/30	#82	4
			"A Lover's Concerto"♦	5/7	#95	5
12/31	AB/TV	Blues Magoos	"We Ain't Got Nothin' Yet"✔	12/10	#5	14

✔First hit by a performer   *Only hit by a performer   ♦Last hit by a performer

BANDSTAND APPEARANCE	AB/TV DEBUT	ARTIST	SONG(S) PERFORMED	DATE APPEARED ON CHART	PEAK CHART POSITION	WEEKS ON CHART
1/7		Neil Diamond	"You Got to Me"	1/28	#18	8
1/7	AB/TV	Electric Prunes	"I Had Too Much to Dream Last Night"✔	12/10/66	#11	14
1/14	AB/TV	Youngbloods	"Grizzly Bear"✔	12/17/66	#52	10
1/14	AB/TV	Mike Williams	"Lonely Soldier"*	7/9/66	#69	5
1/21	AB	Buffalo Springfield	"For What It's Worth"	1/28	#25	10
1/21		Otis Redding	"Try a Little Tenderness"	12/3/66	#25	10
1/28		Standells	"Dirty Water"✔	4/22	#11	16
2/4	AB/TV	Young-Holt Trio	"Wack Wack"✔	12/3/66	#40	8
2/4		Tommy Roe	"It's Now Winter's Day"	12/24/66	#23	11
2/11		Mojo Men	"Sit Down I Think I Love You"	2/4	#26	11
2/11	AB/TV	Jimmy Castor	"Hey Leroy, Your Mamma's Callin' You"✔	12/31	#31	9
2/18	AB	P.J. Proby	"Niki Hokey"♦	1/28	#23	10
2/18	AB/TV	Fifth Dimension	"Go Where You Wanna Go"✔	1/7	#16	10
2/25	AB	McCoys	"I Got to Go Back"	1/7	#69	5
2/25	AB	Felice Taylor	"It May Be Winter Outside (But in My Heart It's Spring)"	1/14	#42	6
3/11	AB	Beatles (films)	"Penny Lane"	2/25	#1	10
			"Strawberry Fields Forever"	2/25	#8	9
3/18		Marvin Gaye	"Little Darlin' I Need You"	8/20/66	#47	7
4/1		Turtles	"Happy Together"	2/11	#1	15
4/8		Lesley Gore	"California Nights"	2/4	#16	14
4/15		Martha & the Vandellas	"Jimmy Mack"	2/25	#10	14
4/15	AB/TV	Nitty Gritty Dirt Band	"Buy for Me the Rain"✔	4/8	#45	7
4/22		Gene Chandler	"Girl Don't Care"	2/25	#66	9
4/22		Blues Magoos	"Pipe Dream"	3/18	#60	6
4/29	AB/TV	Don Grady & Yellow Balloon	"Yellow Balloon"♦	4/1	#25	10
4/29	AB/TV	Brenton Wood	"The Oogum Boogum Song"✔	4/15	#34	12
5/6		Electric Prunes	"Get Me to the World on Time"♦	4/1	#27	8
5/6		Brenda Holloway	"Just Look What You've Done"	4/22	#69	5
5/13		Jerry Butler	"I Dig You Baby"	1/21	#60	9
5/20	AB/TV	Seeds	"Can't Seem to Make You Mine"	4/29	$41	7
5/27	AB	Buckinghams	"Kind of a Drag"✔	12/31/66	#1	13
			"Mercy Mercy Mercy"	6/17	#5	12
6/3	AB/TV	Jefferson Airplane	"Somebody to Love"✔	4/1	#5	15
			"White Rabbit"	6/24	#8	10
6/10	AB/TV	The Grass Roots	"Let's Live for Today"	5/13	#8	12
6/10		? & the Mysterians	"Can't Get Enough of You, Baby"	3/25	#56	6
			"Girl (You Captivate Me)"♦	6/10	#98	2
6/17		Johnny Rivers	"Tracks of My Tears"	6/17	#10	9
6/17	AB/TV	Don & the Goodtimes	"I Could Be So Good to You"✔	4/22	#56	7
6/24		Fifth Dimension	"Up, Up and Away"	6/3	#7	12
7/8	AB	Five Americans	"Western Union"	3/4	#5	12
			"Zip Code"	8/12	#36	7
7/15		Tommy Roe	"Little Miss Sunshine"	6/10	#99	1
7/15		Impressions	"You Always Hurt Me"	3/4	#96	2
7/22	AB/TV	Bee Gees (film)	"New York Mining Disaster 1941"✔	5/27	#14	7
7/22	AB/TV	The Doors	"Light My Fire"✔	6/3	#1	17
7/29	AB	The Byrds	"Have You Seen Her Face"	6/10	#74	4
			"Lady Friend"	8/19	#82	2
7/29	AB/TV	The Forum	"The River Is Wide"*	7/8	#45	8
8/5		James Brown	"Cold Sweat"	7/15	#7	12
8/5	AB/TV	Sam & Dave	"Soothe Me"	6/17	#56	7
			"Soul Man"	9/9	#2	15
8/12	AB	Supremes	"Reflections"	8/12	#2	11
8/12		Mamas & Papas	"12:30"	8/26	#20	6
8/19		The Platters	"Washed Ashore"	7/1	#56	8
8/26		Bobby Vee	"Come Back When You Grow Up"	7/22	#3	16
9/2	AB/TV	Sunshine Company	"Happy"✔	7/15	#50	10
9/2		Brenton Wood	"Gimme Little Sign"	8/12	#9	15
9/16	AB/TV	Lewis & Clarke Expedition	"I Feel Good"*	8/26	#64	4
9/16		Brenda Holloway	"You've Made Me So Very Happy"♦	9/9	#39	10
9/23	AB/TV	Strawberry Alarm Clock	"Incense and Peppermints"✔	8/26	#49	7
9/30	AB/TV	Charles Wright & the Watts 103rd St. Rhythm Band	"Spreadin' Honey"✔	9/9	#73	10
9/30		The Grass Roots	"Things I Should Have Said"	8/12	#23	8
10/7	AB	Merry Go Round	"You're a Very Lovely Woman"♦	9/9	#94	3
			"Live"	4/29	#63	4
10/21		The Grass Roots	"Wake Up, Wake Up"	10/28	#68	5
10/28	AB	Billy Joe Royal	"Hush!"	9/30	#52	8
11/4		Don & the Goodtimes	"Happy and Me"♦	7/29	#98	1
11/11	AB/TV	Van Morrison	"Brown Eyed Girl"✔	7/15	#10	16

BANDSTAND APPEARANCE	AB/TV DEBUT	ARTIST	SONG(S) PERFORMED	DATE APPEARED ON CHART	PEAK CHART POSITION	WEEKS ON CHART
11/18		Strawberry Alarm Clock	"Tomorrow"	12/30	#23	10
11/25		Paul Revere & the Raiders	"Peace of Mind"	11/18	#42	6
12/2	AB	Candymen	"Georgia Pines"♦	11/18	#81	5
12/2		Brenton Wood	"Baby You Got It"	11/25	#34	7
12/9		Sunshine Company	"Back on the Street Again"	10/21	#36	7

BANDSTAND APPEARANCE	AB/TV DEBUT	ARTIST	SONG(S) PERFORMED	DATE APPEARED ON CHART	PEAK CHART POSITION	WEEKS ON CHART
12/9		Glen Campbell	"By the Time I Get to Phoenix"	10/28	#26	11
12/16	AB/TV	American Breed	"Bend Me, Shape Me"	12/2	#5	14
12/16	AB/TV	Pink Floyd	(no hits until 1973)			
12/23	AB	Bruce Channel	"Mr. Bus Driver"♦	12/23	#90	2
12/23		Beatles (film)	"Hello Goodbye"	12/2	#1	11
12/30	AB	Rose Garden	"Next Plane to London"	10/21	#17	14
12/30	AB/TV	The Who (film)	"I Can See for Miles"	10/14	#9	11

1 · 9 · 6 · 8

BANDSTAND APPEARANCE	AB/TV DEBUT	ARTIST	SONG(S) PERFORMED	DATE APPEARED ON CHART	PEAK CHART POSITION	WEEKS ON CHART
1/6	AB	Kenny O'Dell	"Beautiful People"	11/18/67	#38	7
1/6		Turtles	"She's My Girl"	11/11/67	#14	10
1/13	AB	Box Tops	"Cry Like a Baby"	3/2	#2	15
1/13		Jimmie Rodgers	"Child of Clay"♦	9/23/67	#31	8
1/20		Joe Simon	"No Sad Songs"	1/6	#49	7
1/20		American Breed	"Green Lite"	2/24	#39	7
1/27	AB	John Fred & the Playboy Band	"Hey Hey Bunny"♦	2/24	#57	6
			"Judy in Disguise (With Glasses)"	11/25/67	#1	16
2/3		James Brown	"I Got the Feelin'"	3/16	#6	12
2/10	AB/TV	Blue Cheer	"Summertime Blues"✔	3/2	#14	13
2/10		Joe Tex	"Men Are Gettin' Scarce"	2/10	#33	7
2/17	AB	Music Explosion	"Little Bit O' Soul"✔	5/13/67	#2	16
			"Sunshine Games"♦	9/9/67	#63	5
3/2	AB/TV	Iron Butterfly		(no hits until later in year)		
3/9	AB/TV	1910 Fruitgum Co.	"Simon Says"	1/27	#4	14
			"May I Take a Giant Step"	4/20	#63	8
3/9		Brenton Wood	"Lovey Dovey Kinda Lovin'"♦	2/3	#99	2
3/16		Bobby Vee	"Maybe Just Today"	2/10	#46	6
			"My Girl/My Guy Medley"	4/27	#35	9
3/23		Sunshine Company	"Look, Here Comes the Sun"♦	2/10	#56	5
3/23	AB	Tommy Boyce & Bobby Hart	"I Wonder What She's Doing Tonight"	12/23/67	#8	14
				4/6	#53	6
			"Goodbye Baby"			

BANDSTAND APPEARANCE	AB/TV DEBUT	ARTIST	SONG(S) PERFORMED	DATE APPEARED ON CHART	PEAK CHART POSITION	WEEKS ON CHART
4/6	AB/TV	Lemon Pipers	"Green Tambourine"✔	12/16/67	#1	13
			"Rice Is Nice"	3/9	#46	7
4/6		Kenny O'Dell	"Springfield Plane"♦	2/24	#94	2
5/4	AB/TV	Dyke & the Blazers	"Funky Walk Part 1"	4/13	#67	5
			"We Got More Soul"	5/18	#35	10
5/4	AB/TV	Steppenwolf	"Born to Be Wild"✔	7/13	#2	13
5/11		Byrds	"You Ain't Goin' Nowhere"	5/11	#74	5
5/25		Strawberry Alarm Clock	"Sit with the Guru"	3/16	#65	5
6/1	AB	Irish Rovers	"The Unicorn"✔	3/23	#7	12
			"Whiskey on a Sunday"	6/22	#75	7
6/8	AB	The People	"I Love You"	4/6	#14	18
6/8		B.J. Thomas	"The Eyes of a New York Woman"	6/22	#28	14
6/15	AB/TV	Albert King	"Cold Feet"✔	2/3	#67	4
6/15	AB/TV	Merilee Rush	"Angel of the Morning"✔	5/4	#7	16
6/22		Tommy Boyce & Bobby Hart	"Alice Long"♦	7/6	#27	10
7/6	AB/TV	Jon & Robin & the In Crowd	"Dr. John, the Medicine Man"♦	3/16	#85	4
7/20		Joe Tex	"I'll Never Do You Wrong"	5/18	#59	5
			"Keep the One You Got"	8/10	#52	5
7/27	AB	Eternity's Children	"Mrs. Bluebird"♦	7/13	#69	7
8/3		Merilee Rush	"That Kind of Woman"	8/31	#76	6

✔ First hit by a performer   ✱ Only hit by a performer   ♦ Last hit by a performer

BANDSTAND APPEARANCE	AB/TV DEBUT	ARTIST	SONG(S) PERFORMED	DATE APPEARED ON CHART	PEAK CHART POSITION	WEEKS ON CHART
8/3		The Vogues	"Turn Around, Look at Me" "My Special Angel"	6/15 9/7	#7 #7	15 10
8/10		McCoys	"Jesse Brady"♦	10/26	#98	2
8/17		American Breed	"Anyway That You Want Me"♦	8/3	#88	4
8/31	AB/TV	Ohio Express	"Down at Lulu's"	8/3	#33	9
9/7	AB/TV	Patti Drew	"Workin' on a Groovy Thing"	8/3	#62	11
9/7		The Grass Roots	"Midnight Confessions"	8/31	#5	15
9/14	AB	O.C. Smith	"Little Green Apples"	8/17	#2	17
9/21	AB	Jay & the Techniques	"Baby, Make Your Own Sweet Music"♦	4/13	#64	8
9/28	AB/TV	Clarence Carter	"Slip Away"✔ "Funky Fever"	7/13 6/1	#6 #88	16 3
10/5	AB/TV	Eddie Floyd	"I've Never Found a Girl (To Love Me Like You Do)" "Bring It on Home to Me"	7/27 10/19	#40 #17	9 13

BANDSTAND APPEARANCE	AB/TV DEBUT	ARTIST	SONG(S) PERFORMED	DATE APPEARED ON CHART	PEAK CHART POSITION	WEEKS ON CHART
10/5		Iron Butterfly	"In-a-Gadda-Da-Vida"✔	8/24	#30	17
10/12		Johnny Nash	"Hold Me Tight" "You Got Soul"	9/14 12/14	#5 #58	15 7
10/19	AB/TV	Al Wilson	"The Snake"✔	8/3	#27	10
11/2		The Grass Roots	"Bella Linda"	11/23	#28	9
11/9	AB/TV	Andy Kim	"Shoot 'em Up Baby" "Rainbow Ride"	9/7 12/21	#31 #49	10 7
11/16	AB/TV	Avant-Garde	"Naturally Stoned"*	8/31	#40	10
11/30		Merilee Rush	"Reach Out"	12/7	#79	4
12/21		Al Martino	"I Can't Help It"	12/28	#97	3
12/28		Brian Hyland	"Tragedy"	1/11/69	#56	10
12/28	AB	Spanky & Our Gang	"Yesterday's Rain"	12/7	#94	3

I · 9 · 6 · 9

BANDSTAND APPEARANCE	AB/TV DEBUT	ARTIST	SONG(S) PERFORMED	DATE APPEARED ON CHART	PEAK CHART POSITION	WEEKS ON CHART
1/11		Dorsey Burnette	"The Greatest Love"♦	1/25	#67	6
1/25	AB	Classics IV	"Stormy" "Traces"	10/26/68 2/8	#5 #2	15 12
2/15	AB/TV	Willie Mitchell	"30-60-90"♦	2/1	#69	5
2/22	AB/TV	Tyrone Davis	"Is It Something You've Got"	3/22	#24	7
3/1	AB	Arthur Conley	"Ob-La-Di, Ob-La-Da"♦	1/4	#51	6
3/15		1910 Fruitgum Co.	"Indian Giver"	1/25	#5	13
3/22		Sir Douglas Quintet	"Mendocino"	1/18	#27	15
3/22		Neil Diamond	"Brother Love's Travelin' Salvation Show"	2/22	#22	13
3/29		Ohio Express	"Sweeter than Sugar"	3/1	#96	1

BANDSTAND APPEARANCE	AB/TV DEBUT	ARTIST	SONG(S) PERFORMED	DATE APPEARED ON CHART	PEAK CHART POSITION	WEEKS ON CHART
4/5		Betty Everett	"There'll Come a Time" "I Can't Say No to You"	1/18 4/26	#26 #78	11 4
4/5	AB/TV	Bubble Puppy	"Hot Smoke and Sassafrass"	2/15	#14	12
4/26	AB/TV	Spiral Staircase	"No More than Yesterday"✔	4/5	#12	15
5/3	AB/TV	Linda Ronstadt				(no hits in this period; 2 hits in 1967, 1 in 1968 and more from 1970 on.)
5/10		Tommy Roe	"Heather Honey"	4/26	#29	8
5/10	AB/TV	Smoke Ring	"Not Much"*	2/15	#85	4
5/17	AB/TV	DeeDee Warwick	"Foolish Fool"	3/22	#57	8
5/17		Ventures	"Hawaii Five-O" "Theme from A Summer Place"	3/8 6/28	#4 #83	14 5
5/24		Solomon Burke	"Proud Mary"	5/3	#45	7
5/24	AB/TV	Guess Who	"These Eyes" "Laughing"	4/5 7/12	#6 #10	14 11

BANDSTAND APPEARANCE	AB/TV DEBUT	ARTIST	SONG(S) PERFORMED	DATE APPEARED ON CHART	PEAK CHART POSITION	WEEKS ON CHART
5/31	AB/TV	Dorsey Burnette		(no hits until 1970)		
5/31		Classics IV	"The River Is Wide"	4/12	#31	11
			"I'd Wait a Million Years"	7/5	#15	15
6/7	AB/TV	Oliver	"Good Morning Starshine"✔	5/24	#3	13
6/7		Ronnie Dove	"I Need You Now"♦	5/31	#93	2
6/14	AB/TV	Jerry Smith	"Truck Stop"*	5/10	#71	7
6/14	AB/TV	Tony Joe White	"Polk Salad Annie"✔	7/5	#8	12
6/28		Spiral Staircase	"No One for Me to Turn To"	8/30	#52	7
7/5		The Impressions	"Seven Years"	4/26	#84	4
			"Choice of Colors"	6/28	#21	11
7/5		Jerry Butler	"Moody Woman"	5/31	#24	10
			"What's the Use of Breaking Up"	8/30	#20	10
7/19	AB/TV	Peppermint Rainbow	"Don't Wake Me Up in the Morning, Michael"♦	6/14	#54	9
7/19		Andy Kim	"Baby I Love You"	5/24	#9	16
7/26	AB/TV	Cat Mother & the All-Night News Boys	"Good Old Rock 'n' Roll"*	6/28	#21	8
8/2	AB/TV	Underground Sunshine	"Birthday"*	7/19	#26	10
8/9		Junior Walker & the All-Stars	"What Does It Take (To Win Your Love)"	5/17	#4	16
8/16		Guess Who	"Undun"	10/18	#22	10
8/16	AB/TV	Isaac Hayes	"Walk On By"✔	8/23	#30	12
			"By the Time I Get to Phoenix"	8/30	#37	8
8/23		Steppenwolf	"Move Over"	8/16	#31	9
8/23	AB/TV	Smith	"Baby It's You"✔	9/6	#5	15
8/30	AB/TV	Peaches & Herb	"Let Me Be the One"	8/16	#74	4

BANDSTAND APPEARANCE	AB/TV DEBUT	ARTIST	SONG(S) PERFORMED	DATE APPEARED ON CHART	PEAK CHART POSITION	WEEKS ON CHART
9/6	AB	Edwin Hawkins Singers	"Oh Happy Day"*	4/26	#4	10
9/13	AB/TV	Creedence Clearwater Revival	"Bad Moon Rising"	5/3	#2	14
			"Green River"	8/2	#2	14
9/13		Stevie Wonder	"My Cherie Amour"	5/31	#4	14
			"Yester-Me, Yester-You, Yesterday"	10/18	#7	14
9/20		Creedence Clearwater Revival	"Commotion"	8/2	#30	8
			"Down on the Corner"	10/25	#3	15
9/27	AB	The Association	"Goodbye Columbus"	2/15	#80	11
10/11		The Grass Roots	"Heaven Knows"	11/8	#24	10
10/25	AB/TV	Three Dog Night	"Easy to Be Hard"	8/9	#4	13
			"Eli's Coming"	10/25	#10	14
11/1	AB	Joe South	"Games People Play"	1/10/70	#12	12
			"Don't It Make You Wanna Go Home"	8/23	#41	12
11/1		Andy Kim	"So Good Together"	9/27	#36	9
11/8		Cass Elliott	"It's Getting Better"	6/7	#30	19
			"Make Your Own Kind of Music"	10/18	#36	9
11/15	AB/TV	Cufflinks	"Tracey"✔	9/13	#9	12
			"When Julie Comes Around"	12/13	#41	9
11/15	AB/TV	Dorothy Morrison	"All God's Children Got Soul"✔	10/11	#95	1
11/22		Turtles	"Love in the City"	10/11	#91	2
			"Lady-O"	12/6	#78	4
11/29	AB/TV	Thomas & Richard Frost	"She's Got Love"*	10/25	#83	4
12/13		Oliver	"Jean"	8/16	#2	14
			"Sunday Mornin'"	11/22	#35	9

✔First hit by a performer   *Only hit by a performer   ♦Last hit by a performer

THE '70s

The Pointer Sisters, 1978

There was another new *Bandstand* set for the seventies, as there has been roughly every five years or so, but despite its more colorful, neon-Deco-Moderne look, it was still set up in the same basic way. And still the show itself stuff functioned in the same way as before.

What should be mentioned, however, is that in the late sixties a trend began among record buyers that would have some effect on *Bandstand*'s music-industry influence. There was a strong movement away from buying singles and toward buying albums that lasted through much of the seventies. The Beatles may have started the trend—until they came along, no one bought albums in significant quantities, aside from those of Elvis Presley—but they were far from the only ones to keep the trend going or to benefit from it (one thinks of the Doors' first album, the Who's ''rock opera'' *Tommy*, Jimi Hendrix's *Are You Experienced?*, and the Kinks' concept album *Arthur*, among others). Psychedelic bands in particular took full advantage of the album format's greater freedom to stretch song-form past its conventional, 45 RPM limits.

Blondie, 1979

Labelle, 1976

The rock audience had achieved full self awareness, with its own magazines like *Rolling Stone* and *Crawdaddy*, which took a far more serious look at the music and culture of youth than the teen magazines did. And the music reflected it: From 1970 to 1974, and especially after 1972, among the most popular bands were British progressive rock groups, who orchestrated rock rhythms with classical, symphonic arrangements, and who set mystical, hyperliterate lyrics to their intricate, bombastic music. Phil Spector had called his Wall of Sound productions "little symphonies for the kids," but progressive rock took that idea very seriously. Ironically, while progressive rock was in no way designed for conventional popularity, as in radio play—the standard progressive rock tune was between six and ten minutes long—the music *did* become enormously popular. Since little of it could be featured on *Bandstand*, the show drifted away from this particular segment of the pop mainstream.

The seventies in general marked a period of intensive and widespread compartmentalization and fragmentation of the music and its audience. This made it perhaps a bit more delicate for *Bandstand* in terms of slotting hit-bound artists into the show, but basically there was still AM radio and there were still hits and there was still plenty for *Bandstand* to showcase and chronicle.

Then in the mid-seventies came the disco movement, and suddenly *Bandstand* was right back in the thick of it again, with dancing taking center stage as it hadn't since the beginning of the previous decade. Disco dancing was a direct reaction against the formless workouts that passed for dancing in the sixties—just as the Frug and Boogaloo and Twist were direct reactions against the more formal ballroom-style dances of the fifties.

Throughout the decade—as it had been throughout the show's whole history, there was no better place to watch the pop culture pendulum swing back and forth than every Saturday afternoon on *American Bandstand*.

And for once it seemed some other people began to recognize that fact, too. On August 4, 1976, Dick Clark got his very own star on the Hollywood Boulevard "Walk of Fame."

Tony Orlando & Dawn, 1972.

Fleetwood Mac, 1975.

Until disco, there was no single popular musical movement in the spotlight; so *Bandstand* just continued to present the hitmakers of the day. There were the one-hit and two-hit wonders, like R.B. Greaves with "Take a Letter Maria," R. Dean Taylor with the marvelous mini-drama "Indiana Wants Me," and Norman Greenbaum with the funky hard-rocker "Spirit in the Sky." And then, in February 1970, there was the *Bandstand* debut of the Jackson Five, with their first two hits, "I Want You Back" and "ABC." In that first year of the decade, there were classic instances of traditional soul, like Tyrone Davis's "Turn Back the Hands of Time," Chairmen of the Board's "Give Me Just a Little More Time," Freda Payne's "Band of Gold," the Spinners' "It's a Shame," and the Staple Singers' "Heavy Makes You Happy." There were the sounds of soul turning to the more dauntingly syncopated, low-down sounds of funk, as in Charles Wright and the Watts 103rd Street Rhythm Band's "Express Yourself." The Jackson Five defined the best possibilities of bubblegum-soul. There were even hard-rocking, blue-eyed soul, like the white band Rare Earth's two great Motown covers, "Get Ready" and "(I Know) I'm Losing You," and bubblegum pop with the likes of Gary Puckett and Andy Kim, David Cassidy, Bobby Sherman, and the Osmonds. Country-rock emerged with Poco (who streamlined the innovations of sixties bands like the Buffalo Springfield and the Byrds) and country-pop, as represented by Jerry Reed's toetapper, "When You're Hot You're Hot."

Honey Cone's "Want Ads," Sugarloaf's "Green-Eyed Lady," or Blues Image's "Ride Captain Ride" may not be as well-remembered by many today as, say, Smokey Robinson and the Miracles' "Tears of a Clown," but they were all parts of the soundtracks of people's lives in those days, and they were all introduced on *Bandstand*. So too were the novelties, like Les Crane's hysterically pretentious reading of "Desiderata," and the Hillside Singers' "I'd Like to Teach the World to Sing," which—like the

T-Bones' hit "Whatever Shape Your Stomach's In" in the mid-sixties—started out as a TV commercial jingle (in this case for Coca-Cola; the group's only other hit, "We're Together," came from a McDonald's jingle).

Other notable discs that made their debuts on *Bandstand* in the early seventies included: Memphis soul man Joe Tex's "I Gotcha," a rollicking tune that caused some controversy because certain excitable schoolkids thought they heard Tex grunting "I told you not to play with my erection" when the line was actually "my *affection*" (this kind of confusion was a frequent phenomenon due to the less than state-of-the-art production techniques of pop records and the low-fi sound of car radios and transistors); Dennis Coffey and the Detroit Guitar Band's "Scorpio," a laconically funky instrumental that a decade later would become one of the favorites of the South Bronx break dancers who helped spearhead the "hip hop" movement; Love Unlimited's "Walkin' in the

Bonnie Pointer, 1979.

Bread, 1972

147

Jim Croce, 1972.

Rain with the One I Love," in May 1972, the first of twenty-two hits by Barry White and his various assemblages, and one of the earliest harbingers of the disco sound to come (along with Isaac Hayes's "Theme from *Shaft*," which had debuted on the show six months earlier); Millie Jackson's "Ask Me What You Want" in May 1972, the first of eight hits for the sassy soul talk-singer who was a protean influence on eighties rap music; "I'm Movin' On" in June 1972, the only solo hit by ex-Steppenwolf leader John Kay; the first of Michael Jackson's many solo hits in July 1972, "Rockin' Robin" (a cover of the Bobby Day original that had premiered on *Bandstand* over a decade earlier), "I Wanna Be Where You Are," and "Ben"; Jim Croce's first hit, "You Don't Mess Around with Jim" in August 1972; Harry Chapin's first hit, "Taxi," the same month; Rick Springfield's "Speak to the Sky," his first hit back in September 1972 (his first stab at music stardom ended after a few more hits in 1976, then resumed in earnest in 1981 with the smash "Jessie's Girl"); Steely Dan's first of fifteen hits, "Do It Again," which they played on the show in January 1973 (especially notable since they never toured); Electric Light Orchestra's American network TV debut in July 1973 with the first of their twenty-two hits, "Roll Over Beethoven" (one of the few genuine examples of *pop*-oriented "classical rock"); and Aerosmith, with the first of their

Gary Puckett & the
Union Gap, 1970.

148

thirteen hits, "Dream On" in December 1973. "Dream On" is an example of how to scale a progressive rock arrangement (given the tune's stately harpsichord interludes) down for proper pop consumption, and give it a healthy hard-rock shot-in-the-arm to boot. On the other hand, there were B.W. Stevenson's brilliant hard-rocking yet melodic chart debuts with "Shambala" (later covered by Three Dog Night, a real bubblegum tribute) and "My Maria" in August 1973; Britisher David Essex's first U.S. hit, the daringly minimal and theatrical "Rock On" in March 1974; and George McCrae's first hit, the number-one "Rock Your Baby" in July 1974.

"Rock Your Baby" is as good a place as any to move into the disco era. The tune was one of the first disco hits, and kicked off the considerable string of hits that the Miami-based company T.K. Records had in the seventies. T.K. brought us K.C. and the Sunshine Band's disco anthems and Timmy Thomas's "Why Can't We Live Together," a spookily minimal, slow-cooking groove consisting of nothing more than organ and rhythm-box with Thomas's yearning vocal. Disco began as an underground movement in black dance clubs and some gay clubs and black roller-rink discodromes before moving out into the mainstream. The steady-rolling, easy-loping groove of "Rock Your Baby" was classic roller-disco, just as its shimmering Farfisa organ background mirrored the heat of the summer of its release.

From there, the disco floodgates gradually opened wider and wider, and then the sound simply kept gushing through the end of the decade, when the name *disco* was dropped in favor of the more generic *dance music*, which still prevails as of this writing. But disco didn't break wide open in the snap of a finger. Many other black-music styles were still making their own marks. For instance, on the very same show where George McCrae introduced "Rock Your Baby," Chaka Khan and Rufus did *their* first hit, the classic "Tell Me Something Good"—a sort of Sly Stone tribute that was not disco

but *funk*, as in dangerously sharp, hip-slipping syncopations and big, deep spaces in the beat and arrangement (whereas the disco beat was metronomic and mechanical, relentless at all times). Still, "Tell Me Something Good" aptly demonstrated that funk's prime imperative was the same as disco's—to get you to dance. The same could generally be said about ex-Temptation Eddie Kendricks's "Keep On Truckin'" and "Boogie Down" (records introduced on the show in late 1973 and early 1974) and Kool and the Gang's "Hollywood Swinging" and "Jungle Boogie" (also done on the show in early 1974)—they were soulful funk, funky soul, in their own way pointing the way to the disco era soon to come.

Later in 1974, the disco floodgates creaked open still wider, as the Hues Corporation did their seminal "Rock the Boat" on *Bandstand* (and how ironic that a disco classic should have

The Jackson Five, 1970.

Melanie, 1976.

Orders''—two classic disco divas with definitive disco hits. And a few months after *that*, in May 1975, frequent talk-show guest and socialite Monte Rock III jumped on board the disco bandwagon as Disco Tex with his Sex-O-Lettes, and they did their hit, ''I Wanna Dance wit'Choo'' on *Bandstand*.

By the late summer of 1975, disco had not only arrived but taken up full-time residence. K.C. and the Sunshine Band came on the show at the end of August and did the first of their hits, ''Get Down Tonight.'' The next month saw the Bostonian group Tavares begin their hit-making career with the soul-disco gem ''Only Takes a Minute.'' In March 1976, former *Bandstand* teen idol Frankie Avalon returned to the show, having jumped on the disco wave himself with a remake of one of his first hits, ''Venus.'' July 1976 saw the emergence of two more female singers: Vicki Sue Robinson, with ''Turn the Beat Around,'' and Maxine Nightingale, with ''Right Back Where We Started From.'' The next month marked the appearance of the preeminent disco diva: Donna Summer launched her mammothly successful career on the show by moaning her way through the orgastic ''Love to Love You Baby.'' And, speaking of super*sexy* disco classics, in September 1976 came Labelle

the word *rock* in its title, when alienated hard-line rock fans would soon launch the inane Disco Sucks movement); a few months following, B.T. Express launched their career with ''Do It (Till You're Satisfied)''; a short time later, Gloria Gaynor bowed with ''Never Can Say Goodbye'' and Carol Douglas with ''Doctor's

Dick Clark with the legendary Chuck Berry.

The Beach Boys come back, 1979.

fame); in July, Rick James appeared to do his first smash, "You and I," and the next month, Evelyn "Champagne" King did the first of *her* hits, "Shame." In December, there was Sylvester —whose falsetto voice and Little Richard–style makeup and clothing caused gender-confusion among his fans, making him a *male* disco diva—with his first charttopper, "Dance."

In January 1979, the disco wave was cresting, as the Village People appeared on *Bandstand* with "YMCA." Through it all, smooth pop-soul balladry was still in style, as Peaches and Herb proved with "Reunited" a week later on the show. It was disco classic time again, with Alicia Bridges coming onto the show to do her "I Love the Nightlife." And then there was stupendous,

Donna Summer, the first ever substitute host, May, 1978.

with "Lady Marmalade," with its unforgettable chorus "Voulez-vous coucher avec moi ce soir?" (French for "Would you like to sleep with me tonight?"). How times had changed! These lyrics would clearly have been unthinkable on network television when *Bandstand* was young. Then in October Rick Dees and His Cast of Idiots parodied disco as they hitched a ride to the top of it, with "Disco Duck."

It is 1977 . The world keeps moving; *Star Wars* premieres, and disco keeps getting stronger. In February, Brick appeared with their first hit, "Dazz." In April, Thelma Houston performed the unforgettable "Don't Leave Me This Way." And Cerrone unveiled the lushly orchestrated Euro-disco subgenre with his first hit, "Love in C-minor." In May, Shalamar launched their highly successful career with their first hit, "Uptown Festival." September saw the Brothers Johnson doing *their* first hit on the show, stretching the confines of disco with gorgeous melodic bal-ladry and progressive rock instrumental inter-ludes in "Strawberry Letter #23."

In 1978, black pop continued to pull disco beyond its basics, and again it was all brought to you on *Bandstand*: Raydio with their first hit, "Jack and Jill" in March (they were led by none other than Ray Parker, Jr., later of "Ghostbusters"

151

A visit from Bo Diddley.

beyond-category black music based in disco and funk but reaching the heights of symphonic pop splendor, as the Jacksons appeared on *Bandstand* in February with the incredible "Shake Your Body."

Of course, in the midst of all that disco and related black music, many other representatives of the wide pop music spectrum made their appearances on *Bandstand* as well. In 1973 and 1974, teen idols the DeFranco Family did their hits, "Heartbeat," "Abra-Ca-Dabra," and "Save the Last Dance for Me." In 1974, Jim Stafford unveiled his laconically funny novelty wonders, "Spiders and Snakes" and "My Girl Bill." On March 15, 1975, Billy Swann—a Memphis rockabilly singer whose career spanned many years —finally got a big hit with the loping, organ-backed "I Can Help," an uncanny rock 'n' roll complement to George McCrae's "Rock Your Baby." The following week Barry Manilow kicked off his extraordinary career by debuting his first hit, "Mandy," on *Bandstand*. Tex-Mex country rocker Freddy Fender crooned his first hit, "Before the Next Teardrop Falls."

A few more first hits that had their debut on *Bandstand*: the Captain and Tennille's "Love Will Keep Us Together" in May 1975; Melissa Manchester's "Midnight Blue" in July 1975;

The Boomtown Rats, featuring Bob Geldof, 1979.

Midwestern pop rocker Dwight Twilley with "I'm On Fire" in July 1975; Nat King Cole's daughter Natalie with "This Will Be" in October 1975; former Raspberries leader Eric Carmen with his first solo hit, "All by Myself," in January 1976; TV and future movie star John Travolta with "Let Her In" in April; teen idol Shaun Cassidy with his first, a cover of the Phil Spector classic "Da Doo Ron Ron" in March 1977; Debby Boone with "You Light Up My Life" in September 1977; Eddie Money with the first of his hard-rocking hits, "Baby Hold On," in April 1978; and Bonnie Tyler with "It's a Heartache" in August 1978.

And still *more* notable appearances on *Bandstand* through the seventies: Swedish pop giants Abba, in their U.S. TV debut, with their third U.S. hit, "S.O.S.," on November 15, 1975; Larry Groce with his hilarious novelty record, "Junkfood Junkie," in March 1976; Queen's seminal early music video, "Bohemian Rhapsody," in April 1976; John Sebastian, who'd been on the show ten years earlier with his band the Lovin' Spoonful, with his theme from the popular TV show (of which John Travolta was a star) "Welcome Back, Kotter," in June 1976; a concert film of Elton John and Kiki Dee doing a duet on "Don't Go Breakin' My Heart" in September 1976; British teen idols the Bay City Rollers with their top-ten "You Made Me Believe in Magic" in July 1977; Frankie Valli of the Four Seasons with

his smash hit theme from the hit movie *Grease* in September 1978.

Meanwhile, punk and new wave had begun on the underground scenes—not unlike disco had—in New York and London in the mid-seventies. In March 1979, *Bandstand* became one of the first network shows to feature a new-wave rock band—Talking Heads, with their hit version of Al Green's "Take Me to the River." In June of that year, Blondie furthered the new-wave cause with their phenomenal disco-rock-pop crossover, "Heart of Glass"—the first song to stem the cries of the disco backlash that had been heard from the alienated and entrenched reactionary rock audience. And in December 1979, new wave was back again, with Britisher Joe Jackson and "Is She Really Going Out with Him?" That tune was really just a pop song, with music nowhere near as hard edged and radical sounding as new wave was supposed to be. With a title like that, it was a basic teen-drama love song—the kind of thing *Bandstand* had been spotlighting for years. In fact, watching Jackson perform it as the seventies were about to become the eighties, one really had to wonder—to the tune of "Is She Really Going Out with Him?"—"Have things really, really changed *that* much?"

Dick Clark really says it best: "The hits kept coming, and we kept playing them, and that was that."

The Talking Heads, 1979.

THE KIDS

Dance contest winners, 1978.

Joanne Orgel, one of the first seventies regulars to come aboard, must hold some kind of *Bandstand* record. She was on the show for ten years, from 1971 to 1981. Obviously, since the intense focus on the regulars and the attendant demand to become one had fallen off since the show's move to the West Coast, the age limitations on a regular had been relaxed somewhat.

"I grew up watching the show all the time," says Joanne, who now works as an executive secretary for MCA-Universal, "wearing a hole in the living room rug learning to dance from it.

So I finally wrote to Dick Clark's people and managed to get on when I was fourteen or so, and they must have liked me because they invited me back and I just kept going. For ten years. It was just great—always a lot of fun, all of us kids got along well together. I mean, I basically grew up on that show, so I have a lot of memories connected with *American Bandstand*.

"My only problem was that I never really had a regular dancing partner. The longest one I had was for around two years, but I guess when you're on for the long term like I was, nobody else can stay with you *that* long."

However, unlike many regulars since the late-fifties/early-sixties era, Joanne *did* get fan mail: "It was mainly from guys, and usually said the same thing—'I hope you don't think I'm crazy, I mean I like Farrah Fawcett but I don't write her letters, *but* . . .' Or, 'I think you're the best dancer on the show. . . .' I was very flattered and surprised by it all."

One thing Joanne remembers extremely well from her *Bandstand* days is Kentucky Fried Chicken. "Let me explain. They would tape the shows every six weeks, on a weekend, and they'd do three shows a day, six shows in a weekend. During the break midway through the day, they'd give us all lunch, and it was always Kentucky Fried Chicken. I always said you knew another six weeks had gone by when you began to get a craving for Colonel Sanders!"

Deb-E Chaffin joined the show's regulars in 1972, and soon became known as "Queen of *Bandstand*" during her six years on the show. Since her *Bandstand* days, she's done professional dancing and acting, appearing in prime-time TV shows like "Cheers" and "Hardcastle and McCormack."

"I'd always been a big fan of *Bandstand* from watching it on TV," says Deb-E, "because dancing is in my blood. You see, my parents had been dance instructors for eighteen years, and *they'd* always watched the show. Watching *Bandstand* and being a dance fanatic were sort of passed on from generation to generation in my family. So it was only a matter of time

before I actually got onto the show itself, right? In 1972 I was fourteen—I was old enough, so I went for it and I got on, and I stayed until 1978 and loved every minute of it.

"I remember I felt very new and nervous and out of place my first time on the show, but everyone—the crew and Dick Clark and all, not just the other kids—seemed to go out of their way to make everything easier. The crew were just amazing, they were so efficient that they just made everything seem like no big deal. I mean, they could shoot three complete shows between nine and five on a Saturday, with forty-five-minute breaks between each shooting, and it would always go like clockwork.

"After I'd done three weekend taping sessions, which amounts to eighteen or twenty shows, Dick Clark began talking to me on the set, and that was when I began to feel like a regular, before I was even aware that there still were actual regulars on the show. Then at the next taping, they asked me if I wanted to be a regular! Of course I said, 'Absolutely!'

"It was like a family atmosphere on the show after a while. Everyone knew everyone else, we were all pals. Dick Clark was fantastic, completely professional at all times but still just as nice and regular and straightforward as he appears to be on TV. Dick and I became really good friends, actually. How close did we get? Well, in 1974 Dick was asked to be on "Dating Game" with his daughter, and he came up to me and said, 'Look, they want me to bring my daughter on and have me ask three questions for her, and then pick a guy for her. But my daughter's only five years old! You're the closest thing I have to a daughter otherwise. Wanna do it?' I said, 'Sure!' It was great. I ended up going to Lima, Peru, with a very nice medical student.

"I met my partner, Luis Novoa, in 1972, while we were out on the beach. Luis was trying to become a dancer on *Bandstand*, which we were shooting at the time he just happened to be there. He just came over and said, 'Hey, can I

Skateboarding is definitely not as easy as it looks!

155

dance with you?' And we danced and we hit it off together and then we became regular partners on *Bandstand*. We were just good friends, but on camera we'd act like we were in love, make goo-goo eyes at each other and dance nose to nose on slow songs, just to see if anyone watching the show would react to it. Did they ever! We got dozens of letters from people saying things like 'Are you two engaged? When's the wedding? It's so lovely to see two attractive young people so much in love.' We couldn't believe it! In 1978, Luis and I won third place in the *Bandstand* dance contest, and that seemed like a perfect cue to leave the show, so we did. Dick, who I think of as a second father, brought out a big farewell cake and made speeches and all—it was a pretty emotional moment.

''I still get recognized sometimes as someone who used to be on *Bandstand*. I was in a store shopping for clothes for my husband and the salesman comes over and says, 'Hey, I know you—you're Deb-E from *American Bandstand*.' I was working on ''Hardcastle and McCormack'' and this cameraman comes over to me and

says, 'Aren't you Deb-E Chaffin of *American Bandstand*?' Then once I was on Rate-a-Record on *Bandstand*, and gave this record 'Billy Don't Be a Hero'' by Bo Donaldson and the Heywoods an 85. A few weeks later I was at a concert and one of the guys in the group taps me on the shoulder and says, 'Hey, you're that girl Deb-E who gave our record an 85 on *Bandstand*! Here!' And he gives me two tickets to their upcoming concert. Unbelievable.''

Luis Novoa has gone on to a successful show business career since leaving the show: He's made numerous appearances in the highly rated NBC prime time series *St. Elsewhere*, and has

acted in such films as *Pee Wee's Big Adventure* with rising comic star Pee Wee Herman. Asked if he used *Bandstand* as a career stepping stone, Luis replies, ''It looks that way now, but the way it actually was—believe it or not—was that I always watched the show, and still do today whenever I get a chance, because I've always been into dancing. Up until I went on the show at around age 14 or 15, I was a typical kid —I knew what I liked but was kind of aimless about career goals. In the back of my mind I felt that I'd love to have a career as a dancer, but I never thought I'd be able to do it—until I got on *Bandstand*. In a way *Bandstand* did definitely serve as a career stepping stone for me, but I was on the show, having fun, *first*—and *then*, later, I decided to pursue dancing and acting as a career.''

In fact, Luis got on the show much the same way many other regulars have in the seventies and eighties: ''I was out dancing at a club one night and someone from Dick's office approached me and said I was a good dancer and would I like to be on *Bandstand*? I said, 'Are you *kidding*? I only watch it every single week!' At the time I was dancing on a local show, on Channel 9, so this was the biggest thrill for me yet. After that, I would come into Burbank from Glendale and never missed a single taping, from 1971 or 1972 through 1978.''

Damita Jo Freeman appeared in the film *Private Benjamin* with Goldie Hawn, and was in the TV series based on the movie as well. She choreographed the closing ceremonies of the 1984 Summer Olympics in Los Angeles, working with two hundred break dancers and a hundred other dancers. She's also done choreography for the Alvin Ailey American Dance Theater, Diana Ross, Shalamar, the Fifth Dimension, the Spinners, Wilson Pickett, and others. And she says it all started for her on *Bandstand*.

''I had always hung around with these people who later became known as the Lockers. We were like the original break dancers, the original

More contest winners, 1979.

Damita Jo Freeman with Dick Clark.

157

pop-and-lockers. I mean people are saying now that all that stuff happened only recently, but you can bet you could've turned on *Bandstand* back in 1973 or 1974 and you would've seen me and my pals Little Joe Chisholm or Scoobie Doo working all that stuff out. We used to do the Robot and the Runaway and all kinds of things. At first most of the other kids thought we were just weird, but then it caught on. I remember I used to sit back in the stands with Dick Clark's daughter Cindy during breaks in the tapings, and she'd say, 'That's a strange kind of dancing you do—it looks like fun, but it also looks like you're having a fit!' That's what I think most of the other kids thought, too, but after a few weeks they'd start coming up to us and saying, 'Hey, how do you do that robot stuff anyway?' After a while I got so well known for it that Dick Clark let me choreograph the Spinners when they came on the show, which was one of the biggest thrills of my life. After that I got to choreograph one of the *Bandstand* anniversary specials and some other shows Dick produced. By then I was becoming a professional, so I left *Bandstand* and moved on. But it all started there.'' And it continues apace: Damita Jo has been keeping very busy, most recently working with Lionel Richie on his 1984 tour.

As we've seen, not only did Damita Jo's

impressive career get started there, but the street-dance phenomenon, which takes in break dancing and moonwalking and popping and locking and other variations, got its first nation-wide display on *Bandstand*.

Sue Bowser joined the *Bandstand* regulars in 1974. She stayed through 1980, and since leaving the show has appeared in TV shows like ''Sheriff Lobo,'' ''The Love Boat,'' ''Happy Days,'' and ''CHiPs,'' as well as movies like *Stripes, Rocky III, Scarface,* and *The Wild Life.*

''I always enjoyed watching *Bandstand,* but I was never a freak about it,'' she says, ''and while I always wanted to get into show biz, I never thought of myself as much of a dancer. In fact, I got onto *Bandstand* through an accident, really. I wasn't planning to go on the show, but this guy, a friend of a friend of a friend, needed a partner to go with at the last minute, and I ended up being the one to get picked to go with him. I watched the show one week, and then I began getting nervous until the taping the next week. The last couple of nights before the taping I couldn't even sleep at all. But then once I got into the studio everyone there was so friendly and efficient—the producer Larry Klein and the director Barry Glazer, and Dick Clark, and all the rest of the regulars. They all knew what they were doing so well and seemed to enjoy it, it was like this was a really cool place to be. So all of a sudden I forgot my nervousness and just began to ham it up for the cameras, and it just went from there.

''Then I met Deb-E Chaffin and I was just in awe of her—she was so beautiful and such a great dancer and so poised and all. I always tried to copy her look and her style. She used to tell me after a while that when she left the show she'd groom me to be the next Queen of *Bandstand*, and I'd always go 'Yeah, right, a dork like me, huh?' The thing was, I didn't become a decent dancer for a while because for my first couple of years on the show I couldn't get a steady dancing partner. In the town I come from in the Valley, for whatever reason, most of the kids are not into dancing,

Rate-A-Record—
one of *Bandstand*'s
greatest traditions.

and they'd always tease me about going to *Bandstand*. Then I began to notice this cute guy on the show, always dancing with some other girl. I went to Disneyland with some girlfriends one day and there was this guy. So, to make a long story short, I stole this guy from his girlfriend at Disneyland and we eventually became partners on *Bandstand*! And that was David Rosney, and we became inseparable on the show. He taught me everything I know about dancing, really. To this day I really cannot dance with anyone else but David, and whenever we get back together for the heck of it we start dancing again and when he starts twirling me it all comes right back and I feel like I can hear Dick Clark announcing the Spotlight Dance.''

Kim Schreier came on *Bandstand* in 1977 and stayed until 1982. In that time, she became known as ''the Animal.'' ''I guess,'' she explains, laughingly, ''I was just a wild, crazy person —and a real camera hog! I admit it! I was the first person on the show to wear spandex, and I used to wear these see-through plastic pants with Danskins on underneath. I'd do my hair in this wild blonde Afro, and get onto the dance floor and just go for as much camera as I could.

Once I began dressing a little bit wild, I started getting fan mail about it. So I just went even wilder. I remember the first time I ever went to a taping of *Bandstand*. This guy who was a friend of a friend gave me an extra ticket he had for the show and once we got into the studio I just left him I don't know where, and I just went for the camera. That's all I saw.''

Like many of the seventies *Bandstand* regulars, the Animal grew up around Hollywood and had an inbred desire to make it in show biz. And, like some of those regulars, she did, having had roles in ''Happy Days'' on TV and in such films as *Ice Pirates* and *Johnny Dangerously*.

And therein lies the major difference between how the kids *and* the times had changed from *Bandstand*'s early days in Philadelphia to more current times. At the beginning the regular kids suddenly found incalculable fame thrust upon them and in most cases didn't really know what to do with it. They left the show, grew up, and found that often they had achieved the highest points in their lives as kids. Nowadays, the kids are sharper, more goal-oriented. So for the show-biz types, *American Bandstand* can well be a stairway to heaven.

In the early seventies, there were the abundant freestyle dances, holdovers from the sixties, many of which remained popular with a lot of kids through the decade.

With the advent of disco, however, dancing reverted to the formal traditions of touch-dancing. There were the New York Hustle and the Latin Hustle, which were more graceful and gliding updates, in a way, of the jitterbugging that had been seen on the early *Bandstand*—as in the Jitterbug, the male would spin his female partner, and as in the Lindy, the male would athletically and acrobatically toss the female up into the air and spin her. Besides the strenuous side to the Hustle, it was a return to the "old days" in another way: There were set patterns of steps to be mastered, like the fox-trot or even the line for the Stroll. While you were spinning around, your feet had to be moving correctly —otherwise the total effect of the dance would be lost.

Both Sue Bowser and Deb-E Chaffin recall practicing their twirls long and hard. Says Sue Bowser, "Sometimes David would spin me so fast and so long I felt like I might drill right through the dance floor with my high heels." Which brings up another point of interest: These kids did their demanding dances in high heels, where their fifties predecessors did theirs in flats.

Kim "the Animal" Schreier, on the other hand, was "totally into freestyle stuff. I didn't have the discipline to learn the intricate formal couples dances, and I was such a camera hog I hardly ever had any regular partners anyway!"

Then of course there were Damita Jo Freeman and her friends, who pioneered the street-dance revolution that is still sweeping the country and the world. But not all the regulars were swept up in it back then. Deb-E Chaffin recalls, "I never went in for that popping and locking and robot stuff—I thought it was just too weird and unfeminine looking."

But Damita Jo Freeman adds, "After I'd been moonwalking on the show a few times, I got a call. They said, 'Michael's calling—he'd like you to show him some of this new dancing you do.' I said, 'Michael? Michael who?' They said, 'Michael *Jackson*.' I said, 'Of the . . .?' They said, 'The Jackson *Five*!' I said, 'Oh. Oh yeah. Well, okay . . .' Can you *believe* me? What nerve, huh?

"Anyway, that wasn't the only stuff we did.

We could do traditional types of dancing, like the jazzier stuff, and we could even do classical dancing for couples if we wanted, I bet, but we just never really got into that. One thing, though, my original partner, Little Joe, was the one who got the Bump going when disco music came out. He would just be bumping and bumping all the time."

Up through 1973 or 1974, until disco came in and changed everything, there was an abundance of sixties-holdover looks on the show among the regulars. Straight and simple hair for girls, semilong and rather unkempt hair for guys, and more and more big Afros. Girls wore the natural, peasant, or granny looks, guys wore open-necked shirts with dickies, or turtlenecks with bandannas, Indian or safari coats or Edwardian jackets, with much more color and print in evidence than in the mid-sixties. And of course there were bell-bottomed trousers everywhere.

With the birth of disco, styles changed within a year or so. While many kids still dressed rather casually—something intensified across the board in 1972, when the show's dress code was changed to allow girls to wear slacks —there were also more guys in leisure suits or more formal suits. Semiformal three-piece affairs with vests became rather commonplace. One of the biggest items in the disco era was the "twirl" skirt, which was usually flared and

pleated, designed so that it would swirl dramatically away from the body back and forth when the female dance partner was spun around or twirled in the air.

At the same time, the much more athletically strenuous moves being worked out by Damita Jo Freeman and her cohorts demanded more functional clothing. So did the camera-hogging techniques of a Kim Schreier. As she's already mentioned, Kim opted for eye-catching, form-fitting spandex in a rainbow of mix-and-match colors, sometimes with athletic shorts or a halter top in bright contrasting colors to go with it, and that look spread.

Damita Jo and her crew sported, in her own words, "Hot pants with boots to match, a turtleneck, colorful socks with big bright stripes, and wedgies for shoes, and the applecaps —big oversize newsboy's type of caps, you know? There was another friend of ours, Campbell Lock, who the Lockers were named after, and he used to have this thirties poor-little-boy look, with the oversize applecap and knickers with big suspenders. Then I began wearing knit bell-bottoms stuffed into my boots to get the knicker look, because I couldn't afford knickers myself. Later on, we began wearing the baggy pants which were great for the splits and drops we'd begun working into our dances."

It's interesting to note that the seventies were the first decade where the denizens of *Bandstand* did not have a "uniform" style of dress. Just as the music embodied many different forms, so did the clothes. The world had finally reached a point where you could wear what you wanted, and it was perfectly OK. The Individual Triumphant.

Following page— dance contest 1979.

163

1 • 9 • 7 • 0

BANDSTAND APPEARANCE	AB/TV DEBUT	ARTIST	SONG(S) PERFORMED	DATE APPEARED ON CHART	PEAK CHART POSITION	WEEKS ON CHART
1/17		1910 Fruitgum Co.	"The Train"♦	8/23/69	#57	10
1/17		Ohio Express	"Sausalito"♦	9/6/69	#86	2
1/24		Joe South	"Walk a Mile in My Shoes"	1/3	#12	11
1/31	AB/TV	R.B. Greaves	"Take a Letter, Maria"✔	10/18/69	#2	15
			"Always Something There to Remind Me"	1/24	#27	8
2/7	AB	Sandpipers	"Come Saturday Morning"	12/20/69	#17	20
2/7	AB/TV	Evie Sands	"Any Way That You Want Me"✔	8/16/69	#53	17
2/14	AB/TV	David Ruffin	"I'm So Glad I Fell for You"	12/6/69	#53	7
2/21	AB/TV	Jackson Five	"I Want You Back"✔	11/15/69	#1	19
			"ABC"	3/14	#1	13
3/7	AB/TV	George Baker Selection	"Little Green Bag"✔	3/21	#21	13
3/14	AB/TV	Gladys Knight & the Pips	"You Need Love Like I Do"	3/21	#25	8
			"Friendship Train"	10/25/69	#17	14
3/28	AB	Gary Puckett & the Union Gap	"Young Girl"	3/2	#2	15
			"Woman, Woman"✔	11/18/69	#4	17
			"Let's Give Adam and Eve Another Chance"♦	3/7	#41	7
4/4		Oliver	"Angelica"♦	4/4	#97	3
4/4	AB/TV	Friends of Distinction	"Love or Let Me Be Lonely"	3/7	#6	13
4/11		Tommy Roe	"Stir It Up and Serve It"	2/28	#50	6
			"Pearl"	6/20	#50	9
4/18	AB/TV	Norman Greenbaum	"Spirit in the Sky"✔	2/28	#3	15
4/18	AB/TV	Cold Blood	"You Got Me Hummin'"*	1/24	#52	6
4/25		B.J. Thomas	"Raindrops Keep Falling on My Head"	11/1/69	#1	22
			"I Just Can't Help Believing"	6/20	#9	13
5/2	AB/TV	Turley Richards	"Love Minus Zero—No Limit"✔	4/4	#84	3
			"I Heard the Voice of Jesus"	6/13	#99	3
5/9	AB/TV	Crabby Appleton	"Go Back"*	5/9	#36	14
5/9		The Grass Roots	"Baby Hold On"	5/9	#35	10
			"Walking Through the Country"	2/14	#44	8
5/16	AB/TV	Chairmen of the Board	"Give Me Just a Little More Time"✔	1/17	#3	15
			"Dangling on a String"	5/2	#38	9
5/23	AB/TV	Jack Blanchard & Misty Morgan	"Tennessee Birdwalk"✔	2/28	#23	13
			"Humphrey the Camel"♦	6/27	#78	6
5/30		Bobbi Martin	"For the Love of Him"	3/14	#13	14
			"Give a Woman Love"♦	7/11	#97	1
6/6		Charles Wright & the Watts 103rd St. Rhythm Band	"Express Yourself"	8/15	#12	15
			"Love Land"	4/11	#16	17
6/13	AB/TV	Melanie	"Lay Down (Candles in the Rain)"✔	4/4	#6	17
			"Peace Will Come"	8/22	#32	7
6/20	AB/TV	Mac Davis	"Whoever Finds This, I Love You"✔	5/16	#53	8
6/20	AB/TV	Feather	"Friends"*	5/2	#79	5
6/27		Trini Lopez	"If I Had a Hammer"	1/27/63	#3	14
7/4	AB/TV	Blues Image	"Ride Captain Ride"✔	5/9	#4	15
7/11	AB/TV	Alive & Kicking	"Tighter, Tighter"✔	6/6	#7	14
			"Let It Come"♦	9/26	#69	5
7/11		The Impressions	"Check Out Your Mind"	5/16	#28	12
			"Baby Turn On to Me"	9/5	#56	8
7/18		Tyrone Davis	"Turn Back the Hands of Time"	3/21	#3	13
			"I'll Be Right Here"	6/27	#53	9
7/18	AB/TV	Flaming Ember	"Mind, Body and Soul"✔	9/26	#26	14
7/25	AB/TV	Rare Earth	"Get Ready"✔	3/14	#4	20
			"(I Know) I'm Losing You"	8/1	#7	14
8/1		Norman Greenbaum	"Canned Ham"	6/13	#46	6
8/1	AB/TV	Robin McNamara	"Lay a Little Lovin' on Me"	5/30	#11	15
			"Got to Believe in Love"	10/3	#80	5
8/8	AB	Ron Dante & the Detergents	"Leader of the Laundromat"✔	12/5/64	#19	8
			"Double-O-Seven"♦	3/6/65	#89	3
8/15	AB/TV	Arkade	"Sing Out the Love"✔	8/22	#99	1
8/22		Gene Chandler	"Groovy Situation"	7/11	#12	15
8/22		Andy Kim	"It's Your Life"	7/25	#85	4
8/29	AB/TV	R. Dean Taylor	"Indiana Wants Me"✔	9/5	#5	15
8/29	AB/TV	Paul Kelly	"Stealin' in the Name of the Lord"✔	7/4	#49	9
9/5		Gary Puckett	"I Just Don't Know What to Do with Myself"✔	10/31	#61	4
9/5	AB/TV	Bert Sommer	"We're All Playin' in the Same Band"*	8/8	#48	8
9/19	AB/TV	Bobby Bloom	"Montego Bay"✔	9/12	#8	16
10/3		The Grass Roots	"Come On and Say It"	9/19	#61	6
10/3	AB/TV	Spinners	"It's a Shame"	7/25	#14	15
10/10	AB/TV	Poco	"Better Think Twice"✔	10/3	#72	8
10/17	AB/TV	O'Kaysions	"Girl Watcher"✔	8/17/68	#5	14
			"Love Machine"♦	11/23/68	#76	6

✔First hit by a performer   *Only hit by a performer   ♦Last hit by a performer

BANDSTAND APPEARANCE	AB/TV DEBUT	ARTIST	SONG(S) PERFORMED	DATE APPEARED ON CHART	PEAK CHART POSITION	WEEKS ON CHART
10/17	AB/TV	The Moments	"Love on a Two-Way Street"	4/11	#3	15
			"If I Didn't Care"	8/22	#44	8
10/24		Mark Lindsay	"Silver Bird"	6/13	#25	10
			"And the Grass Won't Pay No Mind"	9/19	#44	12
11/7		Brian Hyland	"Gypsy Woman"	9/5	#3	20

BANDSTAND APPEARANCE	AB/TV DEBUT	ARTIST	SONG(S) PERFORMED	DATE APPEARED ON CHART	PEAK CHART POSITION	WEEKS ON CHART
11/4	AB/TV	Freda Payne	"Deeper and Deeper"	9/12	#24	12
			"Band of Gold"✔	4/25	#3	20
12/5	AB/TV	The Carpenters	"We've Only Just Begun"	9/12	#2	17
			"Close to You"	6/20	#1	17
12/12		Gene Chandler	"Simply Call It Love"	11/7	#75	7
12/26		The Grass Roots	"Temptation Eyes"	12/26	#15	18

I • 9 • 7 • I

BANDSTAND APPEARANCE	AB/TV DEBUT	ARTIST	SONG(S) PERFORMED	DATE APPEARED ON CHART	PEAK CHART POSITION	WEEKS ON CHART
1/9		Cass Elliott	"A Song That Never Comes"♦	8/1/70	#99	1
1/9	AB/TV	Dave Mason	"Only You Know and I Know"✔	8/1/70	#42	10
1/16	AB/TV	King Floyd	"Groove Me"✔	10/17/70	#6	20
1/16		Ike & Tina Turner (film)	"Proud Mary"	1/30	#4	13
1/23	AB	The Cowsills	"The Rain, the Park, and Other Things"✔	9/30/67	#2	16
1/30	AB/TV	Redeye	"Games"✔	11/7/70	#27	14
			"Red Eye Blues"♦	4/24	#78	6
1/30		Andy Kim	"Be My Baby"	11/7/70	#17	11
			"I Wish I Were"	3/28/70	#62	6
2/6		Jerry Reed	"Amos Moses"	10/31/70	#8	24
2/6		Dionne Warwick	"The Green Grass Starts to Grow"	12/5/70	#43	9
			"Who Gets the Guy"	3/20	#57	5
2/13	AB	Bobby Sherman	"Cried Like a Baby"	2/13	#16	9
			"Julie, Do Ya Love Me"	8/1/70	#5	15
2/13	AB/TV	Little Sister (Sly Stone's sister, Vanetta Stewart)	"Somebody's Watching You"♦	12/12/70	#32	13
2/20	AB/TV	The Mob	"I Dig Everything About You"✔	1/23	#83	3
			"Give It to Me"♦	3/13	#71	4
2/27	AB/TV	Joey Scarbury	"Mixed Up Guy"✔	1/16	#73	4
3/6		Bobby Goldsboro	"Watchin' Scotty Grow"	12/26/70	#11	13
3/6	AB	Henry Mancini	"Theme from Love Story"	1/16	#13	11
3/13	AB/TV	Wadsworth Mansion	"Sweet Mary"*	12/26/70	#7	14
3/20	AB	Rufus Thomas	"Push and Pull"	12/19/70	#7	14
3/27		Chairmen of the Board	"Pay to the Piper"	11/14/70	#13	13
			"Chairman of the Board"	2/13	#42	8

BANDSTAND APPEARANCE	AB/TV DEBUT	ARTIST	SONG(S) PERFORMED	DATE APPEARED ON CHART	PEAK CHART POSITION	WEEKS ON CHART
4/3	AB	Sammi Smith	"Help Me Make It Through the Night"✔	1/16	#8	16
4/10	AB	Tommy James	"Adrienne"	3/20	#93	3
			"Church Street Soul Revival"	12/19/70	#62	7
4/17		Little Richard	"Greenwood, Mississippi"♦	9/5/70	#85	5
5/1	AB/TV	Helen Reddy	"I Don't Know How to Love Him"✔	2/20	#13	20
			"Crazy Love"	8/7	#51	9
5/8		Mike Nesmith	"Nevada Fighter"♦	4/17	#70	4
5/8	AB/TV	The Bells	"Stay Awhile"	3/6	#7	14
			"I Love You, Lady Dawn"♦	6/26	#64	5
5/15	AB/TV	Staple Singers	"Heavy Makes You Happy"	2/6	#27	12
			"You've Got to Earn It"	7/31	#97	2
5/15		Bobby Bloom	"We're All Goin' Home"	6/26	#93	4
5/22	AB/TV	Sugarloaf	"Mother Nature's Wine"	6/26	#88	3
			"Green-Eyed Lady"✔	8/15/70	#3	17
5/29		Nitty Gritty Dirt Band	"Mr. Bojangles"	11/21/70	#9	19
			"House on Pooh Corner"	4/24	#53	13
6/5	AB/TV	Paul Humphrey & the Cool-Aid Chemists	"Cool-Aid"*	3/13	#29	16
6/12	AB/TV	Susan Raye	"L.A. International Airport"*	4/17	#54	9
6/12	AB/TV	Hamilton, Joe Frank, & Reynolds	"Don't Pull Your Love"✔	5/22	#4	14
			"Annabella"	8/28	#46	7
7/3		Jerry Reed	"When You're Hot, You're Hot"	5/8	#9	12
			"Ko Ko Joe"	9/4	#54	6
7/10		Smokey Robinson & the Miracles	"Crazy 'bout the La La La"	7/3	#56	7
			"The Tears of a Clown"	10/17/70	#1	16

✔First hit by a performer   *Only hit by a performer   ♦Last hit by a performer

BANDSTAND APPEARANCE	AB/TV DEBUT	ARTIST	SONG(S) PERFORMED	DATE APPEARED ON CHART	PEAK CHART POSITION	WEEKS ON CHART
7/17	AB/TV	Chee Chee & Peppy & Rose-Colored Glass	"Can't Find the Time"✔	4/10	#54	14
			"If It's Alright with You"♦	10/23	#95	4
7/24		Mark Lindsay	"Been Too Long on the Road"	6/12	#98	1
7/31		Lou Rawls	"A Natural Man"	8/28	#17	8
8/7	AB/TV	Honey Cone	"Want Ads"	4/10	#1	16
			"Stick Up"	8/7	#11	12
8/14	AB/TV	Dillards	"It's About Time"*	7/31	#92	2
8/14		Gayle McCormick	"Gonna Be Alright Now"✔	7/10	#84	5
			"It's a Cryin' Shame"	9/18	#44	12
8/21	AB	Osmond Brothers	"One Bad Apple"✔	1/2	#1	15
			"Double Lovin'"	5/15	#14	9
			"Yo-Yo"	9/11	#3	13
8/28		Steppenwolf	"Ride with Me"	7/17	#52	8
8/28	AB/TV	Undisputed Truth	"Smiling Faces Sometimes"✔	6/26	#3	18
9/4		Davey Jones	"Rainy Jane"♦	6/19	#52	9

BANDSTAND APPEARANCE	AB/TV DEBUT	ARTIST	SONG(S) PERFORMED	DATE APPEARED ON CHART	PEAK CHART POSITION	WEEKS ON CHART
9/4		The Grass Roots	"Sooner or Later"	6/5	#9	11
			"Two Divided by Love"	10/9	#16	11
9/18	AB/TV	Bobbie Russell	"Saturday Morning Confusion"♦	7/10	#28	14
9/18		Creedence Clearwater Revival (film)	"Sweet Hitchhiker"	7/17	#6	19
10/2	AB	Bill Withers	"Ain't No Sunshine"✔	7/17	#3	16
			"Grandma's Hands"	10/30	#42	8
10/23	AB/TV	Al Green	"Tired of Being Alone"	7/24	#11	19
			"Let's Stay Together"	12/4	#1	16
10/30		Freda Payne	"You Brought the Joy"	10/2	#52	8
			"Bring the Boys Home"	6/5	#12	13
11/20	AB/TV	Coven	"One Tin Soldier (Legend of Billy Jack)"*	9/18	#26	12
12/25	AB	Les Crane	"Desiderata"*	10/9	#8	12

1 · 9 · 7 · 2

BANDSTAND APPEARANCE	AB/TV DEBUT	ARTIST	SONG(S) PERFORMED	DATE APPEARED ON CHART	PEAK CHART POSITION	WEEKS ON CHART
1/8	AB/TV	J. Geils Band	"Lookin' for a Love"✔	12/4/71	#39	10
1/8		Joe Simon	"Drowning in the Sea of Love"	11/27/71	#11	13
1/15	AB	Bread	"Baby I'm a Want You"	10/23/71	#3	12
			"Everything I Own"	1/29	#5	13
1/22	AB	Hillside Singers	"I'd Like to Teach the World to Sing"✔	11/27/71	#13	12
			"We're Together"	2/26	#100	1
1/22		Tommy James	"Nothing to Hide"	11/27/71	#41	9
			"Tell 'em Willie Boy's a-Comin'"	2/19	#89	4
1/29	AB/TV	Tony Orlando & Dawn	"Runaway/Happy Together"	1/29	#79	4
			"What Are You Doing Sunday"	10/2/71	#39	9
2/12	AB/TV	Climax	"Precious and Few"✔	1/1	#3	15
2/12		Rufus Thomas	"Do the Funky Penguin"♦	12/25/71	#44	10
2/19	AB/TV	Addrisi Bros.	"We've Got to Get It On Again"✔	1/22	#25	12
2/26	AB/TV	Donnie Elbert	"Sweet Baby"	1/22	#92	4
			"I Can't Help Myself"♦	1/29	#22	9
3/4	AB/TV	Frank Mills	"Love Me, Love Me Love"✔	1/29	#46	9

BANDSTAND APPEARANCE	AB/TV DEBUT	ARTIST	SONG(S) PERFORMED	DATE APPEARED ON CHART	PEAK CHART POSITION	WEEKS ON CHART
3/11	AB/TV	Bullet	"Willpower Weak, Temptation Strong"♦	3/11	#96	2
			"White Lies, Blue Eyes"✔	11/6/71	#28	13
3/11		Gayle McCormick	"You Really Got a Hold on Me"♦	1/22	#98	1
3/18		Hamilton, Joe Frank & Reynolds	"Daisy Mae"	12/4/71	#41	11
3/18	AB/TV	Denise LaSalle	"Now Run and Tell That"	2/5	#46	11
			"Trapped by a Thing Called Love"✔	8/21/71	#13	14
3/25		Joe Tex	"I Gotcha"	1/22	#2	21
			"You Said a Bad Word"	5/20	#41	8
4/1	AB/TV	Robert John	"The Lion Sleeps Tonight"	1/1	#3	17
4/8		Helen Reddy	"No Sad Song"	12/4/71	#62	8
4/15		Bobby Vinton	"Every Day of My Life"	1/29	#24	16
4/15	AB/TV	Five Man Electrical Band	"Signs"✔	5/29/71	#3	18
			"Absolutely Right"	10/16/71	#26	8
4/22	AB/TV	Malo	"Suavecito"*	3/4	#18	12
4/29		Al Green	"Look What You Done for Me"	4/1	#4	12

BANDSTAND APPEARANCE	AB/TV DEBUT	ARTIST	SONG(S) PERFORMED	DATE APPEARED ON CHART	PEAK CHART POSITION	WEEKS ON CHART
4/29	AB	Dennis Coffey & the Detroit Guitar Band	"Scorpio"✔	10/30	#6	17
			"Taurus"	2/19	#18	12
5/6		Honey Cone	"The Day I Found Myself"	2/19	#23	11
			"One Monkey Don't Stop No Show"	11/20/71	#15	11
5/13	AB/TV	Gallery	"Nice to Be with You"✔	2/26	#4	22
			"I Believe in Music"	8/12	#22	16
5/13	AB/TV	Millie Jackson	"Ask Me What You Want"✔	3/25	#27	14
			"My Man, a Sweet Man"	8/5	#42	10
5/20		Gladys Knight & the Pips	"Help Me Make It Through the Night"	3/25	#33	8
5/20		Stevie Wonder	"If You Really Love Me"	8/14/71	#8	14
			"Superwoman"	5/20	#33	11
5/27	AB/TV	Love Unlimited	"Walkin' in the Rain with the One I Love"✔	4/1	#14	14
5/27		Peter Yarrow	"Don't Ever Take Away My Freedom"*	4/8	#100	2
6/3	AB	Buffy St. Marie	"Mister Can't You See"	4/1	#38	8
			"He's An Indian Cowboy in the Rodeo"	8/19	#98	2
6/3		Bill Withers	"Lean on Me"	4/15	#1	19
6/10	AB/TV	Dr. Hook & the Medicine Show	"Sylvia's Mother"✔	4/1	#5	15
6/10	AB/TV	Frederick Knight	"I've Been Lonely for So Long"*	4/22	#27	14
6/17		Wayne Newton	"Daddy Don't You Walk So Fast"	4/22	#4	20
6/17	AB	Billy Preston	"Outta Space"	4/22	#2	17
6/24		John Kay	"I'm Movin' On"*	4/22	#52	7
6/24	AB	Joey Heatherton	"Gone"✔	5/27	#24	15

BANDSTAND APPEARANCE	AB/TV DEBUT	ARTIST	SONG(S) PERFORMED	DATE APPEARED ON CHART	PEAK CHART POSITION	WEEKS ON CHART
7/1		Michael Jackson	"Rockin' Robin"	3/11	#2	13
			"I Wanna Be Where You Are"	5/27	#16	11
			"Ben"	8/5	#1	16
7/8	AB/TV	Darrel Gerard	"Butterfly"*	6/10	#78	9
7/22	AB/TV	Loggins & Messina	"Nobody but You"	6/10	#86	2
			"Vahevala"✔	4/15	#84	5
7/29		Helen Reddy	"I Am Woman"	6/24	#1	22
8/5	AB/TV	Looking Glass	"Brandy"✔	6/17	#1	16
8/5	AB/TV	Luther Ingram	"(If Loving You Is Wrong) I Don't Wanna Be Right"	6/3	#3	16
8/12	AB/TV	El Chicano	"Brown Eyed Girl"	6/17	#45	7
8/12	AB/TV	Jim Croce	"You Don't Mess Around with Jim"✔	7/1	#8	13
8/19	AB	Harry Chapin	"Taxi"✔	3/11	#24	16
8/26	AB/TV	Sailcat	"Motorcycle Mama"*	6/10	#12	15
9/9		Staple Singers (film)	"I'll Take You There"	6/10	#1	15
9/16	AB/TV	Rick Springfield	"Speak to the Sky"✔	8/5	#14	13
10/14		Rufus Thomas	"The Funky Chicken"	2/7/70	#28	12
11/4	AB/TV	Bobby Womack	"Sweet Caroline"	8/26	#51	9
			"Harry Hippie"	12/9	#39	12
12/9		The Who (film)	"Join Together"	7/22	#17	10
12/16		Johnny Nash	"I Can See Clearly Now"	9/9	#1	20
12/23	AB/TV	Jimmy Osmond	"Tweedle-Dee"♦	1/13/73	#59	6
			"Long-Haired Lover from Liverpool"✔	4/22	#38	10
12/30		Rick Springfield	"What Would the Children Think?"	11/25	#70	4

1 • 9 • 7 • 3

BANDSTAND APPEARANCE	AB/TV DEBUT	ARTIST	SONG(S) PERFORMED	DATE APPEARED ON CHART	PEAK CHART POSITION	WEEKS ON CHART
1/6	AB/TV	Billy Paul	"Me and Mrs. Jones"✔	11/4/72	#1	16
1/13	AB/TV	Chi-Lites	"We Need Order"	12/2/72	#61	6
1/27	AB/TV	Steely Dan	"Do It Again"	11/18/72	#6	17
2/3	AB/TV	Albert Hammond	"It Never Rains in California"	10/21/72	#5	16
			"If You Gotta Break Another Heart"	3/3	#63	6

BANDSTAND APPEARANCE	AB/TV DEBUT	ARTIST	SONG(S) PERFORMED	DATE APPEARED ON CHART	PEAK CHART POSITION	WEEKS ON CHART
2/10	AB/TV	Austin Roberts	"Something's Wrong with Me"✔	10/14	#12	15
			"If You Gotta Break Another Heart"	2/3	#50	8
2/17		Gallery	"Big City Miss Ruth Ann"♦	12/23	#23	15
3/3	AB/TV	Hurricane Smith	"Oh Babe What Would You Say"✔	12/2/72	#3	15
			"Who Was It?"♦	3/17	#49	9

✔First hit by a performer   *Only hit by a performer   ♦Last hit by a performer

BANDSTAND APPEARANCE	AB/TV DEBUT	ARTIST	SONG(S) PERFORMED	DATE APPEARED ON CHART	PEAK CHART POSITION	WEEKS ON CHART
3/17	AB/TV	Edward Bear	"Last Song"	12/16/72	#3	18
			"Close Your Eyes"	4/14	#27	12
3/31	AB/TV	Raspberries	"I Wanna Be with You"	11/25/72	#3	18
			"Let's Pretend"	3/24	#35	12
4/7	AB/TV	Sylvers	"Wish That I Could Talk to You"	2/3	#77	10
4/21		Tony Orlando & Dawn	"Tie a Yellow Ribbon Round the Old Oak Tree"	2/17	#1	23
4/28	AB/TV	Sam Neely	"Rosalie"	1/27	#43	8
			"Loving You Just Crossed My Mind"✔	9/2/72	#29	12
5/5	AB	Vickie Lawrence	"The Night the Lights Went Out in Georgia"✔	2/10	#1	20
5/12		Dobie Gray	"Drift Away"	2/24	#5	21
5/19		Sylvia	"Pillow Talk"✔	3/24	#3	21
			"Didn't I"♦	7/21	#70	5
6/9	AB/TV	Gunhill Road	"Back When My Hair Was Short"✱	3/31/71	#40	15
6/16	AB/TV	Dr John	"Right Place, Wrong Time"	4/14/72	#9	20
6/23		Three Dog Night	"Joy to the World"	3/13	#1	13
			"Black and White"	8/12	#1	11
			"Shambala"	5/19	#3	16
6/30	AB/TV	Skylark	"Wildflower"✱	2/17	#9	12
7/14	AB/TV	DeFranco Family	"Heartbeat—It's a Lovebeat"✔	9/8	#3	17
7/21	AB/TV	Electric Light Orchestra	"Roll Over Beethoven"✔	4/14	#42	16

BANDSTAND APPEARANCE	AB/TV DEBUT	ARTIST	SONG(S) PERFORMED	DATE APPEARED ON CHART	PEAK CHART POSITION	WEEKS ON CHART
8/11		Bobby "Boris" Pickett & the Crypt Kickers	"Monster Mash"	5/5	#10	20
8/18		Billy Preston	"Will It Go Round in Circles"	3/31	#1	17
8/25	AB/TV	B.W. Stevenson	"My Maria"✔	7/28	#9	16
			"Shambala"	5/12	#66	8
9/8		Curtis Mayfield	"Future Shock"	7/21	#39	10
9/22	AB/TV	Lobo	"How Can I Tell Her"	6/23	#22	12
9/29		Raspberries	"Tonight"	9/1	#69	7
10/6	AB	New Seekers	"Pinball Wizard/See Me, Feel Me"♦	2/24	#29	13
10/6	AB/TV	Willie Hutch	"Slick"	8/11	#65	6
			"Brother's Gonna Work It Out"	5/19	#67	10
10/13	AB/TV	Johnnie Taylor	"I Believe in You"	6/23	#11	16
11/3	AB/TV	Tavares	"Check It Out"✔	9/22	#35	12
11/10		Steely Dan	"My Old School"	11/3	#69	9
12/8		David Gates	"Sail Around the World"	10/20	#50	8
12/15		Billy Preston	"Space Race"	9/22	#4	18
12/15	AB/TV	Aerosmith	"Dream On"✔	10/20	#59	9
12/29	AB/TV	Eddie Kendricks	"Keep On Truckin'"✔	8/25	#1	19
			"Boogie Down"	1/5/74	#2	18

1 • 9 • 7 • 4

BANDSTAND APPEARANCE	AB/TV DEBUT	ARTIST	SONG(S) PERFORMED	DATE APPEARED ON CHART	PEAK CHART POSITION	WEEKS ON CHART
1/5	AB/TV	Ann Peebles	"I Can't Stand the Rain"♦	9/8/73	#38	21
1/5		El Chicano	"Tell Her She's Lovely"♦	11/17/73	#40	10
1/12	AB/TV	Kool & the Gang	"Jungle Boogie"	12/8/73	#3	22
			"Funky Stuff"	9/8/73	#29	12
1/12		Albert Hammond	"Half a Million Miles Away"	12/1/73	#87	5
1/19	AB	Jim Stafford	"Spiders and Snakes"	11/10/73	#3	3
1/26	AB/TV	Harold Melvin & the Blue Notes	"The Love I Lost"	9/29/73	#7	18

BANDSTAND APPEARANCE	AB/TV DEBUT	ARTIST	SONG(S) PERFORMED	DATE APPEARED ON CHART	PEAK CHART POSITION	WEEKS ON CHART
2/2		DeFranco Family	"Abra-Ca-Dabra"	12/29/73	#32	12
2/9		Al Wilson	"Show and Tell"	10/20/73	#1	22
2/9	AB/TV	Terry Jacks	"Seasons in the Sun"✔	1/12	#1	21
2/16	AB	Redbone	"Come and Get Your Love"♦	1/12	#5	23
3/2	AB/TV	Bloodstone	"Outside Woman"	2/23	#34	14
3/16	AB/TV	Natural Four	"Can This Be Real"✔	1/5	#31	10
3/23		Moments	"Sexy Mama"	1/12	#17	13

BANDSTAND APPEARANCE	AB/TV DEBUT	ARTIST	SONG(S) PERFORMED	DATE APPEARED ON CHART	PEAK CHART POSITION	WEEKS ON CHART
3/30	AB	David Essex	"Rock On"✔	11/10/73	#5	25
3/30	AB	The Dells	"I Miss You"	1/19	#60	7
4/6		Chi-Lites	"Homely Girl"	2/9	#54	8
4/13	AB/TV	Maureen McGovern	"The Morning After"✔	6/22	#1	15
4/13	AB	Stories	"If It Feels Good, Do It"	3/30	#88	5
4/20		Tony Orlando & Dawn	"It Only Hurts When I Try to Smile"	3/30	#81	5
4/27		Kool & the Gang	"Hollywood Swinging"	4/20	#6	19
4/27		DeFranco Family	"Save the Last Dance for Me"♦	5/4	#18	13
5/4	AB/TV	Sami Jo	"Tell Me a Lie"✔	2/9	#29	14
5/4	AB/TV	Soul Children	"I'll Be the Other Woman"	2/16	#36	9
5/11	AB/TV	Bo Donaldson & the Heywoods	"Billy Don't Be a Hero"	6/22	#1	19
5/18		Staple Singers	"Touch a Hand, Make a Friend"	2/23	#23	13
5/25		Bill Withers	"The Same Love That Made Me Laugh"	4/13	#50	13
6/8	AB/TV	Rick Chuna	"I'm a Yo-Yo Man"✱	4/27	#61	7
6/8	AB/TV	Crusaders	"Scratch"	4/27	#81	6
6/22		Johnny Nash	"Lovin' You"♦	4/13	#91	3
6/29	AB/TV	William DeVaughn	"Be Thankful for What You Got"✔	5/4	#4	18
7/6		Jim Stafford	"My Girl Bill"	4/20	#12	15
7/6	AB	Ohio Players	"Jive Turkey"	6/15	#47	11
7/13	AB	Main Ingredient	"Just Don't Wanna Be Lonely"	2/2	#10	20
7/13		Andy Kim	"Rock Me Gently"	6/22	#1	19
7/20	AB/TV	George McCrae	"Rock Your Baby"✔	6/1	#1	17
7/20	AB	Rufus (with Chaka Khan)	"Tell Me Something Good"✔	6/15	#3	17

BANDSTAND APPEARANCE	AB/TV DEBUT	ARTIST	SONG(S) PERFORMED	DATE APPEARED ON CHART	PEAK CHART POSITION	WEEKS ON CHART
7/27		Billy "Crash" Craddock	"Rub It In"	6/29	#16	15
7/27	AB	Blue Magic	"Sideshow"	5/18	#8	21
8/3	AB/TV	Fanny	"I've Had It"	6/8	#79	7
8/10		Billy Preston	"Nothin' from Nothin'"	7/13	#1	18
8/17		Little Anthony & the Imperials	"I'm Falling In Love With You"♦	6/15	#84	4
8/31		Eddie Kendricks	"Tell Her Love Has Felt the Need"	8/10	#50	10
9/7		Bloodstone	"That's Not How It Goes"	7/27	#82	6
9/7	AB	Dave Loggins	"Please Come to Boston"✔	6/1	#5	18
9/14		Impressions	"Sooner or Later"	7/6	#68	8
9/21		Smokey Robinson & the Miracles	"Do It Baby"	8/24	#13	15
10/26	AB/TV	Johnny Bristol	"You and I"	11/16	#48	7
10/26		Bo Donaldson & the Heywoods	"Who Do You Think You Are"	7/27	#15	12
11/2		Spinners	"You Don't Love Nobody"	9/21	#15	13
11/16	AB	Carl Carlton	"Everlasting Love"	9/21	#6	15
11/16		Bobby Vinton	"My Melody of Love"	9/21	#3	7
11/30	AB	Lattimore	"Let's Straighten It Out"✔	10/26	#31	12
12/7		Andy Kim	"Baby I'm on Fire"♦	10/26	#28	9
12/7		Al Wilson	"La La Peace Song"	10/5	#30	10
12/14	AB	Hues Corp.	"Rock the Boat" / "Rockin' Soul"	5/25 / 10/12	#1 / #18	18 / 12
12/21		Kool & the Gang	"Rhyme Time People"	1/4/75	#63	8
12/28		Gloria Gaynor	"Never Can Say Goodbye"✔	11/2	#9	17

1 • 9 • 7 • 5

BANDSTAND APPEARANCE	AB/TV DEBUT	ARTIST	SONG(S) PERFORMED	DATE APPEARED ON CHART	PEAK CHART POSITION	WEEKS ON CHART
1/4	AB	Shirley Brown	"Woman to Woman"✔	11/2/74	#22	14

BANDSTAND APPEARANCE	AB/TV DEBUT	ARTIST	SONG(S) PERFORMED	DATE APPEARED ON CHART	PEAK CHART POSITION	WEEKS ON CHART
1/4		Bo Donaldson & the Heywoods	Heartbreak Kid"	11/16/74	#39	7

✔First hit by a performer   ✱Only hit by a performer   ♦Last hit by a performer

BANDSTAND APPEARANCE	AB/TV DEBUT	ARTIST	SONG(S) PERFORMED	DATE APPEARED ON CHART	PEAK CHART POSITION	WEEKS ON CHART
1/11	AB	B.T. Express	"Do It (Til Your Satisfied)"✔	9/28/74	#2	18
1/18		Chi-Lites	"Toby"	3/1	#78	7
1/25		Neil Sedaka	"Laughter in the Rain"	10/19/74	#1	20
1/25		Michael Jackson	"We're Almost There"	3/1	#54	8
2/1	AB	Carol Douglas	"Doctor's Orders"✔	11/30/74	#11	16
2/1	AB/TV	Nigel Olsson	"Only One Woman"✔	3/1	#91	6
2/8		Maureen McGovern	"We May Never Love This Way Again"	1/25	#83	4
2/8	AB	Lamont Dozier	"Let Me Start Tonite"♦	1/4	#87	5
3/1		Sugarloaf	"Don't Call Us, We'll Call You"	12/7/74	#9	21
3/8		Smokey Robinson	"Baby That's Backatcha"✔	4/26	#26	11
3/15	AB	Billy Swann	"I Can Help"	9/28/74	#1	18
			"I'm Her Fool"	3/15	#53	4
3/22	AB/TV	Barry Manilow	"Mandy"✔	11/16/74	#1	16
			"It's a Miracle"	3/1	#12	13
3/22	AB	Minnie Riperton	"Lovin' You"✔	1/18	#1	18
3/29	AB/TV	Polly Brown	"Up in a Puff of Smoke"✱	1/4	#16	13
4/5	AB/TV	Freddy Fender	"Before the Next Teardrop Falls"✔	2/1	#1	21
4/12	AB	Jose Feliciano	"Chico and the Man"	1/25	#96	2
4/26	AB	Sammy Johns	"Chevy Van"	2/1	#5	17
5/3		B.J. Thomas	"Another Somebody Done Somebody Wrong Song"	2/1	#1	18
5/3	AB	Elvin Bishop	"Fooled Around and Fell in Love"	3/8	#3	17
5/10	AB/TV	Captain & Tennille	"Love Will Keep Us Together"✔	4/19	#1	23
5/10	AB/TV	Charlie Kulis	"Runaway"✱	3/15	#46	8
5/24		Evie Sands	"You Brought Out the Woman in Me"♦	3/29	#50	18
5/31	AB	Disco Tex & the Sex-O-Lettes	"I Wanna Dance wit'Choo"	4/19	#23	11
6/7	AB/TV	Boomer Castleman	"Judy Mae"✱	5/3	#33	8
6/7	AB/TV	Consumer Rapport	"Ease on down the Road"✱	4/19	#42	12
6/14	AB/TV	Tamiko Jones	"Touch Me Baby"✱	4/5	#60	10
6/28		The Jackson Five	"Dancin' Machine"	3/15	#2	22
7/5	AB	Donald Byrd & the Blackbyrds	"Walkin' in Rhythm"	2/8	#6	17
7/5	AB/TV	Sparks		(no hits until 1982)		
7/5		Al Martino	"To the Door of the Sun"	12/21/74	#17	16
7/12	AB	Gwen McCrae	"Rockin' Chair"✱	5/17	#9	14
7/19	AB/TV	Melissa Manchester	"Midnight Blue"✔	5/10	#6	17
7/19	AB/TV	Bazuka	"Dynomite"✱	4/12	#10	20
7/26	AB/TV	Dwight Twilley	"I'm on Fire"✔	4/26	#16	10
8/2		Spinners	"Games People Play"	8/9	#51	18
8/2		Johnny Rivers	"Help Me Rhonda"	7/12	#22	10
8/9		Hamilton, Joe Frank & Reynolds	"Fallin' in Love Again"	6/21	#1	17
8/9		Willie Hutch	"Love Power"♦	11/1	#41	6
8/16		Joe Simon	"Music in My Bones"♦	8/23	#92	4
8/23		Freddy Fender	"Wasted Days and Wasted Nights"	6/21	#8	19
8/30	AB	K.C. & the Sunshine Band	"Get Down Tonight"✔	7/12	#1	15
9/6		Tavares	"Only Takes a Minute"	7/26	#10	18
9/13		B.T. Express	"Give It What You Got"	8/9	#40	6
9/13	AB/TV	Austin Roberts	"Rocky"♦	7/19	#9	17
9/20		Bo Donaldson & the Heywoods	"Our Last Song Together"♦	7/5	#95	2
9/20	AB	Ralph Carter	"When You're Young and in Love"✱	9/6	#95	3
10/4	AB	Faith, Hope & Charity	"To Each His Own"♦	8/16	#50	15
10/18	AB	Natalie Cole	"This Will Be"✔	8/30	#6	17
10/25	AB	Gary Tom's Empire	"7, 6, 5, 4, 3, 2, 1, Blow Your Whistle"✔	6/21	#46	17
10/25	AB/TV	Cotton, Lloyd & Christian	"I Go to Pieces"✱	9/27	#66	5
11/15	AB/TV	ABBA	"S.O.S."	9/6	#15	17
11/15		David Ruffin	"Walk Away from Love"	11/8	#9	15
12/6	AB	Hudson Brothers	"Lonely School Year"	11/22	#57	5
12/13	AB	People's Choice	"Do It Anyway You Wanna"	8/23	#11	16
12/20		Smokey Robinson & the Miracles	"Love Machine"♦	10/25	#1	28

1·9·7·6

BANDSTAND APPEARANCE	AB/TV DEBUT	ARTIST	SONG(S) PERFORMED	DATE APPEARED ON CHART	PEAK CHART POSITION	WEEKS ON CHART
1/3		Staple Singers	"Let's Do It Again"	12/27/75	#1	15
1/3	AB/TV	C.W. McCall	"Convoy"*	12/6/75	#1	16
1/10	AB/TV	David Geddes	"Last Game of the Season"♦	11/15/75	#18	18
1/17		Captain & Tennille	"Lonely Nights"	1/24	#3	19
1/31		Smokey Robinson	"Quiet Storm"	1/17	#61	7
1/31		Eric Carmen	"All by Myself"✔	12/20/75	#2	19
2/21	AB/TV	Gary Wright	"Dream Weaver"✔	1/3	#2	30
2/28		Natalie Cole	"Inseparable"	12/13/75	#32	17
2/28	AB/TV	Jonathan Cain (later of Journey)	"It's Time to Say Goodbye"*	1/17	#44	9
3/6		Frankie Avalon	"Venus" (disco version)	1/24	#46	11
3/13	AB/TV	Larry Santos	"We Can't Hide It Anymore"*	2/14	#34	10
3/20		Sylvers	"Boogie Fever"	2/14	#1	21
3/20	AB/TV	Larry Groce	"Junkfood Junkie"*	1/10	#9	15
3/27		Marilyn McCoo & Billy Davis, Jr.	"Hope We Get to Love in Time"	3/27	#97	2
4/3		Johnnie Taylor	"Disco Lady"	2/7	#1	19
4/10	AB	John Travolta	"Let Her In"✔	5/1	#10	20
4/17		Supremes	"Gonna Let My Heart Do the Walkin'"	5/29	#40	14
4/17	AB/TV	Michel Polnareff	"If You Only Believe"✔	2/21	#48	7
4/24		Al Wilson	"I've Got a Feeling"	3/27	#29	10
4/24	AB/TV	Queen (video)	"Bohemian Rhapsody"	1/3	#9	24
5/1	AB	Commodores	"Sweet Love"	12/27/75	#5	23
5/1		Melissa Manchester	"Better Days"	5/1	#71	5
5/8	AB/TV	Dorothy Moore	"Misty Blue"✔	8/21	#3	22
5/8	AB/TV	Pratt & McClain	"Happy Days"✔	4/24	#5	14
5/15		Hamilton, Joe Frank & Reynolds	"Every Day Without You"	4/3	#62	7
5/22		Kool & the Gang	"Love and Understanding"	3/20	#77	8
5/29		Fifth Dimension	"Love Hangover"♦	4/3	#80	4
5/29		Jim Stafford	"Jasper"	4/3	#69	6
6/5		Aretha Franklin	"Something He Can Feel"	6/12	#28	12
6/5	AB	Cate Brothers	"Union Man"✔	2/7	#24	20
6/12	AB	Brass Construction	"Movin'"	4/3	#14	16
6/12		John Sebastian	"Welcome Back"	3/27	#1	14
6/19	AB	Rhythm Heritage	"S.W.A.T. Theme"✔	11/13/71	#1	24
			"Barretta Theme"	4/10	#20	13
6/26	AB	Manhattans	"Kiss and Say Goodbye"	4/17	#1	26
7/10	AB	Vicki Sue Robinson	"Turn the Beat Around"✔	4/10	#10	25
7/17	AB	Maxine Nightingale	"Right Back Where We Started From"✔	2/14	#2	20
7/31		Sylvers	"Cotton Candy"	6/26	#59	7
8/7	AB/TV	Cyndi Greco	"Making Our Dreams Come True"*	5/8	#25	12
8/14	AB/TV	England Dan & John Ford Coley	"I'd Really Love to See You Tonight"✔	6/12	#2	24
8/21	AB	Donna Summer	"Love to Love You Baby"✔	12/6/75	#2	18
8/28	AB/TV	Starbuck	"Moonlight Feels Right"✔	4/17	#3	22
9/4	AB	Labelle	"Lady Marmalade"✔	1/4/75	#1	18
9/11		John Travolta	"When I'm Away from You"	10/30	#38	6
9/11		Spinners	"Rubberband Man"	9/11	#2	21
9/18	AB	Elton John & Kiki Dee (film)	"Don't Go Breakin' My Heart"*	7/3	#1	20
9/25	AB	Walter Murphy Band	"A Fifth of Beethoven"✔	5/29	#1	20
10/2	AB/TV	Rick Dees & His Cast of Idiots	"Disco Duck"✔	8/14	#1	25
10/2		Four Tops	"Catfish"	10/30	#71	6
10/16	AB	Ritchie Family	"Best Disco in Town"	8/28	#17	20
10/23	AB	Lady Flash	"Street Singin'"*	7/17	#27	12
10/30	AB	Flash Cadillac & the Continental Kids	"Did You Boogie"♦	8/28	#29	14
10/30		Marilyn McCoo & Billy Davis, Jr.	"You Don't Have to Be a Star, Baby"	9/11	#1	26
11/6		Sylvers	"Hot Line"	8/28	#29	14
11/6		Rick Springfield	"Take a Hand"	8/21	#41	9

✔First hit by a performer   *Only hit by a performer   ♦Last hit by a performer

BANDSTAND APPEARANCE	AB/TV DEBUT	ARTIST	SONG(S) PERFORMED	DATE APPEARED ON CHART	PEAK CHART POSITION	WEEKS ON CHART
12/4	AB	Judy Collins	"Send in the Clowns"	6/26	#36	11
12/11		Jermaine Jackson	"Let's Be Young Tonight"	9/18	#55	13

BANDSTAND APPEARANCE	AB/TV DEBUT	ARTIST	SONG(S) PERFORMED	DATE APPEARED ON CHART	PEAK CHART POSITION	WEEKS ON CHART
12/18		Walter Murphy Band	"Flight 76"	11/13	#44	10
12/18		Johnny Bristol	"Do It to My Mind"♦	11/27	#43	11

1 · 9 · 7 · 7

BANDSTAND APPEARANCE	AB/TV DEBUT	ARTIST	SONG(S) PERFORMED	DATE APPEARED ON CHART	PEAK CHART POSITION	WEEKS ON CHART
2/19	AB	Brick	"Dazz"✔	10/23/76	#3	21
2/19		Queen (video)	"Tie Your Mother Down"	3/19	#49	6
2/26	AB/TV	Jennifer Warnes	"Right Time of the Night"✔	1/29	#6	22
3/5		Rufus	"At Midnight"	2/12	#36	12
3/5	AB	Parker McGee	"I Just Can't Say No to You"*	1/29	#42	7
3/12	AB	Emotions	"I Don't Want to Lose Your Love"	11/6/76	#51	12
3/19	AB/TV	The Babys	"If You've Got the Time"✔	3/19	#88	2
3/19		Lattimore	"Somethin' 'bout 'Cha"♦	2/5	#37	10
3/26	AB	Sons of Champlin	"Here is Where Your Love Belongs"♦	2/5	#8	5
4/2	AB/TV	The Rubinoos	"I Think We're Alone Now"♦	2/5	#45	12
4/2		Thelma Houston	"Don't Leave Me This Way"	12/18/76	#1	24
4/9	AB	Enchantment	"Gloria"✔	1/29	#25	13
4/9	AB	Shaun Cassidy	"Da Doo Ron Ron"✔	5/14	#1	22
4/16		James Darren	"You Take My Heart Away"♦	3/19	#52	9
4/16		England Dan & John Ford Coley	"It's Sad to Be Lonely"	5/7	#21	16
4/23		Sylvers	"High School Dance"	4/23	#17	17
4/23	AB	Cerrone	"Love in C-minor"✔	2/26	#36	8
4/30	AB	Andrew Gold	"Lonely Boy"	3/19	#7	21
5/7	AB	Hot	"Angel in Your Arms"✔	2/19	#6	27
5/7		Ohio Players	"Feel the Beat" / "O-H-I-O"♦	1/29 / 7/23	#61 / #45	5 / 12
5/14	AB	Rose Royce	"I Wanna Get Next to You"	2/26	#10	17
5/21	AB	Yvonne Elliman	"Hello Stranger"	3/19	#15	16

BANDSTAND APPEARANCE	AB/TV DEBUT	ARTIST	SONG(S) PERFORMED	DATE APPEARED ON CHART	PEAK CHART POSITION	WEEKS ON CHART
5/21	AB	Crown Heights Affair	"Dancin'"	2/19	#42	13
5/28	AB/TV	Alan O'Day	"Undercover Angel"✔	4/2	#1	25
5/28	AB	Shalamar	"Uptown Festival"✔	3/12	#25	17
6/4	AB	T-Connection	"Do You Wanna Do"✔	3/12	#46	17
6/4		Addrisi Bros.	"Slow Dancin' Don't Turn Me On"	4/9	#20	15
6/11	AB	Carrie Lucas	"I Gotta Keep Dancin'"	4/30	#64	8
6/11		Hues Corp.	"I Caught Your Act"♦	4/30	#92	2
6/18	AB/TV	Peter McCann	"Do You Wanna Make Love"*	4/23	#5	22
6/25		Dave Mason	"So High"	5/28	#89	3
6/25		Starbuck	"Everybody Be Dancin'"	4/16	#38	8
7/2	AB/TV	Pablo Cruise	"Whatcha Gonna Do"✔	4/16	#6	26
7/9	AB/TV	Bay City Rollers	"You Made Me Believe in Magic"	6/4	#10	17
7/16		Joe Tex	"Ain't Gonna Bump No More"♦	4/16	#12	18
7/16	AB	Cat Stevens (film)	"Old Schoolyard"	6/25	#33	10
7/23	AB/TV	Kenny Nolan	"Love's Grown Deep"	4/2	#20	18
7/30	AB	Stephen Bishop	"On and On"	5/7	#11	28
8/6	AB/TV	Andy Gibb	"I Just Want to Be Your Everything"✔	4/23	#1	31
8/13	AB/TV	Sanford-Townshend Band	"Smoke from a Different Fire"*	6/18	#9	18
8/20	AB/TV	LeBlanc & Carr	"Something About You"✔	7/2	#48	6
8/20		Johnny Rivers	"Swayin' to the Music"	6/25	#10	24
8/27	AB	Floaters	"Float On"*	7/9	#2	16

BANDSTAND APPEARANCE	AB/TV DEBUT	ARTIST	SONG(S) PERFORMED	DATE APPEARED ON CHART	PEAK CHART POSITION	WEEKS ON CHART
9/3	AB/TV	Dean Friedman	"Ariel"*	4/16	#26	22
9/17	AB	Brothers Johnson	"Strawberry Letter #23"	7/2	#5	19
9/24	AB/TV	Paul Nicholas	"Heaven on the 7th Floor"✔	8/20	#6	23
9/24	AB/TV	Debby Boone	"You Light Up My Life"✔	9/3	#1	25
10/1	AB	Leif Garrett	"Surfin' USA"✔	8/27	#20	15
			"Runaround Sue"	11/12	#13	14
10/22	AB/TV	Ronnie McDowell	"The King Is Gone"	9/10	#13	12

BANDSTAND APPEARANCE	AB/TV DEBUT	ARTIST	SONG(S) PERFORMED	DATE APPEARED ON CHART	PEAK CHART POSITION	WEEKS ON CHART
10/29		Shaun Cassidy	"That's Rock 'n' Roll"	7/23	#3	23
			"Hey Deanie"	11/12	#7	16
11/12		Dorothy Moore	"I Believe You"♦	8/6	#27	15
12/3	AB/TV	Village People	(no hits until 1978)			
12/7		The Babys (video)	"Isn't It Time?"	10/8	#13	16

1 • 9 • 7 • 8

BANDSTAND APPEARANCE	AB/TV DEBUT	ARTIST	SONG(S) PERFORMED	DATE APPEARED ON CHART	PEAK CHART POSITION	WEEKS ON CHART
1/7	AB	Odyssey	"Native New Yorker"✔	11/12/77	#21	19
1/7		Alan O'Day	"Started Out Dancing, Ended Up Making Love"♦	10/1/77	#73	6
1/14	AB	Peter Brown	"Do Ya Wanna Get Funky with Me"✔	9/17/77	#18	14
1/14	AB	High Energy	"You Can't Turn Me Off"✔♦	9/17/77	#12	22
1/21	AB	Samantha Sang	"Emotion"✔	11/19/77	#3	27
1/21		Bill Withers	"Lovely Day"♦	12/10/77	#30	12
1/28		Sylvers	"Any Way You Want Me"♦	11/26/77	#72	9
2/4	AB	LTD	"Back in Love Again"	10/15/77	#4	19
2/11		Yvonne Elliman	"If I Can't Have You"	1/28	#1	22
2/11		David Gates	"Goodbye Girl"	12/17/77	#15	24
2/18	AB/TV	Gene Cotton	"Before My Heart Finds Out"	2/4	#23	14
3/4		Spinners	"If You Wanna Do a Dance"	7/29	#49	6
3/11		Cerrone	"Supernature"	1/21	#70	5
3/18		War	"Galaxy"	1/7	#39	9
3/25	AB	Raydio	"Jack and Jill"✔	1/7	#8	21
4/1	AB/TV	Jay Ferguson	"Thunder Island"✔	11/12/77	#9	21
4/1		Captain & Tennille	"I'm on My Way"	4/22	#74	6
4/8	AB	Ashford & Simpson	"Don't Cost You Nothing"	3/11	#79	9

BANDSTAND APPEARANCE	AB/TV DEBUT	ARTIST	SONG(S) PERFORMED	DATE APPEARED ON CHART	PEAK CHART POSITION	WEEKS ON CHART
4/22	AB/TV	Eddie Money	"Baby Hold On"✔	2/25	#11	20
4/22		Millie Jackson	"If You're Not Back in Love by Monday"♦	11/19/77	#43	11
4/29	AB/TV	Wild Cherry	"I Love My Music"♦	2/25	#69	8
5/6	AB/TV	Bobby Arvon	"Until Now"*	12/3/77	#72	16
5/13	AB/TV	Robert Palmer	"Every Kind of People"	3/25	#16	18
5/13	AB	Chic	"Everybody Dance"	4/22	#38	10
5/20	AB/TV	Joey Travolta	"I Don't Wanna Go"*	6/3	#43	8
5/27		Donna Summer	"Last Dance"	5/13	#3	21
5/27	AB	Brooklyn Dreamers	"Music, Harmony, and Rhythm"	3/25	#57	8
6/3	AB/TV	Jimmy "Bo" Horne	"Dance Across the Floor"*	6/3	#43	8
6/3		K.C. & the Sunshine Band	"It's the Same Old Song"	5/13	#35	10
6/10	AB/TV	Walter Egan	"Magnet and Steel"	5/27	#8	22
6/24	AB/TV	Tuxedo Junction	"Chattanooga Choochoo"	4/22	#32	17
7/1		Pablo Cruise	"Love Will Find a Way"	6/3	#6	18
7/8		Rare Earth	"Warm Ride"♦	4/29	#39	11
7/22	AB	Rick James	"You and I"✔	7/1	#13	17
7/29		High Energy	"Love Is All You Need"♦	3/4	#89	5

✔First hit by a performer   *Only hit by a performer   ♦ Last hit by a performer

BANDSTAND APPEARANCE	AB/TV DEBUT	ARTIST	SONG(S) PERFORMED	DATE APPEARED ON CHART	PEAK CHART POSITION	WEEKS ON CHART
8/12	AB	Love & Kisses	"Thank God It's Friday"*	5/6	#22	16
8/19	AB/TV	Bonnie Tyler	"It's a Heartache"✔	3/25	#3	21
8/26	AB	Evelyn "Champagne" King	"Shame"✔	6/17	#9	19
8/26	AB/TV	Snail	"The Joker"♦	9/23	#93	2
9/2		Burton Cummings	"Break It to Them Gently"	7/15	#85	5
9/2	AB/TV	Nick Gilder	"Hot Child in the City"✔	6/10	#1	31
9/9	AB	Frankie Valli	"Grease"	5/27	#1	22
9/16	AB	Foxy	"Get Off"✔	7/22	#9	21

BANDSTAND APPEARANCE	AB/TV DEBUT	ARTIST	SONG(S) PERFORMED	DATE APPEARED ON CHART	PEAK CHART POSITION	WEEKS ON CHART
9/30	AB/TV	Stonebolt	"I Will Still Love You"✔	8/5	#29	14
10/28		David Gates	"Took the Last Train"	8/12	#30	14
12/9	AB	Sylvester	"Dance"✔	8/19	#19	18
12/16		Eric Carmen	"Change of Heart"	9/16	#19	15
12/16	AB	Pointer Sisters	"Fire"	11/11	#2	23
12/30	AB	Chanson	"Don't Hold Back"*	11/11	#26	16
12/30	AB	Justin Heyward	"Forever Autumn"*	10/7	#47	12

1 · 9 · 7 · 9

BANDSTAND APPEARANCE	AB/TV DEBUT	ARTIST	SONG(S) PERFORMED	DATE APPEARED ON CHART	PEAK CHART POSITION	WEEKS ON CHART
1/6		Village People	"YMCA"	10/21/78	#2	26
1/13		Peaches & Herb	"Reunited"	3/17	#1	23
1/20	AB	Livingston Taylor	"I Will Be in Love with You"	10/21/78	#30	14
1/20	AB	Grace Jones		(no hits until the 80s)		
1/27	AB	Alicia Bridges	"I Love the Nightlife"✔	7/8/78	#5	31
1/27	AB	Dan Hartman	"Instant Replay"✔	10/14/78	#29	17
			"This Is It"	2/24	#91	3
2/3		Nigel Olsson	"Dancin' Shoes"	12/16/78	#18	16
2/3		Melissa Manchester	"Don't Cry Out Loud"	11/18/78	#10	23
2/10		The Jacksons	"Shake Your Body (Down to the Ground)"	2/17	#7	22
2/17	AB/TV	The Raes	"A Little Lovin'"*	12/16/78	#61	4
2/17	AB/TV	Bonnie Pointer	"Free Me from My Freedom"♦	2/17	#58	14
2/24	AB	Eddie Rabbit	"Every Which Way but Loose"	1/20	#40	11
3/3	AB/TV	Roger Voudouris	"Get Used to It"*	3/17	#21	19
3/10	AB/TV	Bobby Caldwell	"What You Won't Do for Love"✔	12/23/78	#9	20

BANDSTAND APPEARANCE	AB/TV DEBUT	ARTIST	SONG(S) PERFORMED	DATE APPEARED ON CHART	PEAK CHART POSITION	WEEKS ON CHART
3/10	AB	Herbie Mann	"Superman"♦	1/13	#26	18
3/17	AB/TV	Talking Heads	"Take Me to the River"	11/4/78	#26	17
3/17		Brooklyn Dreams	"Make It Last"♦	2/24	#69	4
3/24	AB	Sister Sledge	"He's the Greatest Dancer"	2/10	#9	19
3/24	AB	Gary's Gang	"Keep On Dancin'"*	2/11	#41	10
4/7	AB/TV	Linda Clifford	"Bridge over Troubled Waters"	3/24	#41	6
4/7		Shalamar	"Second Time Around"	12/9/78	#8	23
4/14	AB/TV	Arpeggio	"Love and Desire"*	3/10	#70	5
4/14	AB	Edwin Starr	"Contact"	2/10	#65	7
4/21	AB/TV	Fabulous Poodles	"Mirror Star"*	4/28	#81	4
4/28	AB	Farragher Bros.	"Stay the Night"*	2/24	#50	7
5/5	AB	Bachman-Turner Overdrive	"Heartaches"♦	2/24	#60	7
5/12	AB/TV	Blondie	"Heart of Glass"✔	2/17	#1	21
5/12	AB	G.Q.	"Disco Nights"✔	3/17	#12	18
			"I Do Love You"	6/30	#20	17
5/19	AB/TV	Badfinger	"Love's Gonna Come at Last"	4/7	#69	4

BANDSTAND APPEARANCE	AB/TV DEBUT	ARTIST	SONG(S) PERFORMED	DATE APPEARED ON CHART	PEAK CHART POSITION	WEEKS ON CHART
5/19	AB/TV	Narada Michael Walden	"I Don't Want Nobody Else"✔	3/31	#47	11
5/26		Carrie Lucas	"Dance with You"♦	5/12	#70	7
6/2	AB	Anita Ward	"Ring My Bell"✔	5/12	#1	21
6/16	AB	Cheryl Barnes (video)	"Easy to Be Hard"✱	4/28	#64	7
6/23	AB	McFadden & Whitehead	"Ain't No Stoppin' Us Now"✔	4/28	#13	18
7/14	AB	Alton McClain & Destiny	"It Must Be Love"	4/7	#32	12
7/21	AB	David Naughton	"Makin' It"✱	3/31	#5	24
7/28		Maxine Nightingale	"Lead Me On"	5/26	#5	23
8/4		Robert John	"Sad Eyes"	5/19	#1	27
8/11		Nick Gilder	"Rock Me"♦	6/16	#57	6
8/18		Maureen McGovern	"Different Worlds"♦	7/7	#18	16

BANDSTAND APPEARANCE	AB/TV DEBUT	ARTIST	SONG(S) PERFORMED	DATE APPEARED ON CHART	PEAK CHART POSITION	WEEKS ON CHART
9/1		Jennifer Warnes	"I Know a Heartache When I See It"	6/30	#19	22
9/8		Bonnie Pointer	"Heaven Must Have Sent You"	6/16	#11	23
9/15		Beach Boys	"Good Timing"	4/28	#40	10
9/22	AB/TV	Patrick Hernandez	"Born to Be Alive"✱	6/23	#16	19
10/6		Smokey Robinson	"Cruisin'"	10/6	#4	25
10/6	AB	Mary MacGregor	"Good Friends"	8/11	#39	12
12/15		Lauren Wood	"Please Don't Leave"✱	9/22	#24	14
12/22	AB/TV	Joe Jackson	"Is She Really Going Out with Him"	6/9	#21	15
12/29	AB/TV	Terry Desario with K.C.	"Yes, I'm Ready"✔	11/17	#2	23
12/29		Captain & Tennille	"Do That To Me One More Time"	10/20	#1	27

✔First hit by a performer   ✱Only hit by a performer   ♦Last hit by a performer

THE '80s

'80s ANYTHING GOES

We're still in the middle of the eighties as this book is coming out, so it's difficult to step back and get a perspective on what this decade is all about. Let's see . . . there've been mega-mega-superstars like Michael Jackson and Prince, and the revivals of rockabilly (via the Stray Cats), and, as this book goes to press, sixties psychedelia (on a more underground level musically thus far, though in terms of fashion, sixties-inspired designers like Stephen Sprouse are all the rage). Disco metamorphosed into "dance music," or, as Dick Clark puts it, "Those who say disco died in the late seventies are wrong. It never went away. It's still around, whatever name you give it: The basic idea is still people making music to get other people to dance." And then there was the "new music" trend, which seems to have started merely because somewhere someone got tired of having every new band with a recording contract called a "new wave" band. New wave may have conjured up too many negative associations with punk rock, and eventually the name *new music* stuck. And then there was the rise of music video, which gave birth to its own superstars like Duran Duran. This phenomenon also brought about the only major change in *Bandstand*'s format in some thirty years: Since the early eighties, each *Bandstand* features a "video showcase" in which one promotional videoclip is shown.

But let us remember that *Bandstand* actually began—thirty years before it added a video showcase—as a showcase for short musical films on television. So goes that old French proverb: "*Plus ça change . . .*"

Devo, 1980

THE MUSIC

Toni Basil, 1982.

One thing hasn't changed: *Bandstand* has continued to present future stars performing their very first hits, before most of the country was fully aware of who these people were, or would be. The very first broadcast of the decade, on January 5, 1980, featured a handsome young man named John Cougar performing his first hit, ''I Need a Lover (Who Won't Drive Me Crazy),'' which he wrote but which became a much bigger hit in a version by Pat Benatar. Cougar would later become a big enough star to stop relying on the phony surname a manager had given him, and revert to his given last name, Mellencamp.

A Flock of Seagulls, 1982.

West Coast new-music act the Motels appeared the following week, long before any of their tunes actually made the charts. The third week saw British new wavers the Boomtown Rats with their first hit, "I Don't Like Mondays" —which was based on the explanation given by a young California girl who'd recently holed herself up in a school tower and started shooting strangers with a rifle.

On January 26, 1980, Prince was among the guests. This was a particularly fascinating *Bandstand* episode, because for one thing Prince has lately become one of the biggest stars in music, and this appearance occurred when his first really big single, "I Wanna Be Your Lover," was just entering the charts (he'd had an earlier, but minor, hit in "Soft and Wet"). But more importantly, Prince has become near-legendary as the Greta Garbo of rock, an ultrareclusive star who since 1982 has refused to be interviewed by the press. His *Bandstand* appearance constitutes the only recorded public interview he's ever given. Here's how it went:

Prince, attired in a loose, peach-colored shirt open to the navel, and skintight gold spandex tights (his bass player, Andre Cymone, wore see-through plastic pants with black bikini briefs on underneath), led his band through an incredible lip-synch of "I Wanna Be Your Lover." Any viewer would've sworn they were playing live. Prince pranced and strutted with uncontainable energy, and at times, showing early instances of his famed erotic exhibitionism, stroked his crotch and wiggled his behind into the camera. Then the tune ended, and Dick Clark

Irene Cara, 1980.

Laura Branigan, 1982.

P (*nervous pause—he was twenty-one at the time and about to tell a lie*): Um, nineteen.

DC: And how many years ago did you make these demos and have offers on them?

P (*looks flustered, almost angry, pauses, then suddenly holds four outstretched fingers in DC's face, as if to say "four"*).

DC: And why did you turn those offers down?

P: Um . . . they wouldn't let me produce myself.

DC: And you were fifteen at the time? Did they think you didn't know what you were doing?

P: Don't know . . .

DC: Were you ever disappointed that you didn't let them do that to you?

P: No.

DC: Somebody told me that you played all the instruments on your album, is that true?

P (*pause, supercilious look*): Maybe.

DC: No, you're shy, you're too modest . . . Come on, how many instruments *do* you play?

P: Hmm . . . (*grimaces, looks at floor, fidgets*).

DC (*to audience*): In moments we'll be with you—

came out to chat with the band. And like *that*, Prince became another person altogether—painfully shy, tongue-tied, awkward.

DICK CLARK (*approaching stage*): Al-*right*! Man . . . where'd you learn to do this in *Minneapolis*?

PRINCE (*looking haughty, with sarcastic inflection*): Uh, where?

DC: I mean, this is not the kind of music that comes from Minneapolis, Minnesota.

P (*fidgets nervously, looks away at floor, smiles uneasily, throws head back, grits teeth, puts hands on hips in apparent annoyance*): . . . No.

DC: I said something before you came out here, to the effect that you made a couple of demonstration records when you were a teenager, you're barely more than that now, are you?

The Motels. 1982.

P: Thousands.

DC: Thousands? Literally, *do* you play all the instruments?

P: ·Umm . . . a lot.

DC: If that is the case, then you have these other people with you to travel, to tour. Do you have any travel plans?

P: We have a tour coming up . . . in a few weeks.

DC: Well, we'll look forward to it. We thank you very much for joining us. Now what's the name of your next song?

P: Uh . . . "Why You Wanna Treat Me So Bad."

DC: Okay, ladies and gentlemen, this is Prince!

And with that, Prince, with a fire in his eyes, strutted and shimmied as he led his band through another stunning example of his thoroughly unique fusion of black-funk and white-rock styles. But everyone in the studio, and all those in the viewing audience at home, could not have forgotten the bizarre, schizoid way Prince behaved. Those who were fortunate enough to have caught *Bandstand* that day got a good idea of just why Prince has been so reclusive.

As *Bandstand* producer Larry Klein explains, "Everyone thought Prince was being standoff-ish to Dick that time. People kept asking us, 'How did that kid get the nerve to treat Dick that way?' But they misinterpreted what I think was just basic shyness on Prince's part. *Incredible* shyness—I mean awkwardness like I've never seen in a human being before, especially after he'd given this virtual striptease of a performance, but there you go. The guy just has trouble in conversation with strangers. But I just want it clear that Prince was not being arrogant or

The Go-Go's, 1981.

Cyndi Lauper, 1984.

And then on May 17, 1980, something strange and magical happened. Public Image Ltd. appeared on *Bandstand*. They were led by a singer named John Lydon, who a few years earlier had fronted original British punk rockers the Sex Pistols under the name Johnny Rotten. Sitting in the bleachers with the kids, Dick Clark introduced them this way: ''This is something interesting and special—ladies and gentlemen, please greet Public Image Ltd.!''

The band's guitarist Keith Levene, bassist Jah Wobble, and drummer Martin Atkins were set up at their instruments. But as the band's non-hit (they never had a hit, their music being much too abrasively avant-garde) ''Poptones'' began to play in the background, the cameras found John Lydon seated with his head in his hands at the lip of the stage. He then got up with a typically mad gleam in his eye, and

mean to us, and that he didn't anger or offend us or anything.''

A month after that interview with Prince, Pat Benatar appeared on *Bandstand* to deliver her first hit, ''Heartbreaker.'' In March, it was the Romantics with their first, ''What I Like About You.''

Madness, 1984.

began exhorting kids in the studio audience to come up and join him onstage. Lyrics were being sung on the playback track, but Lydon ignored the opportunity to lip-synch. From time to time he *would* lip-synch halfheartedly, but just as often he sneered into the camera or, at one point, put nose drops up his nostrils and then let them run back out his nose. But mostly, he kept grabbing kids from the bleachers and dragging or pushing them onstage, until the stage was full of confused, excited, clapping and laughing and shouting kids milling about the band. As the song began to fade out, he ran up on top of one of the elevated platforms flanking the stage. At that point, Dick Clark came walking out onstage.

DICK CLARK: Hello up there, Johnny, you alright? Feeling okay?
JOHN LYDON (*still on podium*): Yeah, I'm alright.
DC: Would you like the audience up here or in their seats?

Rod Stewart, 1982.

JL (*"come on" wave of arm*): No, they're welcome up here. Tell everyone to come on up and dance.
DC: Okay, they can all come, everybody out! One more time, here is Public Image Ltd.!

Another of their tunes, "Careering," started up on tape, and again Lydon barely made any attempt at lip-synching. Instead, he led his bandmates in trading their instruments, and at one point he gave a guitar to an audience member. Lydon then went over to Dick Clark's podium and lip-synched into the mike there. Benevolent chaos ruled as the tune, and the picture, finally faded out.

"Lydon came up to me before that taping," says Dick Clark, "and said, 'Don't expect me to do the usual lip-synching stuff. I'm getting over the flu, I feel bloody horrible, blah-blah-blah . . .' Basically he let it be known that we'd better let him do what he liked or there might be trouble.

Adam Ant, 1981.

Following page—
Night Ranger, 1983.

187

Lionel Richie, 1982

I told him I didn't like threats, but that as long as he didn't hurt anyone, he'd be guaranteed the run of the place. And that's what we gave him. You saw what happened—controlled anarchy.''

Call it controlled anarchy or benevolent chaos, but whatever it was, it was ultimately a stunning testament to the indomitable resilience of *Bandstand*—and Dick Clark. Lydon had just recently turned an episode of Tom Snyder's ''Tomorrow'' show into an embarrassing shambles. Many so-called sophisticates who normally never watched a show as ''square'' as *Bandstand* did tune in that day, just for the pleasure of seeing Johnny Rotten demolish the show. Instead, they saw Lydon's low-key mayhem as a slightly out-of-the-norm *Bandstand* performance, somewhat off-the-wall fun, but basically just another passing phenomenon to be glimpsed through *Bandstand*'s window. Not even Johnny Rotten himself could fluster that unflappable crew. Basically, neither Lydon's crazi-

Shalamar, 1984.

ness nor the show's steadiness triumphed over the other—rather, they found a peaceful accord, which was the *real* triumph.

A month after *that*, there was more bad-boy weirdness as those futuristic spuds from Akron, Devo, appeared on *Bandstand* with their video for ''Girl U Want'' and a performance of ''Snowball'' (''Whipit,'' their big hit single, had yet to be released). The ''Girl U Want'' video is actually a bit of a satire on an *American Bandstand*—like show, in which an off-camera emcee/ military officer is seen electronically controlling the performers, dancers, and audience members (the latter of whom sit in bleachers, just like on *Bandstand*). Marvelously, Dick Clark took note of this in his pre-performance comments with Devo, chuckling, ''Hmmm, that looked vaguely familiar in spots!'' Before Devo performed ''Snowball,'' there was this inspired bit of repartee between Dick and Devo singer Mark Mothersbaugh:

DC: You came from Akron, Ohio, right?
MM: Correct—where the rubber meets the road.

And while Devo did ''Snowball,'' their performance was shot in psychedelically colored, solarized, special-effects-laden fashion—a *Bandstand* rarity.

Who else appeared on *Bandstand* in the eighties? Chaka Khan and Rufus; Kool and the Gang; Sister Sledge; Ray, Goodman and Brown;

Jose Feliciano; Tommy James; Madness; the Jam; the Spinners; Jermaine Jackson; Barry White; Judy Collins; Bernadette Peters; Stephanie Mills; the Whispers; Helen Reddy; Stanley Clarke; Kim Carnes; Alabama; Dave Edmunds and Nick Lowe with Rockpile; Loverboy; Rupert Holmes; Juice Newton; Deniece Williams; Sheena Easton; Billy Preston; Teena Marie; Lakeside; Adam and the Ants; the Busboys; Gladys Knight and the Pips; the Sugarhill Gang; Richard ''Dimples'' Fields; Ronnie Milsap; Rod Stewart; James Ingram; Patti Austin; Quarterflash; Tommy Tutone; the Go-Go's; the Blasters; Huey Lewis and the News; George Duke; the Fleshtones; Oingo Boingo; Ashford and Simpson; Haircut 100; Squeeze; A Flock of Seagulls; Sparks; Stray Cats; Men at Work; the English Beat; X; Bryan Adams; Lionel Richie; ABC; Hall and Oates; Toni Basil; Laura Branigan; the Alarm; Scandal; Billy Idol; the Gap Band; Wall of Voodoo; the Time; the Greg Kihn Band; Night Ranger; Jeffrey Osborne; Wham (with ''Young Guns'' and ''Wham Rap,'' a full year before they became huge with ''Wake Me Up Before You Go-Go''); DeBarge; Tyrone Davis; Jefferson Starship; the Bangles; Bananarama; Red Rider; Irene Cara; Bow Wow Wow; Thompson Twins;

Following Page (clockwise): Smokey Robinson, c. 1981; Nick Lowe, 1983; The Gap Band, 1982; Huey Lewis and the News, 1983.

Men at Work, 1982.

191

Hall & Oates, 1982.

Def Leppard; Simple Minds; Naked Eyes; the Temptations; Heaven 17; Mitch Ryder; Champaign; James Brown; Bonnie Tyler; Marshall Crenshaw; Michael Sembello; the Mary Jane Girls; Midnight Star; Madonna; Cyndi Lauper; Paul Young; Shannon; Bon Jovi; Golden Earring; Christine McVie; Berlin; Yarbrough and Peoples; Sergio Mendes; Wang Chung; Slade; LaToya Jackson; and more, many more.

Now, we defy anyone, anywhere, to find us a performance list for a network TV show that's *that* hip, *that* commendably blind to color and category in this age of ever-increasing compartmentalization of popular music.

Here's what Mike Peters, singer/guitarist with Irish protest-rockers the Alarm, thinks about *American Bandstand*:

"We'd been told by lots of other groups about what a great show *Bandstand* was to do. And they were right! We got on *Bandstand* before we even got on "Top of the Pops" back in the U.K.! We were so proud of that we put that in our record company bio. We'll always be grateful to *American Bandstand*. They were so nice and professional and efficient, and Dick Clark and his wife Kari and everyone else make it like a real family atmosphere on the show—they make you feel a part of it all. It's very lovely in that regard.

"Public Image and the English Beat had both told us how easy and fun the show was and how much it helped your career to be on it. It was fantastic getting to meet the kids in the studio audience, I mean that's never happened on any other pop TV shows we've done or heard of.

"In fact, something really interesting happened right before our taping, something that really increased my respect for the show and for Dick Clark. Just before we were going on, a bunch of kids were screaming for us, and Dick came over and jokingly said, 'Why are those animals screaming like that?' I said, 'They're not animals, they're people.' And he looked at me like 'yeah, you're right.' And *then*—and this was what *really* impressed me—when he introduced us he told that whole story of what had just happened right on the air, and at the end of it he said, 'Mike's right, it's the *people* that make this show work—that's what it's all about.' And he thanked me! He didn't have to do that.

"*Bandstand* was one of the first things we ever saw in America, and it was probably the best intro to the country we could have ever had. Not to put anyone down, but I wish more of America could live up to that intro! Seriously, it's the best pop TV show I ever saw. It's geared more to the bands and the kids than to the producers or the host or anything. They let the groups talk a bit, which is really nice. It's also more traditional than a lot of the other new shows about these days—in fact, a lot of those new ones are just copying what *Bandstand*'s

Bananarama, 1982.

been doing for thirty years. I mean, *that's* incredible. It's stood the test of time. That's gotta say something right there. And yet, despite the history and tradition, it doesn't just rest on those laurels, the show is still around and it's still up to date. Fantastic! I think every band should get to go on *American Bandstand*."

Julian Lennon, 1985.

New Year's Rockin' Eve—Dick Clark, Melissa Walker, Robert Frias, 1984.

Current or recent regulars include Rob Frias, Becky King, Robert Martinez, Curly Newsome, Leslie Nivens, Kim Kearney, Carl Haller, Cathy Ricard, Kelly Niland, Bob Thibedeau, Cathy Stevens, Dawn Sheppard, Artis Smith, Kristen Crocker, and Dexter Manning.

Dawn Sheppard:

"My partner, Artis Smith, and I originally wanted to get on the show to be in the dance contest. We'd like to become professional dancers one day. We started on the show in 1981. I've always loved dancing, so of course I've always watched the show for as long as I can remember. I learned a lot from watching people like Damita Jo Freeman, Deb-E Chaffin, Sue Bowser. It's a good professional move to be on the show for us, I think, but aside from that it's just a whole lot of fun, and so easy because Dick Clark and all his people are just so professional and together, it's a pleasure to work with them."

Rob Frias:

"I've always enjoyed dancing, so I've been watching *Bandstand* for some time. All of a sudden I started seeing these familiar faces on the show—all these same kids I'd see in all the

clubs I'd go dancing in around here. So I made the calls and wrote the letters to get on the show. That was December 1982. From going to the show, and hanging out with those kids I'd seen in the clubs, I began to get a lot more serious about dancing. I've been playing baseball and tennis all my life, and may get into UCLA on a baseball scholarship, but dancing to me is now as much an athletic pursuit as anything else.

"The first time I was on the show I was totally nervous. I froze up and really couldn't get into the dancing. But after that first time, you loosen up and you're not so hyper-conscious of who's looking at you, and before you know it you're in there pushing for camera position with everyone else. Basically it's a lot of fun, everyone is so easy to work with. The only real pressure is the pressure you put on yourself the first time you're on the show. That, and the jostling for the camera, which does get a little crazy at times. You won't see it on TV, but it's there.

"You know what I'd like to see? I'd like to see the show get to be more like it was in the old days, when they had all the regulars and everyone knew who they were.

"I'd say my most unforgettable moment on the show," Rob concludes, "was when Patti Smyth and Scandal were on. She came over and sat on my lap while she lip-synched one song, and she was really singing! It was great! Then I saw her at the taping for the 1984–85 "New Year's Rockin' Eve," and she remembered me!"

Not unlike the regulars of the seventies, the current crop of *Bandstand* kids are far less naïve than their predecessors of the fifties and sixties. Like Dawn Sheppard (who is representative of this generation), they are more mature for their age than the previous participants, more aware of post–Me Generation socioeconomic pressures, more career-oriented and more goal-oriented, often seeing *Bandstand* as much as a stepping stone to a show-biz career as it is something fun to do. Being products of an intensely media-conscious age, for them being on TV every week is not such a big deal in itself. What's important is what that appearance can *do* for them.

But while times have certainly changed, *Bandstand* for the most part has not. The kids still get to show how hip they are by their dress and their dancing, just as *Bandstand* still gets to show how hip *it* is by its selection of records and artists. The specifics may change with the times, but overall, boys will be boys and girls will be girls. And as long as *Bandstand* is *Bandstand* —which just might be forever at the rate the show's been going—those boys and girls will be just as integral a part of the show as ever, and we will be able to continue tuning in once a week to see the youth of America in timely yet timeless action.

Nothing changes but the decor . . .

Scenes from a 1981 dance contest.

up and down, and you're sidestepping at the same time with your heels together, like the way Dorothy clicked her heels in *Wizard of Oz*. Then your head goes to the other shoulder and you sidestep back while waving your arms up and down.

"The Bird comes from the movie *Purple Rain*, it's exactly what the Time were doing in that song in the movie. It's basically another sort of sidestep dance, but the movement is much more exaggerated, and centered more in the hips than in the feet and shoulders. And then you flap your arms like a bird. It's a really fun dance to do, especially to that song 'The Bird,' which they've just started playing on the show."

One wonders why there haven't been many new dances lately. Are the eighties kids less creative? Or are they just taking it easy, and not worrying about having to adhere to specific formulas? Well, we've still got five years to go in this decade; it will be interesting to see how things develop.

In many ways the trends of the past twenty or thirty years have come to constitute much of what might be considered "current" culture in the eighties. Thus, on *Bandstand* these days you're liable to see swinging Jitterbug-style dancing *à la* the fifties, lots of sixtiesish freestyle movement, plenty of disco-era holdovers, and the breaking/popping/locking that began in the seventies on *Bandstand* but didn't "break" (pardon the pun) until the early eighties.

So far, the dances that we can say, with reasonable accuracy, have been created this decade include the Smurf and the Bird. Rob Frias explains:

"The Smurf is a sort of sidestep dance, and then there's the ET, which is very, very similar. Basically, you put your head on your shoulder and kind of swing one way and your arms go

THE FASHIONS

What holds true for the dances in this decade goes double, triple, *quadruple* for the clothes. Fashion is known for recycling its past all the time anyway, but this holds true for the eighties in a totally unprecedented way. The entire panoply of styles seen throughout the history of *Bandstand* have all resurfaced at the same time, in only slightly altered form: there are rockabilly and fifties greaser styles, mock-"innocent" early sixties looks, throwbacks to the psychedelic era, plenty of people in disco twirl skirts and polyester suits, and loads of folks in the loose, casual, functional athletic gear that first came into style with *Bandstand*'s proto-hip-hop dancers of the mid-seventies. The latest fashion trends? Oversized, man-cut sweaters and suits for women (that look an awful lot like the stuff the *guys* wore in the fifties!), huge belts accessorizing slim silhouettes, Michael Jackson's Sgt. Pepper epaulet coats, Prince's Edwardian ruffles . . . just tune in *Bandstand* and see for yourself. It's all there.

Anyone who has ever subscribed to the notion that you can't go home again has obviously never watched *American Bandstand*. These kids have been "coming home" for more than thirty years —and they're likely to continue this way forever.

TOP 100 CHART SONGS PERFORMED AND OTHER IMPORTANT
APPEARANCES ON *AMERICAN BANDSTAND*, 1980s.

I · 9 · 8 · 0

BANDSTAND APPEARANCE	AB/TV DEBUT	ARTIST	SONG(S) PERFORMED	DATE APPEARED ON CHART	PEAK CHART POSITION	WEEKS ON CHART
1/5	AB/TV	John Cougar Mellencamp	"I Need a Lover"✔	10/13/79	#28	14
			"Small Paradise"	2/16	#87	3
1/5		Electric Light Orchestra (video)	"Last Train to London"	12/8/79	#39	11
1/12		Richie Furay	"I Still Have Dreams"*	10/27/79	#39	11
1/12	AB/TV	The Motels	(no hits until 1982)			
1/19	AB/TV	Boomtown Rats	"I Don't Like Mondays"✔	2/2	#73	5
1/19	AB/TV	Rupert Holmes	"Him"	1/19	#6	17
1/26	AB	Patrice Rushen	"Haven't You Heard"	1/26	#42	9
1/26	AB/TV	Prince	"I Wanna Be Your Lover"✔	11/24/79	#11	16
2/2	AB	Nicolette Larson	"Let Me Go, Lover"	1/12	#35	11
2/2		Jackie DeShannon	"I Don't Need You Anymore"♦	3/8	#86	5
2/9	AB	Tom Johnston	"Savannah Nites"*	11/17/79	#34	12
2/16		Rufus	"Do You Love What You Feel"	11/24/79	#30	15
3/1	AB	Manhattan Transfer	"Twilight Zone / Twilight Zone"	4/19	#30	12
3/1	AB/TV	Pat Benatar	"Heartbreaker"✔	12/22/79	#23	18
3/8		Bonnie Pointer	"I Can't Help Myself"♦	12/22/79	#40	13
3/22	AB/TV	Cindy Bullens	"Trust Me"♦	1/12	#90	3
3/22		Kool & the Gang	"Ladies Night"	10/6/79	#8	24
			"Too Hot"	1/19	#5	18
3/29	AB/TV	Romantics	"What I Like About You"✔	2/16	#49	8
3/29	AB	Ray, Goodmann & Brown	"Special Lady"✔	1/26	#5	18
4/5		Kenny Nolan	"Us and Love"	2/2	#44	8
4/5		Sister Sledge	"Got to Love Somebody"	1/19	#64	5
4/19		Tommy James	"Three Times in Love"	1/26	#19	16
5/3		Felix Cavalieri	"Only a Lonely Heart Sees"	3/1	#36	11
5/10	AB/TV	Photoglo	"We Were Meant to Be Lovers"✔	3/29	#31	14
5/17	AB/TV	Robbie Dupree	"Steal Away"✔	4/12	#6	23
5/17	AB/TV	Public Image Ltd.	"Poptones" / "Careering"	(never made charts)		
5/24		Jermaine Jackson	"Let's Get Serious"	3/29	#9	23
5/24		Mary MacGregor	"Dancing Like Lovers"♦	5/3	#72	4
5/31		Peter Mclan	"Solitaire"	4/5	#52	7
6/7	AB/TV	Cretones	"Real Love"*	5/3	#79	6
6/21	AB	Bernadette Peters	"Gee Whiz"✔	3/29	#31	13
6/21	AB	Devo	"Snowball" / "Girl U Want" (video)	(neither of these records made the charts)		
6/28	AB/TV	Rocky Burnette	"Tired of Toein' the Line"*	5/10	#8	19
7/5	AB	Stephanie Mills	"Sweet Sensation"	6/14	#52	6
7/12		Whispers	"Lady"	4/19	#28	11
7/19		Temptations	"Power"	5/10	#43	9
8/9	AB/TV	Kim Carnes	"More Love"	5/31	#10	19
8/16	AB/TV	Ali Thompson	"Take a Little Rhythm"	6/14	#15	17
8/23		Pete Townshend (video)	"Let My Love Open the Door"✔	6/14	#9	19
8/30	AB	Pure Prairie League	"Let Me Love You Tonight"	5/10	#10	17
9/6	AB	Billy Preston & Syreeta	"One More Time for Love"♦	6/14	#52	10
9/6		Dave Mason	"Save Me"♦	7/12	#71	3
9/13	AB	Larry Graham	"One in a Million You"✔	6/28	#9	20
9/13	AB/TV	Benny Mardonnes	"Into the Night"*	6/14	#11	20
9/20		Spinners	"Cupid/I've Loved You for a Long, Long Time"	5/17	#4	19
10/18	AB	Irene Cara	"Fame"✔	6/14	#4	26
10/18		Livingston Taylor	"First Time Love"♦	7/26	#38	10
12/13	AB	Jimmy Hall	"I'm Happy That Love Has Found You"✔	9/27	#27	17

✔ First hit by a performer   *Only hit by a performer   ♦ Last hit by a performer

1·9·8·1

BANDSTAND APPEARANCE	AB/TV DEBUT	ARTIST	SONG(S) PERFORMED	DATE APPEARED ON CHART	PEAK CHART POSITION	WEEKS ON CHART
1/3	AB	Tierra	"2-gether"✔	11/8/80	#18	21
1/10		Kool & the Gang	"Celebration"	10/25/80	#1	30
1/10		John Cougar Mellencamp	"Ain't Even Done with the Night"	1/31	#17	21
1/17	AB/TV	Rockpile	"Teacher Teacher"	11/22/80	#51	12
1/31	AB	Fred Knoblock & Susan Anton	"Killing Time"*	11/22/80	#28	18
2/7	AB/TV	Firefall	"Stayin' with It"	1/24	#37	9
2/14	AB/TV	Phil Seymour	"Precious to Me"*	1/24	#22	16
2/14	AB	Taste of Honey	"Sukiyaki"	3/7	#3	24
2/21	AB/TV	Loverboy	"Turn Me Loose"	1/31	#35	17
2/21		Rupert Holmes	"I Don't Need You"	4/4	#56	7
2/28	AB	Association	"Dreamer"♦	1/31	#66	5
3/7	AB	James Taylor & J.D. Souther	"Her Town Too"*	3/14	#11	14
3/14		Jermaine Jackson	"You Like Me, Don't You"	4/18	#30	9
3/21	AB/TV	Juice Newton	"Angel of the Morning"	2/21	#4	22
3/28	AB/TV	Sheena Easton	"Morning Train"✔	2/14	#1	21
4/4	AB	Lakeside	"Fantastic Voyage"	1/31	#55	8
4/11		Sister Sledge	"All American Girls"	3/21	#79	5
4/11	AB/TV	Michael Damian	"She Did It"*	5/30	#69	6
4/25		Dr. Hook	"That Didn't Hurt Too Bad"	4/11	#69	4
4/25		Ray Parker, Jr., & Raydio	"A Woman Needs Love"	3/7	#4	27
5/9		Bill Medley	"Don't Know Much"	2/28	#88	4
5/16	AB/TV	Franke & the Knockouts	"Sweethearts"✔	3/7	#10	19
5/23		Rick Springfield	"Jessie's Girl"	3/28	#1	32
5/30	AB	Don McLean	"Yesterday Once More/Nothing Remains the Same"	2/14	#95	2
6/6		Gary U.S. Bonds	"This Little Girl"	4/25	#11	18
6/6		Kim Carnes	"Bette Davis Eyes"	3/28	#1	26
6/20	AB/TV	John O'Banion	"I Love You Like I Never Loved Before"*	3/28	#24	13
6/20	AB/TV	Get Wet	"Just So Lonely"	4/25	#39	9
7/25	AB/TV	Lee Ritenour	"Is It You"✔	4/25	#15	16
8/22		Manhattan Transfer	"Boy from New York City"	5/23	#7	21
8/29	AB	Frankie Smith	"Double Dutch Bus"*	5/16	#30	19
9/5	AB	Sugarhill Gang	"Eighth Wonder"	2/7	#82	9
			"Rapper's Delight"✔	11/10/79	#36	12
9/19		Jacksons (video)	"The Triumph (Can You Feel It)"	5/2	#77	5
10/17	AB	Ronnie Milsap	"There's No Gettin' over Me"	6/27	#5	20
12/19	AB/TV	Chilliwack	"My Girl (Gone, Gone, Gone)"	9/26	#12	19
12/26	AB	Rod Stewart	"Young Turks"	10/17	#5	19
12/26	AB	James Ingram	"Just Once"✔	8/15	#17	23
			"One Hundred Ways"	12/19	#14	21

1·9·8·2

BANDSTAND APPEARANCE	AB/TV DEBUT	ARTIST	SONG(S) PERFORMED	DATE APPEARED ON CHART	PEAK CHART POSITION	WEEKS ON CHART
1/2	AB	Patti Austin	"Every Home Should Have One"	11/21/81	#62	8
1/9	AB/TV	Quarterflash	"Harden My Heart"	10/17/81	#3	24
1/16		Del Shannon	"Sea of Love"	12/12/81	#33	12
1/16		Del Shannon	"Sea of Love"	12/12/81	#33	12
1/16	AB/TV	Sneaker	"More than Just the Two of Us"✔	10/31/81	#34	15
			"Don't Let Me In"	2/27	#63	5
1/23	AB/TV	The Go-Go's	"Our Lips Are Sealed"✔	8/29/81	#20	30
			"We Got the Beat"	1/30	#2	19
1/23	AB/TV	Stevie Woods	"Just Can't Win 'em All"	1/23	#38	12

✔First hit by a performer   *Only hit by a performer   ♦Last hit by a performer

BANDSTAND APPEARANCE	AB/TV DEBUT	ARTIST	SONG(S) PERFORMED	DATE APPEARED ON CHART	PEAK CHART POSITION	WEEKS ON CHART
2/6		Kool & the Gang	"Steppin' Out"	12/12/81	#89	2
2/6		Jennifer Warnes	"Could It Be Love"♦	12/5/81	#47	10
2/13		Carl Carlton	"She's a Bad Mama Jama♦	8/22/81	#22	21
2/13	AB	Lulu	"If I Were You"♦	11/21/81	#44	11
2/20	AB/TV	Henry Paul Band	"Keepin' Our Love Alive"*	12/12/81	#50	10
3/6	AB/TV	Chris Christian	"I Want You, I Need You"✔	10/3/81	#37	12
3/6		Chubby Checker	"Runnin'"♦	2/20	#91	5
3/13		Sheena Easton	"When He Shines"	4/3	#30	15
3/20	AB/TV	Buckner & Garcia	"Pac Man Fever"*	1/9	#9	19
3/27	AB/TV	Huey Lewis & the News	"Do You Believe in Love"✔	2/6	#7	17
3/27	AB/TV	Greg Guidry	"Goin' Down"✔	2/13	#17	16
4/3	AB	Player	"If Looks Could Kill"♦	1/23	#48	9
4/3	AB	Deniece Williams	"It's Gonna Take a Miracle"	4/3	#10	17
4/17	AB	Skyy	"Call Me"*	1/16	#26	11
4/24		John Cougar Mellencamp	"Hurts So Good"	4/24	#2	28
4/24		Ray Parker, Jr.	"The Other Woman"	3/20	#4	21
5/1		Taste of Honey	"I'll Try Something New"	3/13	#41	8
5/1	AB	George Duke	"Shine One"♦	3/20	#38	11
5/8	AB/TV	Karla Bonoff	"Personally"	5/1	#19	18
5/8	AB	Atlantic Starr	"Circles"✔	3/27	#38	11
5/15		War	"You Got the Power"	4/3	#66	6
5/22	AB	Richard "Dimples" Fields	"If It Ain't One Thing . . . It's Another"✔	4/3	#47	10
5/29		Patrice Rushen	"Forget Me Not"	5/1	#23	16
6/5		Motels	"Only the Lonely"✔	6/5	#9	23
6/12		Ashford & Simpson	"Street Corner"	6/5	#56	10
6/26	AB/TV	Haircut 100	"Love Plus One"✔	5/15	#37	17
7/3		Franke & the Knockouts	"Without You"♦	4/3	#24	15
7/10	AB/TV	Paul Davis	"Love or Let Me Be Lonely"♦	7/17	#40	10
8/7	AB/TV	Flock of Seagulls	"I Ran"✔	7/10	#9	22
8/14		Loverboy	"When It's Over"	4/10	#26	15
8/21	AB	Chris Atkins	"How Can I Live Without Her"*	8/7	#71	7
8/21		Eddie Money	"Think I'm in Love"	7/31	#16	17
8/28		Sparks	"I Predict"✔	5/15	#60	7
9/4		Jermaine Jackson	"Let Me Tickle Your Fancy"	7/24	#18	15
9/11	AB/TV	Stray Cats	"Rock This Town"✔	9/18	#9	21
9/11	AB	Dazz Band	"Let It Whip"	4/24	#5	23
9/18	AB/TV	Men at Work	"Who Can It Be Now"✔	7/10	#1	27
10/9		Kim Carnes	"Voyeur"	8/21	#29	12
10/16	AB	Hall & Oates	"Your Imagination"	6/19	#33	11
			"Maneater"	10/16	#1	23
			"Did It in a Minute"	3/20	#9	16
			"I Can't Go for That"	11/14/81	#1	21
10/23		Lionel Richie	"Truly"	10/9	#1	18
10/23	AB/TV	ABC	"The Look of Love"✔	9/11	#18	25
10/30	AB/TV	Janet Jackson	"Young Love"✔	12/18	#64	6
10/30	AB/TV	Laura Branigan	"Gloria"✔	7/10	#2	36
11/13	AB/TV	Toni Basil	"Mickey"✔	9/4	#1	27
11/13		Chilliwack	"Whatcha Gonna Do"	10/23	#41	13
11/20	AB/TV	Steel Breeze	"You Don't Want Me Anymore"✔	8/28	#16	21
11/20		Sylvia	"Nobody"	8/28	#15	20
12/4	AB	America	"Right Before Your Eyes"	11/27	#45	13
12/4	AB/TV	Scandal	"Goodbye to You"✔	11/13	#65	11
12/11		Kim Carnes	"Does It Make You Remember?"	11/6	#36	13
12/11	AB	Little River Band	"The Other Guy"	11/20	#11	18
12/18	AB/TV	Billy Idol	"Hot in the City"✔	7/3	#23	17
			"White Wedding"	5/21/83	#36	13
12/18	AB	The Gap Band	"You Dropped a Bomb on Me"	8/14	#31	13

BANDSTAND APPEARANCE	AB/TV DEBUT	ARTIST	SONG(S) PERFORMED	DATE APPEARED ON CHART	PEAK CHART POSITION	WEEKS ON CHART
1/1	AB/TV	Adam Ant	"Desperate but Not Serious"	3/12	#66	8
			"Goody Two Shoes"	12/11/82	#12	14
1/1		Billy Joel (video)	"Allentown"	12/18/82	#17	16
1/8		Lee Ritenour	"Cross My Heart"	(failed to chart)		
			"Keep It Alive"			
1/8	AB/TV	Bobby Nunn	"She's Just a Groupie"	(failed to chart)		
			"Never Seen Anything Like You"			
1/15	AB	Bus Boys	"The Boys Are Back in Town"	(failed to chart)		
			"American Worker"			
1/15		Ray Parker, Jr.	"Bad Boy"	1/15	#85	4
			"The People Next Door"			
1/22		Juice Newton	"Heart of the Night"	12/18/82	#25	10
			"Queen of Hearts"	6/20/81	#2	19
1/22	AB/TV	Wall of Voodoo	"Mexican Radio"	3/19	#58	9
			"Tomorrow"	(failed to chart)		
1/29	AB	Yarbrough & Peoples	"Heartbeats"	1/15	#100	5
			"Feels So Good"	(failed to chart)		
1/29	AB	Con Funk Shun	"Ms. Got the Body"	(failed to chart)		
			"Love's Train"			
2/5	AB	The Time	"The Walk"	10/9/82	#88	3
			"777-9311"			
2/5	AB/TV	Charlene	"I've Never Been to Me"	3/27/82	#3	14
			"I Want to Go Back There Again"	(failed to chart)		
2/12	AB/TV	Greg Kihn Band	"Jeopardy"	3/5	#2	22
			"I Fall to Pieces"	(failed to chart)		
2/12	AB/TV	Night Ranger	"Don't Tell Me You Love Me"	3/26	#40	11
			"Sing Me Away"	4/9	#54	9
2/19		Phil Everly	"Who's Gonna Keep Me Warm Tonight"	(failed to chart)		
2/19	AB	Jeffrey Osborne	"On The Wings of Love"	11/20/82	#29	7
			"Eenie Meenie"	3/19	#76	5
2/26	AB/TV	Chas Jankel	"Glad to Know You"	(failed to chart)		
			"I'll Get Over It If You Get Over Her"			
2/26	AB/TV	Kelly Groucutt	"Am I a Dreamer?"	(failed to chart)		
			"You Don't Need to Hold Me Tight"			
3/5	AB/TV	Wham! U.K.	"Young Guns Go for It"	(failed to chart)		
			"Wham Rap"			
3/5		Tyrone Davis	"Are You Serious"	(failed to chart)		
			"A Little Bit of Love"			
3/12	AB	DeBarge	"All This Love"	5/28	#17	19
			"I Like It"	3/26	#31	17
3/12	AB/TV	Sonny Charles	"Put It in a Magazine"	1/22	#40	8
			"Always on My Mind"	(failed to chart)		
3/19	AB/TV	Lanier & Company	"After I Cry Tonight"	(failed to chart)		
			"I Just Got To Have You"			
3/19	AB/TV	Jefferson Starship	"Winds of Change"	3/19	#38	11
			"Jane"	11/24/79	#13	11
3/26		The Bangles	"I Want You"	(failed to chart)		
			"Real World"			
3/26		Sparks (with Jane Wiedlin (Go-Go's))	"Cool Places"	4/16	#49	12
			"Popularity"	(failed to chart)		
4/2		Marty Balin	"What Love Is"	2/19	#63	6
			"Born to Be a Winner"	2/26	#92	3
4/2	AB/TV	Bananarama	"Really Sayin' Somethin'"	(failed to chart)		
			"Na Na Hey Hey"	5/7	#100	2
4/9	AB/TV	Oxo	"Whirly Girl"	4/2	#28	14
			"My Ride"	(failed to chart)		
4/9		Stephen Bishop	"It Might Be You"	4/2	#25	20
4/16		Laura Branigan	"Solitaire"	4/2	#7	17
			"Deep in the Dark"	(failed to chart)		
4/16	AB/TV	Bryan Adams	"Straight from the Heart"	4/16	#10	19
			"Cuts Like a Knife"	6/25	#15	14
4/23	AB/TV	The English Beat	"I Confess"	(failed to chart)		
			"Save It for Later"	5/21	#98	3
4/23	AB/TV	Red Rider	"Human Race"	(failed to chart)		
			"Winner Take All"			
4/30		Irene Cara	"Flashdance...What a Feeling"	4/16	#1	25
4/30	AB/TV	Felony	"The Fanatic"	2/12	#42	12
			"What a Way to Go"	(failed to chart)		
5/7	AB/TV	Bow Wow Wow	"Do You Want to Hold Me"	4/23	#77	4
			"Aphrodisiac"	(failed to chart)		
5/7	AB/TV	Thompson Twins	"Lies"	3/12	#30	16
			"Love on Your Side"	4/30	#45	9
5/14		Nick Lowe	"Wish You Were Here"	(failed to chart)		
			"Raging Eyes"			
5/14		Jose Feliciano	"Lonely Teardrops"	(failed to chart)		
			"One Night"			
5/21	AB	Patrick Simmons	"It's So Wrong"	4/16	#30	13
			"Don't Make Me Do It"	6/18	#75	5
5/21	AB/TV		"Photograph"	4/16	#12	17
			"Rock of Ages"	6/11	#16	15
5/28	AB/TV	Simple Minds	"Promised You a Miracle"	(failed to chart)		
			"Somewhere, Someone, Summertime"			
5/28	AB/TV	Naked Eyes	"Always Something There to Remind Me"	3/12	#8	22
			"Fortune and Fame"	(failed to chart)		
6/4		The Hollies	"Stop in the Name of Love"	7/2	#29	12
			"Casualty"	(failed to chart)		
6/4	AB/TV	Robert Hazard	"Escalator of Life"	3/5	#58	9
			"Change Reaction"	(failed to chart)		
6/11		Walter Egan	"Fool Moon Fire"	4/9	#46	10
			"Star of My Heart"			
6/11		Temptations	"Love on My Mind Tonight"	4/16	#88	3
			"Surface Thrills"	(failed to chart)		
6/18	AB/TV	Heaven 17	"Temptation"	(failed to chart)		
			"Live So Fast"			

✔First hit by a performer   ✳(Only hit by a performer)   ◆Last hit by a performer

BANDSTAND APPEARANCE	AB/TV DEBUT	ARTIST	SONG(S) PERFORMED	DATE APPEARED ON CHART	PEAK CHART POSITION	WEEKS ON CHART
6/25		Dave Edmunds	"Slipping Away"	5/14	#39	15
			"Information"	(failed to chart)		
7/2		Mitch Ryder	"When You Were Mine"	7/16	#87	4
			"Thrill of it All"	(failed to chart)		
7/9	AB	Champaign	"Try Again"	4/2	#23	20
			"Let Your Body Rock"	(failed to chart)		
7/23	AB/TV	Rockats	"Burnin'"	(failed to chart)		
			"Make a Move"			
7/30		James Brown	"Bring It On"	5/28	#98	2
8/6	AB/TV	The Blasters	"Red Rose"	(failed to chart)		
			"Long White Cadillac"			
8/6	AB/TV	Lindsey Buckingham (video)	"Holiday Road"	8/6	#82	5
8/13		Sheena Easton	"Telefone"	8/20	#9	22
			"I Like the Fright"	(failed to chart)		
8/13	AB/TV	Toto (video)	"Waiting for Your Love"	7/2	#73	6
8/20		Stray Cats	"She's Sexy and 17"	8/6	#5	15
			"Something's Wrong with My Radio"	(failed to chart)		
8/20		Donna Summer (video)	"She Works Hard for the Money"	5/28	#3	21
8/27		Jeffrey Osborne	"Don't You Get So Mad"	7/16	#25	14
			"Stay with Me Tonight"	10/15	#30	21
9/3	AB/TV	The Flirts	"Telephone"	(failed to chart)		
			"Jukebox"	8/6	#88	5
9/3	AB/TV	X	"New World"	(failed to chart)		
			"True Love Part II"			
9/3		Electric Light Orchestra	"Rock 'n' Roll is King"	6/25	#19	13
9/17	AB/TV	Amy Holland	"I Hang on Your Every Word"	(failed to chart)		
			"Shake Me, Wake Me"			
9/17	AB	Scott Baio	"Some Girls"	(failed to chart)		
			"She's Trouble"			
10/1		Bonnie Tyler	"Total Eclipse of the Heart"	7/16	#1	29
			"Have You Ever Seen the Rain"	(failed to chart)		
10/1	AB	Frank Stallone	"Far from Over"	7/30	#10	16
10/1		Lionel Richie (video)	"All Night Long"	9/17	#1	24
10/8	AB/TV	Marshall Crenshaw	"Whenever You're on My Mind"	(failed to chart)		
			"Our Town"			
10/8	AB	The Animals	"The Night"	8/13	#48	10
10/8		Shalamar (video)	"Dead Giveaway"	6/25	#22	20
10/15		Paul Anka	"Hold Me Til the Mornin' Comes"	6/18	#40	16
			"Gimme the Work"	(failed to chart)		
10/15		Loverboy (video)	"Queen of the Broken Hearts"	9/17	#34	12
10/22	AB/TV	Michael Sembello	"Maniac"	6/4	#1	22
			"Automatic Man"	9/24	#34	10
10/22	AB/TV	Menudo (video)	"Cannonball"	(failed to chart)		
10/29		Gap Band	"Party Train"	(failed to chart)		
10/29		Huey Lewis & the News	"Heart and Soul"	9/10	#8	21
			"Heart of Rock 'n' Roll"	(chart info not yet available)		
10/29		Billy Joel (video)	"Tell Her About It"	7/30	#1	18
11/5	AB	Mary Jane Girls	"All Night Long"	(failed to chart)		
			"Candy Man"			
11/5	AB/TV	Dave Davies	"Love Gets You"	(failed to chart)		
11/5	AB/TV	The Fixx (video)	"One Thing Leads to Another"	8/27	#4	19
11/12	AB/TV	Michael Stanley Band	"My Town"	10/1	#39	10
			"Hard Times"	(failed to chart)		
11/12	AB	Midnight Star	"Wet My Whistle"	11/26	#61	11
12/3	AB/TV	Glen Shorrock	"Little Girls Get Lonely"	9/24	#69	6
			"Til I Love You"	(failed to chart)		
12/3		James Ingram	"Party Animal"	(failed to chart)		
12/17		Kim Carnes	"Invisible Hands"	10/15	#40	13
			"You Make My Heartbeat"	(failed to chart)		
12/17	AB/TV	Peter Schilling	"Major Tom"	9/24	#14	22
12/24		The Romantics	"Talking In Your Sleep"	10/8	#3	26
			"Rock You Up"	(failed to chart)		
12/24		DeBarge	"Time Will Reveal"	10/15	#18	21
12/31		ABC	"That Was Then, but This Is Now"	(chart info not yet available)		
			"S.O.S."			
12/31	AB/TV	Oingo Boingo	"Wake Up It's 1984"	(chart info not yet available)		

1 · 9 · 8 · 4

BANDSTAND APPEARANCE	AB/TV DEBUT	ARTIST	SONG(S) PERFORMED	DATE APPEARED ON CHART	PEAK CHART POSITION	WEEKS ON CHART
NOTE: Compilations of chart information for the years 1984 and 1985 were not available at the time of this writing. But since most bands appearing on *Bandstand* have hits, bands and songs they performed on the show are listed, where that information is available.						
1/14		Quarterflash	"Take Me to Heart" / "Take Another Picture"			
1/14	AB/TV	Madonna	"Holiday"			
1/21	AB/TV	Eric Martin Band	"Sucker for a Pretty Face" / "Letting It Out"			
1/21		Tavares	"Words and Music"			
3/10	AB/TV	Mick Fleetwood's Zoo	"Angel" / "You Might Need Somebody"			
3/10	AB	Eurythmics (video)	"Here Comes the Rain Again"			
3/10		Grace Slick	"All the Machines"			
3/17	AB/TV	Cyndi Lauper	"Girls Just Want to Have Fun" / "Time After Time"			
3/17		John Lennon (video)	"Nobody Told Me"			
3/17	AB/TV	Glen Scarpelli	"Don't Mess Up This Good One"			
3/24	AB/TV	Paul Young	"Come Back and Stay" / "Love of the Common People"			
3/24	AB/TV	Van Halen (video)	"Jump"			
3/24	AB/TV	UB40	"Red Red Wine"			
3/31	AB/TV	Madness	"The Sun and The Rain" / "Keep Moving"			
3/31		Adam Ant (video)	"Strip"			
3/31		K.C.	"Give It Up"			
4/7		Dwight Twilley	"Girls" / "Don't You Love Her"			
4/7		Kool & the Gang (video)	"Tonight"			
4/7		Shalamar	"Dancing in the Streets"			
4/14	AB/TV	The Alarm	"Marching On" / "68 Guns"			
4/14		Billy Idol (video)	"Rebel Yell"			
4/14		Patti Austin	"It's Gonna Be Special"			
4/21	AB	Shannon	"Let the Music Play" / "Give Me Tonight"			
4/21	AB/TV	Golden Earring	"Clear Light Moonlight"			
4/28	AB/TV	Bon Jovi	"Runaway" / "She Don't Know Me"			
4/28	AB/TV	Mr. Mister	"Hunters of the Night"			
5/5	AB/TV	Christine McVie	"Got a Hold on Me" / "Love Will Show Us How"			
5/5	AB/TV	Wire Train	"Chambers of Hello"			
5/12	AB/TV	Berlin	"No More Words" / "Now It's My Turn"			
5/12		Yarbrough & Peoples	"Don't Waste Your Time"			
5/19	AB/TV	Wang Chung	"Don't Let Go" / "Dance Hall Days"			
5/19	AB	Kim Fields	"Dear Michael"			
5/26		The Romantics	"One in a Million" / "Open Your Door"			
5/26	AB	Sergio Mendes	"Olympia"			
6/2	AB/TV	Van Stephenson	"Modern Day Delilah" / "What the Big Girls Do"			
6/2		Paul Young (video)	"Love of the Common People"			
6/9		Laura Branigan	"Self Control" / "Satisfaction"			
6/9		Deniece Williams (video)	"Let's Hear It for the Boy"			
6/16		Bananarama	"Robert DeNiro's Waiting" / "Cruel Summer"			
6/16	AB/TV	Duran Duran (video)	"Reflex"			
6/23	AB	Slade	"Run Runaway" / "My Oh My"			
6/23	AB/TV	R.E.M. (video)	"South Central Rain"			
6/30	AB	LaToya Jackson	"Heart Don't Lie" / "Betcha Gonna Need My Lovin'"			
7/7	AB/TV	Howard Jones	"New Song" / "What Is Love"			
7/7	AB	Dennis Edwards	"Aphrodisiac"			
9/1	AB	New Edition	"Mr. Telephone Man" / "Cool It Now"			
9/1		Flock of Seagulls (video)	"The More You Live the More You Love"			
9/1	AB/TV	Romeo Void	"Girl In Trouble"			
9/8		Scandal	"The Warrior" / "Hands Tied"			
9/8		Peter Wolf (video)	"Lights Out"			
9/8		Patrice Rushen	"Get Off"			
9/15		Janet Jackson	"Don't Stand Another Chance" / "Dream Street"			
9/15	AB	Lindsay Buckingham (video)	"Go Insane"			
9/15		Lakeside	"Make My Day"			
9/22		Gary U.S. Bonds	"Standing in the Line of Fire" / "Sneaking Away"			

✔First hit by a performer   ∗Only hit by a performer   ♦Last hit by a performer

BANDSTAND APPEARANCE	AB/TV DEBUT	ARTIST	SONG(S) PERFORMED	DATE APPEARED ON CHART	PEAK CHART POSITION	WEEKS ON CHART
9/22		Wham (video)	"Wake Me Up Before You Go-Go"			
9/22	AB	Psychedelic Furs	"Heaven"			
9/29	AB/TV	Y&T	"Don't Stop Runnin'" "Lipstick and Leather"			
9/29		The Fixx (video)	"Are We Ourselves"			
9/29	AB	O'Bryan	"Breakin' Together"			
10/6		Sparks	"With All My Might" "Pretending to Be Drunk"			
10/6	AB/TV	Billy Ocean (video)	"Caribbean Queen"			
10/6	AB/TV	Karen Kamon	"Da Do Ron Ron"			
10/13		Billy Ocean	"Caribbean Queen" "Loverboy"			
10/13		Tina Turner (video)	"Better Be Good to Me"			
10/13		Deborah Allen	"Heartache and a Half"			
10/20	AB	John Cafferty & the Beaver Brown Band	"On the Dark Side" "Tender Years"			
10/20	AB	David Bowie (video)	"Blue Jean"			
10/20		Champaign	"Off and On Love"			
10/27		Stephen Stills	"Stranger" "Can't Let Go"			
10/27		Steve Perry (video)	"Strung Out"			
10/27	AB/TV	Prime Time	"I Owe It to Myself"			
11/3		Matthew Wilder	"Bouncin' Off the Walls" "Hey Little Girl"			
11/3	AB	Corey Hart (video)	"It Ain't Enough"			

BANDSTAND APPEARANCE	AB/TV DEBUT	ARTIST	SONG(S) PERFORMED	DATE APPEARED ON CHART	PEAK CHART POSITION	WEEKS ON CHART
11/3	AB	Honeymoon Suite	"New Girl Now"			
11/10	AB	Tommy Shaw	"Girls with Guns" "Lonely School"			
11/10	AB	Maria Vidal (video)	"Body Rock"			
11/10		Dwight Twilley	"Why You Wanna Break My Heart"			
11/17		Sheena Easton	"Strut" "Hard to Say It's Over"			
11/17		Pat Benetar (video)	"We Belong"			
11/17	AB	Sam Harris	"Sugar Don't Bite"			
11/24	AB	Ollie & Jerry	"Breakin'...There's No Stopping Us" "Electric Boogaloo"			
11/24		Hall & Oates (video)	"Out of Touch"			
11/24	AB	Jack Wagner	"All I Need"			
12/8		Bryan Adams	"Run to You" "Kids Just Wanna Rock"			
12/8		Chaka Khan (video)	"I Feel for You"			
12/8	AB	Teena Marie	"Lovergirl"			
12/15		Evelyn "Champagne" King	"Just for the Night" "Out of Control"			
12/15	AB	Honeydrippers (video)	"Sea of Love"			
12/15	AB/TV	Michael Furlong	"Two Hearts"			
12/29		Donna Summer	"Supernatural Love" "I'm Free"			

1 • 9 • 8 • 5

BANDSTAND APPEARANCE	AB/TV DEBUT	ARTIST	SONG(S) PERFORMED	DATE APPEARED ON CHART	PEAK CHART POSITION	WEEKS ON CHART
1/5	AB	Julian Lennon	"Valotte" "Too Late For Goodbyes"			
1/5		Shalamar	"My Girl Love Me"			
1/12		General Public	"Tenderness" "Never You Done That"			
1/12		Rebbie Jackson	"Centipede"			

BANDSTAND APPEARANCE	AB/TV DEBUT	ARTIST	SONG(S) PERFORMED	DATE APPEARED ON CHART	PEAK CHART POSITION	WEEKS ON CHART
1/19		Dan Hartman	"I Can Dream About You" "Second Nature"			
1/19		Kashif	"Ooh Love"			
1/26		Stephanie Mills	"The Medicine Song" "Edge of the Razor"			
1/26		John Hunter	"Tragedy"			

BANDSTAND APPEARANCE	AB/TV DEBUT	ARTIST	SONG(S) PERFORMED	DATE APPEARED ON CHART	PEAK CHART POSITION	WEEKS ON CHART
2/2		Roger Hodgson	"Had a Dream (Sleeping With the Enemy)" "In Jeopardy"			
2/2		Eugene Wilde	"Gotta Get You Home Tonight"			
2/9	AB	John Parr	"Naughty Naughty" "Magical"			
2/9		The Commodores	"Night Shift"			
2/16		The New Edition	"Mr. Telephone Man" "Lost In Love"			
2/16		Autograph	"Turn Up the Radio"			
2/16		Greg Kihn	"Lucky" "They Rock By Night"			
2/23		Animotion	"Obsession" "Let Him Go"			
2/23		The Sylvers	"Falling For Your Love"			
3/2		Jermaine Stewart	"The Word Is Out" "I Like It"			
3/2		The Blasters	"Colored Lights"			
3/9		Limahl	"Never Ending Story" "Only For Love"			
3/9		Bonnie Pointer	"The Beast In Me"			

BANDSTAND APPEARANCE	AB/TV DEBUT	ARTIST	SONG(S) PERFORMED	DATE APPEARED ON CHART	PEAK CHART POSITION	WEEKS ON CHART
3/16		Philip Bailey	"Walkin' On the Chinese Wall" "I Go Crazy"			
3/16		Jeff Lorber	"Step By Step"			
3/23		George Thorogood & the Destroyers	"Gear Jammer" "Long Gone"			
3/23		DeBarge	"Rhythm of the Night"			
3/30		Jeffrey Osborne	"The Borderlines" "Let Me Know"			
3/30		Tears For Fears	"Everyone Wants to Rule the World"			
4/6		Dokken	"Just Got Lucky" "Alone Again"			
4/6		Gladys Knight & The Pips	"My Time"			
4/13		Gap Band	"I Found My Baby"			
4/13		Los Lobos	"Will the Wolf Survive" "Don't Worry Baby"			
4/20		Lady Pank	"Minus Zero" "Hero"			
4/20		Sheena Easton	"Swear"			

✔First hit by a performer   ✷Only hit by a performer   ◆Last hit by a performer

25TH/30TH
ANNIVERSARY

So many stars, so many hits, so many dances, so many good times, so many memories . . . what more is left to say?

Perhaps it's most fitting to leave you with a smile—just as *American Bandstand* has always left its legions of viewers with a satisfied collective grin, every one of the thousands of times over the years that Dick Clark has signed off with his trademark salute. For this occasion, we return to *Bandstand*'s anniversary spectaculars.

Bandstand has held special anniversary shows ever since it went on the air, usually gathering former regulars and performers who had appeared on the show with some frequency, in order to talk over old times and watch kinescopes or videoclips of good times gone by. There was a two-hour twentieth anniversary spectacular; a similar twenty-fifth anniversary show, and a thirtieth anniversary extravaganza. Those specials also featured visits and videograms from celebrities who'd gotten their starts or made themselves more familiar to millions of Americans on *Bandstand*, as well as kinescopes

and clips of highlights from earlier years, and visits with onetime regulars. But the last two anniversary specials also featured "superbands" made up of dozens of music superstars—from Bo Diddley and Chuck Berry to Booker T and Junior Walker to Chuck Mangione and Doc Severinsen and the Pointer Sisters and on and on and on—closing the show with their mammoth renditions of rock 'n' roll classics. On the twenty-fifth anniversary show, they did Chuck Berry's "Roll Over, Beethoven," with Chuck leading them in his inimitable duck-walking style. For the thirtieth anniversary show, in a fascinating piece of television, the onstage superband traded off its live version of "Rock Around the Clock" with Bill Haley and the Comets' original—which was seen and heard on a gigantic video screen hung above the stage.

Previous page— Chubby Checker and Cher, 25th Anniversary Special.

25th Anniversary Super Group.

For the twenty-fifth anniversary, there were some moments that were special indeed. Barry Manilow unveiled his updated, lyrics-added version of Les Elgart's swingin' *Bandstand* theme —the same one that starts off "We're goin' hoppin'/We're goin' hoppin' today/Where things are boppin'/Down Philadelphia way . . ." and that opens and closes every episode of *Bandstand* now. And Stevie Wonder sat at his space-age triple-tiered synthesizer and did his very own treatment of the *Bandstand* theme, as deeply syncopated as his classic "Superstition," with lyrics that went: "Congratulations to *American Bandstand*/Congratulations for twenty-five years/ I have to come and celebrate your anniversary/ Because you helped me get a hit back in 'sixty-three/Well congratulations, Dick Clark and you/ Da da da da da, can you dance to it?/Does it have a good beat, and will you give it a 98?/ Congratulations to *American Bandstand*/Just know that Stevie really loves you."

And now for the *Bandstand* smiles with which we close, from the thirtieth anniversary special. To open the show, Dick Clark noted that he could hardly think of any performers who'd been around as long as *American Bandstand*, but he did come up with a couple. They included George Burns and Bob Hope. Dick said he'd asked them for their thoughts on *Bandstand*.

In his familiar rasp, trademark cigar in hand, George Burns said, "*American Bandstand*? Great show. I've been watching Dick Clark ever since I was a little kid."

Then Dick Clark intoned, "I'm not sure, but, you know, when the world comes to an end and there's that final series of shattering explosions, the smoke will clear and a heavenly voice above it all will proclaim—"

Cut to Bob Hope, smiling and saying, 'I like the beat, and it's *so* easy to dance to!"

Barry Manilow, 25th Anniversary Special.

Scenes from the 30th Anniversary Show. Clockwise from top left: The publicity poster; Chubby Checker and Charlene Tilton; Dick Clark with Kenny Rogers and John Travolta; and Bo Diddley with Al Jardine of The Beach Boys.

The 30th Anniversary continued. This page clockwise: Rod Stewart; Dick Clark arriving at the studio by helicopter; Stevie Wonder.

B. B. King with Dick Clark and the 30th Anniversary cake that looks a lot like B. B.'s guitar.

Chuck Berry and Rod Stewart chat with Dick.

Frankie Avalon and Connie Francis.

A splendid time . . .

. . . Was had by all.

Following pages: Dick Clark on the occasion of the donation of the original *Bandstand* podium and its Record Store backdrop to the Smithsonian Institution.

225

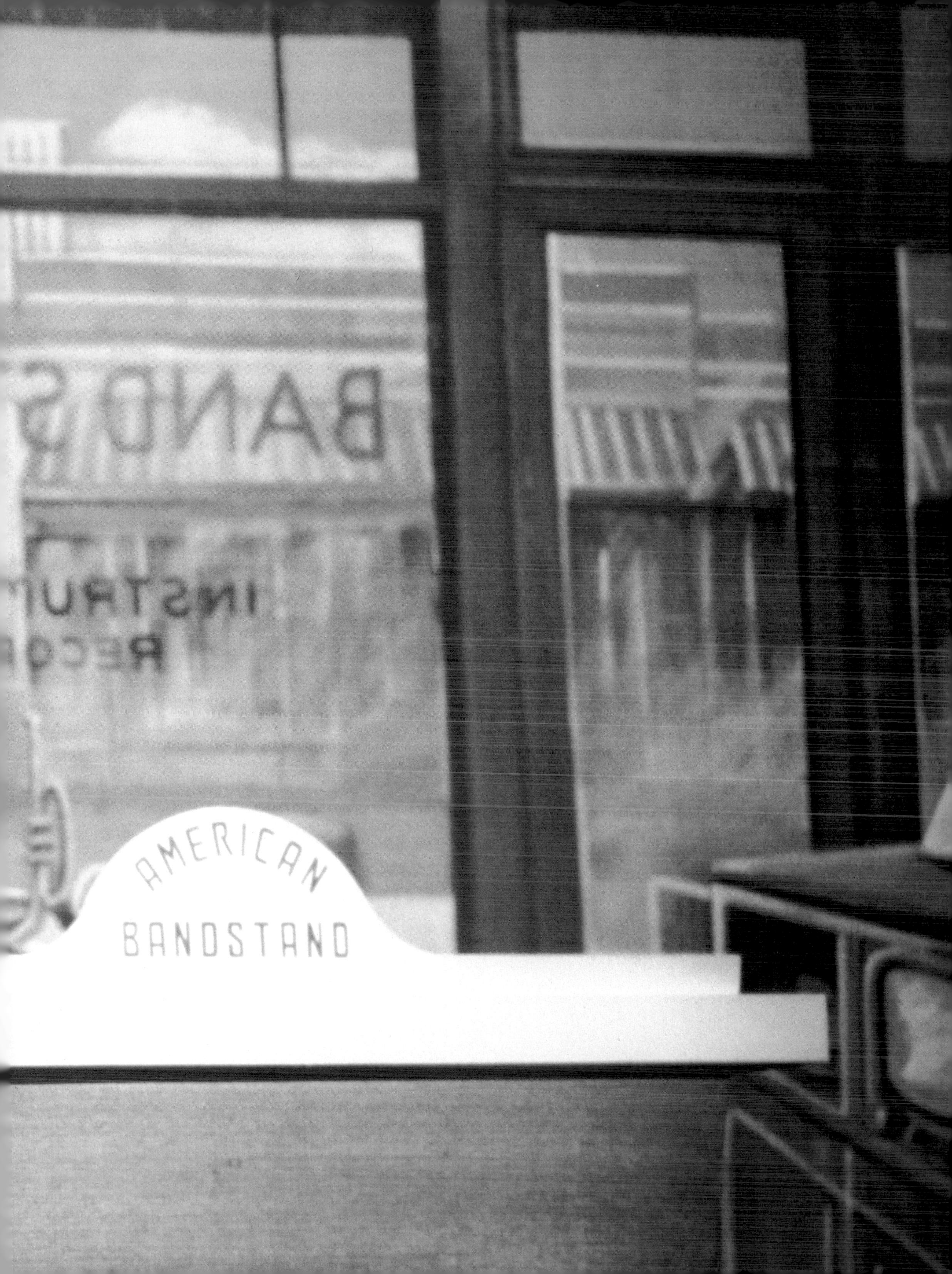
AMERICAN
BANDSTAND

INDEX

PAGE No.	CREDIT	PAGE No.	CREDIT
xv	Photo by Paul Schutzer; *Life Magazine* © Time Inc.	103 (bottom)	Photo © Michael Ochs Archives
2	Photo by Edgar S. Brinker	104 (top)	Photo © Michael Ochs Archives
3 (bottom)	Photo by John Loengard; *Life Magazine* © Time Inc.	106	Photo © Michael Ochs Archives
		107 (top)	Photo © Chuck Boyd
17 (top)	Photo by Paul Schutzer; *Life Magazine* © 1958 Time Inc.	108 (left)	Photo © Michael Ochs Archives
18	Photo by Paul Schutzer; *Life Magazine* © Time Inc.	111 (top)	Photo © Michael Ochs Archives
		(bottom)	Photo by Leon Baron
19 (bottom)	Photo by Edgar S. Brinker	112 (bottom)	Photo by John D. Gregoire
23 (left)	Photo by Paul Schutzer; *Life Magazine* © Time Inc.	120 (top)	Photo by Jules Schick
24 (top)	Photo by John Loengard; *Life Magazine* © Time Inc.	144 (top)	Photo by Michael Putland, © London Features International Ltd.
25 (bottom)	Photo by Edgar S. Brinker	(bottom)	Photo from the collection of Neal Peters
32 (bottom)	Photo by Robert Kelley; *Life Magazine* © Time Inc.	145	Photo from the collection of Neal Peters
33 (top)	Photo by Paul Schutzer; *Life Magazine* © Time Inc.	148	Photos © Michael Ochs Archives
37 (top)	Photo by Paul Schutzer; *Life Magazine* © Time Inc.	149	Photo by Bill Orchard, © RDR Productions 1985
44 (bottom)	Photo by Edgar S. Brinker	150 (top)	Photo © RDR Productions 1985
47	Photos by Edgar S. Brinker	152 (bottom)	Photo © Paul Shefrin
60–61	From *The Official Bandstand Yearbook*, 1957	153	Photo © Ebet Roberts
62 (top)	Photo by Edgar S. Brinker	181	Photo © 1980 Murray Schwartz
63	Photo by Maurice B. Finkel	182 (bottom)	Photo © 1982 Murray Schwartz
64 (top)	Photo by Edgar S. Brinker	184 (top)	Photo © 1982 Murray Schwartz
65 (top)	Photo by Edgar S. Brinker	185	Photo © 1981 Murray Schwartz
66 (middle & bottom)	Photos by Edgar S. Brinker	186 (top)	Photo © Paul Shefrin
90	Photo by Edgar S. Brinker	187 (top)	Photo © 1982 Murray Schwartz
94	Photos by Edgar S. Brinker	(bottom)	Photo © 1981 Murray Schwartz
96	Photos © Michael Ochs Archives	191	Photo © 1982 Murray Schwartz
97 (left)	Photo © Michael Ochs Archives	192	Photos © 1982 Murray Schwartz
(right)	Photo by John D. Gregoire	193 (top three)	Photos © 1982 Murray Schwartz
98 (left)	Photo © Michael Ochs Archives	195 (top)	Photo © 1982 Murray Schwartz
(right)	Photo © Chuck Boyd	(bottom)	Photo © Paul Shefrin
99 (bottom)	Photo © Michael Ochs Archives	199 (top right)	Photo © Neal Preston
100 (bottom)	Photo © Michael Ochs Archives	200	Photos © Neal Preston
101	Photos © Michael Ochs Archives	201	Photos © Neal Preston
102 (left)	Photo © Michael Ochs Archives	202 (top left)	Photo © Neal Preston
		204	Photo © Neal Preston

MICHAEL SHORE was born in Peabody, Massachusetts, in 1956. He graduated with a B.A. in communications from Fordham University in the Bronx in 1978. He was an editor at the *Soho News* in New York from 1979 to 1982, and was an editor at *Home Video* magazine in 1982–83. He is a contributor to *Musician*, *Video Review*, *Rolling Stone*, *Billboard*, and *Music-Sound Output*. His first book, published by William Morrow/Quill in 1984, was *The Rolling Stone Book of Rock Video*.

DICK CLARK, three-time Emmy Award winner, is among the most active of all on-camera and behind-the-scenes television and motion picture personalities.

He is the host and executive producer of *American Bandstand*, which is in its thirty-third consecutive year on the air.

He is the co-executive producer and co-host (with Ed McMahon) of NBC's weekly "TV's Bloopers and Practical Jokes" series.

He is the host of CBS's daytime series, "$25,000 Pyramid" and the syndicated "$100,000 Pyramid."

He is the first personality to simultaneously host series on all three networks.

American Bandstand is the foundation upon which Clark has built his varied entertainment enterprises, in motion pictures, TV, radio, and "live" stage productions.

A native of Mt. Vernon, New York, where he was born on November 30, 1929, Dick Clark became fascinated with radio while attending high school. His imagination was particularly fired up by Martin Block's "Make Believe Ballroom" and Art Ford's "Milkman Matinee," two New York programs that featured recordings introduced by personable hosts, and by such "talkers" as Arthur Godfrey, Garry Moore, Steve Allen, and Dave Garroway. At 13 Clark attended a broadcast of the "Jimmy Durante–Garry Moore Show," and knew then that broadcasting would be his career.

During 1947, Clark's family moved to Utica, New York, where his father had taken a job with a new radio station, WRUN.

That summer, while waiting to enter Syracuse University, Clark got his first job in radio, at WRUN, in the mimeograph and mail rooms. Before summer's end, at 17, he was announcing weather forecasts, station breaks, and news.

During his senior year at Syracuse University, Clark got a full-time announcing job at WOLF, Syracuse, where he disc-jockeyed country and popular music.

After graduation Clark returned to Utica, where he became the television news anchorman at WKTV. In 1952, he auditioned and won a radio and TV announcing position at Philadelphia's WFIL. At WFIL Clark was soon given his own afternoon disc jockey show, the radio version of WFIL-TV's *Bandstand*.

In 1956, he was made full-time host of the TV *Bandstand*.

On August 5, 1957, the program made its debut on the network with the new title *American Bandstand*, and has remained on the network continuously since then.

Clark moved the base of his operations to the West Coast in 1964 and now makes his headquarters in Burbank, California.

In his nonbusiness hours Clark likes to watch movies, read, travel, swim, and listen to his enormous collection of records.

He is a member of the National Board of Directors of the Parkinson's Foundation.

Clark, married to the former Kari Wigton, is the father of two sons and a daughter by previous marriage.

He is 5'9" tall, has brown hair and brown eyes, and weighs 160 lbs. He lives in Malibu, California.